The Clash of Ideas

The Ideological Battles that Made the Modern World—And Will Shape the Future

Edited by

Gideon Rose and Jonathan Tepperman

To Richard Allen—here is
some reading for
my neolibertarian friend,

cheers,

D1241914

FOREIGN AFFAIRS

Foreign Affairs magazine is the leading forum for serious discussion of America's role in the world. It covers a broad range of topics related to U.S. foreign policy and international relations with a mix of non-partisan analysis, reportage, and reviews and criticism. It offers rigorous thinking by knowledgeable observers on important practical issues, presented in a style accessible to both professionals and a general audience. *Foreign Affairs* takes no institutional positions on policy issues and has no affiliation with the U.S. government. All views expressed in its publications and on its website are the sole responsibility of the author or authors.

Subscribe today at www.ForeignAffairs.com/subscribe.

For further information about *Foreign Affairs* or this publication, please write to Foreign Affairs, 58 East 68th Street, New York, NY 10065, or call Communications at 212.434.9888. Visit *Foreign Affairs'* website, www.ForeignAffairs.com.

Contents

This book presents a special selection of new and archival material from *Foreign Affairs*, telling the story of the ideological battles of the past century and the emergence of the modern order. It is meant as is an accompaniment to the January/February 2012 issue of the magazine, which includes the four new pieces published here and heavily trimmed selections from the older articles. This volume presents, in addition to the new articles, the full, original text of all the archival articles, along with related material. The contents are arranged in substantive, rather than strictly chronological, order.

Contents

Contents

Making Modernity Work

The Reconciliation of Capitalism and Democracy

Gideon Rose

Foreign Affairs, January/February 2012

We are living, so we are told, through an ideological crisis. The United States is trapped in political deadlock and dysfunction, Europe is broke and breaking, authoritarian China is on the rise. Protestors take to the streets across the advanced industrial democracies; the high and mighty meet in Davos to search for "new models" as sober commentators ponder who and what will shape the future.

In historical perspective, however, the true narrative of the era is actually the reverse—not ideological upheaval but stability. Today's troubles are real enough, but they relate more to policies than to principles. The major battles about how to structure modern politics and economics were fought in the first half of the last century, and they ended with the emergence of the most successful system the world has ever seen.

Nine decades ago, in one of the first issues of this magazine, the political scientist Harold Laski noted that with "the mass of men" having come to political power, the challenge of modern democratic government was providing enough "solid benefit" to ordinary citizens "to make its preservation a matter of urgency to themselves." A generation and a half later, with the creation of the postwar order of mutually supporting liberal democracies with mixed economies, that challenge was being met, and as a result, more people in more

GIDEON ROSE, Editor of *Foreign Affairs*.

places have lived longer, richer, freer lives than ever before. In ideological terms, at least, all the rest is commentary.

To commemorate *Foreign Affairs'* 90th anniversary, we have thus decided to take readers on a magical history tour, tracing the evolution of the modern order as it played out in our pages. What follows is not a "greatest hits" collection of our most well-known or influential articles, nor is it a showcase for the most famous names to have appeared in the magazine. It is rather a package of 20 carefully culled selections from our archives, along with three new pieces, which collectively shed light on where the modern world has come from and where it is heading.

THE BIRTH OF THE MODERN

In the premodern era, political, economic, and social life was governed by a dense web of interlocking relationships inherited from the past and sanctified by religion. Limited personal freedom and material benefits existed alongside a mostly unquestioned social solidarity. Traditional local orders began to erode with the rise of capitalism in the eighteenth and nineteenth centuries, as the increasing prevalence and dominance of market relationships broke down existing hierarchies. The shift produced economic and social dynamism, an increase in material benefits and personal freedoms, and a decrease in communal feeling. As this process continued, the first modern political ideology, classical liberalism, emerged to celebrate and justify it.

Liberalism stressed the importance of the rule of law, limited government, and free commercial transactions. It highlighted the manifold rewards of moving to a world dominated by markets rather than traditional communities, a shift the economic historian Karl Polanyi would call "the great transformation." But along with the gains came losses as well—of a sense of place, of social and psychological stability, of traditional bulwarks against life's vicissitudes.

Left to itself, capitalism produced long-term aggregate benefits along with great volatility and inequality. This combination resulted in what Polanyi called a "double movement," a progressive expansion of both market society and reactions against it. By the late nineteenth and early twentieth centuries, therefore, liberalism was being challenged by reactionary nationalism and cosmopolitan socialism, with both the right and the left promising, in their own ways, relief from the turmoil and angst of modern life.

The catastrophic destruction of the Great War and the economic nightmare of the Great Depression brought the contradictions of modernity to a head, seemingly revealing the bankruptcy of the liberal order and the need for some other, better path. As democratic republics dithered and stumbled during the 1920s and 1930s, fascist and communist regimes seized control of their own destinies and appeared to offer compelling alternative models of modern political, economic, and social organization.

Over time, however, the problems with all these approaches became clear. Having discarded liberalism's insistence on personal and political freedom, both fascism and communism quickly descended into organized barbarism. The vision of the future they offered, as George Orwell noted, was "a boot stamping on a human face—forever." Yet classical liberalism also proved unpalatable, since it contained no rationale for activist government and thus had no answer to an economic crisis that left vast swaths of society destitute and despairing.

Fascism flamed out in a second, even more destructive world war. Communism lost its appeal as its tyrannical nature revealed itself, then ultimately collapsed under its own weight as its non-market economic system could not generate sustained growth. And liberalism's central principle of laissez faire was abandoned in the depths of the Depression.

What eventually emerged victorious from the wreckage was a hybrid system that combined political liberalism with a mixed economy. As the political scientist Sheri Berman has observed, "The postwar order represented something historically unusual: capitalism remained, but it was capitalism of a very different type from that which had existed before the war—one tempered and limited by the power of the democratic state and often made subservient to the goals of social stability and solidarity, rather than the other way around." Berman calls the mixture "social democracy." Other scholars use other terms: Jan-Werner Müller prefers "Christian Democracy," John Ruggie refers to "embedded liberalism," Karl Dietrich Bracher talks of "democratic liberalism." Francis Fukuyama wrote of "the end of History"; Daniel Bell and Seymour Martin Lipset saw it as "the end of ideology." All refer to essentially the same thing. As Bell put it in 1960, "Few serious minds believe any longer that one can set down 'blueprints' and through 'social engineering' bring about a new utopia of social harmony. At the same time, the older 'counter-beliefs' have lost their intellectual force as well. Few 'classic' liberals insist that the State should play no role in the economy, and few serious conservatives, at least in England and on the Continent, believe that the Welfare State is 'the road to serfdom.' In the Western world, therefore, there is today a rough consensus among intellectuals on political issues: the acceptance of a Welfare State; the desirability of decentralized power; a system of mixed economy and of political pluralism."

Reflecting the hangover of the interwar ideological binge, the system stressed not transcendence but compromise. It offered neither salvation nor utopia, only a framework within which citizens could pursue their personal betterment. It has never been as satisfying as the religions, sacred or secular, it replaced. And it remains a work in progress, requiring tinkering and modification as conditions and attitudes change. Yet its success has been manifest—and reflecting that, its basic framework has remained remarkably intact.

THE ONCE AND FUTURE ORDER

The basic question of modernity has been how to reconcile capitalism and mass democracy, and since the postwar order came up with a good answer, it has managed to weather all subsequent challenges. The upheavals of the late 1960s seemed poised to disrupt it. But despite what activists at the time thought, they had little to offer in terms of politics or economics, and so their lasting impact was on social life instead. This had the ironic effect of stabilizing the system rather than overturning it, helping it live up to its full potential by bringing previously subordinated or disenfranchised groups inside the castle walls. The neoliberal revolutionaries of the 1980s had little more luck, never managing to turn the clock back all that far.

All potential alternatives in the developing world, meanwhile, have proved to be either dead ends or temporary detours from the beaten path. The much-ballyhooed "rise of the rest" has involved not the discrediting of the postwar order of Western political economy but its reinforcement: the countries that have risen have done so by embracing global capitalism while keeping some of its destabilizing attributes in check, and have liberalized their polities and societies along the way (and will founder unless they continue to do so).

Although the structure still stands, however, it has seen better days. Poor management of public spending and fiscal policy has resulted in unsustainable levels of debt across the advanced industrial world, even as mature economies have found it difficult to generate dynamic growth and full employment in an ever more globalized environment. Lax regulation and oversight allowed reckless and predatory financial practices to drive leading economies to the brink of collapse. Economic inequality has increased as social mobility has declined. And a loss of broad-based social solidarity on both sides of the Atlantic has eroded public support for the active remedies needed to address these and other problems.

Renovating the structure will be a slow and difficult project, the cost and duration of which remain unclear, as do the contractors involved. Still, at root, this is not an ideological issue. The question is not what to do but how to do it—how, under twenty-first-century conditions, to rise to the challenge Laski described, making the modern political economy provide enough solid benefit to the mass of men that they see its continuation as a matter of urgency to themselves.

The old and new articles that follow trace this story from the totalitarian challenge of the interwar years, through the crisis of liberalism and the emergence of the postwar order, to that order's present difficulties and future prospects. Some of our authors are distinctly gloomy, and one need only glance at a newspaper to see why. But remembering the far greater obstacles that have been overcome in the past, optimism would seem the better long-term bet.☯

Lenin and Mussolini

Harold J. Laski

Foreign Affairs, September 1923

I

The progress of science in the past century has reduced the world to the unity of interdependence. A civil war in America brings starvation to the cotton towns of Lancashire. An injury to the credit-structure of Germany may involve a panic on the Paris Bourse. Not less notable than this web of complex interweaving is the pace at which change proceeds. Feudal Japan can become, as it were overnight, the modern state. Men are still living to whom the railway was an incredible innovation; and their children will doubtless watch aerial traffic blot out the distance between London and New York.

We pay, of course, the price for scientific development. The complexity that ensues involves a necessary fragility in the machine. The working of our social institutions depends, as never before, upon the maintenance of peace. The mechanisms of civilization are so delicate that they respond like the needle of the compass to every gust of wind; and without their continuous functioning we are, to continue the metaphor, like sailors upon an uncharted sea. We cannot maintain the vast system of inter-relationships we have built unless men are prepared to follow consistently the path of reason in their affairs. We need a minimum of social unity that will at least persuade mankind that the path of social change is a matter for deliberation and argument, not for violence and physical conflict.

HAROLD J. LASKI, Professor in the London School of Economics and Political Science.

Yet our interdependence has not procured a unified outlook. Racial hatred, national suspicion, the war of class and class, all these remain to emphasize to us the error of optimism. Confidence, in fact, is the more dangerous because the weapons that science has placed at the service of destruction are now so powerful that their utilization is incompatible with civilized life. We have learned in the last decade that the impulses of savagery that are loosed by war are utterly destructive of the foundations of a decent existence. If men cease to trust the goodwill of institutions, if, that is, they sacrifice the winning of conviction to the attainment of their desires, civilization could quite easily be reduced to the condition where, as in Mr. Wells' imaginary picture, some aged survivor may tell of an organized and coherent world as a legend which his grandchildren cannot hope to understand. The plain lesson of scientific knowledge is the making of social change in terms of peace. We must utilize our institutions. To destroy them is to destroy ourselves.

Such, at least, seems the plain lesson of recent experience. It implies, of course, the general realization that great events suggest the importance of continuous social reform. The mass of men has now been entrusted with political power; and the governments of the modern state must discover ways and means of translating the will of an electorate which has hardly known the amenities life can offer into terms of statutes. It is possible that so long as the process of legislation can offer proof to the democracy of a good will that results in solid benefit the transition to a new social order will be accomplished in peace. But the good will must be demonstrated; and the benefits must affect those who feel that they have now too small a stake in the present order to make its preservation a matter of urgency to themselves.

Such an attitude is the more important because the desirability of social peace has recently been attacked from what, at first sight, might seem two opposite directions. In Russia, a revolution made in the name of the workers has enthroned in authority men whose boast it is that they hold power without regard to the will of their subjects. In Italy, there developed alongside the constitutional government an extra-legal organization to which, at the first definite challenge, the former was compelled to yield. In Russia, the Bolsheviks have won and maintained power only at the cost of immense bloodshed, in large part, doubtless, the result of foreign intervention. In Italy, the Fascisti met with relatively little opposition at home, and with no external challenge. It is common to both movements that their power is built upon the force they can command. It is common to them, also, that they have rigorously suppressed all opposition to themselves and dismissed as unimportant the forms of constitutionalism. Each has exalted the end it has in view as superior to all problems implied in the means that have been used. Each has declared its own will so clearly identical with the good of the community as to make invalid, on *a priori* grounds, the notion of its critical analysis. Each, that is to say, has abandoned the path of reason and declared, in substance, that a great end transcends the doubts to which its methods have given rise. It is worth while to examine in some detail the principles and possibilities which lie behind this attitude.

II

A revolution in Russia was doubtless implied in the logic of events. No government which is vicious in principle and corrupt in practice can hope, particularly in the atmosphere of military defeat, to retain the allegiance of those who do not share in the benefits of its dishonesty. But the Russian Revolution differs from all its predecessors in that it came in the name of a consistent system of doctrine; and it was largely made by men to whom that system contained the quintessence of social truth. No one can fail to be impressed by the contrast between France in 1789 and the Bolshevik Revolution of November, 1917. At no stage in the drama of Versailles was a body of coherent principles given validity in the event. 1789 was a revolution of occasion; November, 1917, was a revolution of theory. Lenin and his disciples came to do battle in the name of a social philosophy each item of which was built upon historic interpretation. Accident might have defeated their effort, Kerensky might have been a strong man; the Allies might have had a definite policy; the nation might not have been welded into unity by external invasion. But granted that the opportunity was given, Lenin was the first author of an attempt to translate the Marxian creed into the institutions of a state. His was a root-and-branch challenge to western civilization. It was not merely a rejection of social reform; it was not merely an insistence on the over-whelming superiority of communism. It was pre-eminently the argument that communism is so obviously desirable that the cost of its establishment must not be counted; and the methods to that end were drawn from the system inherited by Lenin from Marx.

The theses upon which Lenin has proceeded have at any rate the merit of comparative simplicity. The political institutions of society, he argues, are merely a facade to conceal the real nature of the state's organization. The state is in fact a method of protecting the owners of property; and the true division of men is into those who own and those who do not own possessions other than their power to labor. The life of the state is an eternal struggle between them. They have no interests in common. The class which owns property moulds the civilization of society in the service of its own interests. It controls the government, it makes the laws, it builds the institutions of the commonwealth in accordance with its own desires. It divides the society into free men and slaves; and with the advent of capitalism the last stage of that historic antithesis is reached. Just as the social order of the past has secreted within its womb the germ of its successor, as, for example, feudalism produced capitalism, so does the latter contain within itself the germ of its communist successor. Capitalism, as Marx said, produces its own grave-digger. The conflict between owner and proletariat is an inevitable one, and it is bound to result in the victory of the proletariat. The process is predetermined; and there is nothing in Lenin's writings to suggest that a doubt of ultimate success has ever crossed his mind.

The method he advocates is, of course, the method of Marx. The workers are to assume the reins of power by a revolutionary act; and a dictatorship of iron rigor is to consolidate the new system until the period of transition has been effectively bridged. Lenin has never blinded himself to what this implies. The history of capitalism seems to him the history of a relentless defense of every phase of the rights of property. These were maintained at every point by methods unconnected with morality. If the conflict was extreme, as in the days of June, 1848, or as with the Commune of Paris, the last ounce of misery was wrung from its opponents that capitalism might be secure. A period of comparative quiescence may produce the concession of social reform, but this is merely deception. Once a really vital point is touched by the workers' demands, they are met by armed resistance. This means that only a conscious and violent intervention can realize communism. The proletariat must seize a propitious moment for the revolution; and until the revolution comes it must do all in its power to disturb the existing régime. For communists have only two functions, to prepare for the revolution and to consolidate it successfully when it has been prepared.

The period of consolidation has always seemed to Lenin a period of iron dictatorship. He has had no illusions about the possibility, in such an hour, of democratic governance. Ideals of freedom and equality are bourgeois myths which cannot be admitted until the ground won has been secured. Revolution provokes counter-revolution; and a victorious proletariat must be on its guard against reaction. Revolution, in fact, demands of the revolutionary class that it secure its purpose by every method at its disposal. For compassion or remorse it has neither time nor opportunity. It must disarm antagonism by execution, imprisonment, forced labor, control of the press. For as it cannot allow any effort at the violent overthrow of what it has established, so must it stamp out such criticism as might engender further attack. Revolution is war, and war is founded upon terror. The communist must use, in fact, the methods of capitalism to extinguish capitalism. For as capitalism has made of life itself the cheapest of commodities, there need be no repining at its sacrifice, and the result, in the end, is worth the cost, since it destroys the possibility of future sale. It would be, as Marx said of the Paris Commune, a wanton betrayal of trust to observe the traditional forms of liberalism. The end involved is too great to be nice about the means employed.

Nor, Lenin argues, can revolutionary communism halt at its own frontiers. The best defensive is the offensive method; it must attack other states lest they become centres of attack against itself. Of this attitude the Moscow International has been a not ineffective expression. It has allied itself to every centre of proletarian discontent. It has sought everywhere to create revolutionary working-class organizations hostile to the constitutional weapons of the middle-class state. Communists all over the world have been invited to arm the class-conscious proletariat. They have been invited to do all they could to cut down the army of the state as the chief weapon of defense possessed by the bourgeoisie. They have been urged to form their independent, if hidden, military force and acquire arms by every method. They have been asked to discredit influential democrats to whose word the working-class seemed to respond. For everywhere, Lenin has insisted, a violent struggle is inevitable. In England, for example, the workers might capture Parliament at the polls, but political power is in any case a shadow, and were it used for an attack on property it would inevitably provoke an armed resistance. Lenin, indeed, has gone further, and is openly contemptuous of democracy. It is for him a bourgeois institution intended only to deceive the people. The proletariat will always be deceived; and there can be no reliance save upon the class-conscious minority which accepts his views. For in his eyes there is no place in history for the majority-principle. The record of states is of a clash between determined minorities contending for the seat of power. To introduce considerations of consent, to wait on in the belief that the obvious rightness of communist doctrine will ultimately persuade them to its acceptance, is entirely to ignore reality.

A generation which, like our own, has seen these dogmas applied by armed battalions is unlikely to under-estimate their importance. Nor are they less significant because Lenin has retreated from the full substance of his original position. Compromise may have been made with the peasants; internal difficulties may have called a halt to international propaganda; the pressure of circumstance may have admitted a small measure of private trading. What is here in dispute is not the end the Russian Revolution seeks to serve. The idea of emancipating a people from economic servitude is unquestionably a noble one; and there is a fundamental sense in which the atmosphere of that effort marks a great epoch in the history of mankind. Lenin is quite obviously informed by high sincerity. No work has been too difficult or too dangerous for either himself or his disciples to undertake. They have shrunk from no labor, however hard; and they have pursued throughout impersonal ends.

The question involved is a different one. Capitalism may be all that Lenin believes; and, indeed, the indictment against it is, on any impartial view, a formidable one. The question is whether the overthrow of institutions by violent means is ever likely to serve its intended purpose. It entails, and has entailed in Russia, the suppression of tolerance and kindliness. It has sown cruelty and hatred, anger and suspicion, into the soil of human relations. It has impaired at every point the intellectual heritage of the Russian people. It has been impatient of reason and fanatically hostile to critical enquiry. Its method, in fact, has been that by which every militant religion in past history has propagated its creed. The religion may have been true; but a religion which has sought to enforce its truth by the sword has always been in ultimate conflict with what is most precious in the nature of men.

III

The Italian movement is different in origin, but its ultimate spirit is in no-wise dissimilar. Leninism has been the dictatorship of a party, Fascism is the dictatorship of a man. Its rise is in part due to the endeavor to escape from the disillusion which seized Italy after the Treaty of Versailles, and in part to the ill-considered effort of the left-wing Italian socialists not merely to link themselves to the Third International but also to seize control of industry in some of the great towns. Violence assumed the character of a habit in post-war Italy. D'Annunzio's defiance of the Allies at Fiume awoke everywhere a vivid enthusiasm; and the ultimate expulsion of his troops by the government was a profound blow to the new pride of irredentist victory. Hardly less dissatisfaction was caused by the supineness of the government before the progress of socialism. Its refusal to expel the workers from the occupied factories was taken, not as a wise effort to avoid unnecessary bloodshed—since their surrender was inevitable—but as a failure to accept the challenge of Bolshevism. The older politicians were thoroughly discredited. Giolitti had been opposed to Italy's entrance into the war; Orlando had surrendered to the prestige of President Wilson; Nitti's conversion to the outlook of a "good European" did not square with the inflamed ambitions of victory. There had, moreover, been for many years a profound unreality about the alignment of Italian parties. They were in the control of machines bankrupt of ideas and—the clericals apart—little different from each other. A revivification of political life was essential if Italy was to realize the new possibilities opened by her part in the victory.

It was as the symbol of that revivification that Mussolini came to do battle with the old order. In part he represented the passionate optimism of youth, eager to control what seemed a great destiny, and in part the desire of the small property-owner for security against the advance of socialism. Fascist ideas found a ready acceptance wherever men were ambitious of power or apprehensive of novelty. As a soldier in the late war, Mussolini could claim a part in the victory. As a former member of the Socialist Party, he had the credit which always attaches to those who abandon unpopular views. The small bands of his supporters grew rapidly until they were the one organized and disciplined party in the state. They were able by direct action to drive out the socialists from their municipal strongholds. They met criticism and dissent not by words but by deeds. They destroyed the printing-presses of their opponents. They broke up public meetings. They beat strikers into submission. Where they encountered resistance, they did not hesitate even at assassination to enforce their will. The district authorities were cowed into submission to their local leaders. They infected the army and navy with their spirit; and the government did not dare to challenge their power. Mussolini, as chairman of the central council, exacted and received an iron obedience from his followers. They were organized like an army; they wore a uniform. By the summer of 1922 Mussolini had half a million soldiers under his command. The time had come to move from the atmosphere of influence to the realm of government. He marched to Rome. The cabinet resigned its authority into the King's hands; and the latter had no alternative save to make Mussolini Prime Minister.

He was not even within sight of a parliamentary majority; but the Chambers abdicated before his avowed contempt for them. Either, he asserted, they must accept his will, or he would act without regard to their constitutional power. The ethos of Italy was incarnate in himself; and to oppose him was to invite disaster. The result was a remarkable triumph of dominant personality. The deputies did not hesitate to surrender their authority; if they criticized, they were beaten in the street or subjected to humiliating personal attack. Foreign policy and domestic policy alike were simply the will of Mussolini. His followers became the national militia. It is now a legal offense to publish material which serves to bring either the government or its policies into contempt. Freedom of speech has so far ceased to exist that older statesmen like Giolitti and Orlando have hastened to salute the new star. The Chamber of Deputies has passed a bill by which any party which receives one-quarter of the votes at a general election will secure automatically two-thirds of the seats in the Chamber; and since every Italian Government controls the elections Mussolini has granted himself at least four years of power.

He has openly thrown overboard all pretense of majority-rule. He will obtain power not because the mass of the electorate supports his views, but because his followers will not allow opposition to make itself heard. Government, for him, exists to fulfill needs, not to give effect to wills; and its first requirement is an overwhelming strength incompatible with liberty. For liberty, indeed, Mussolini professes no affection. He has called it a nineteenth-century concept which has exhausted its utility. Liberty, for him, is the parent of anarchy if it implies hostility from opponents, and the proof of disloyalty, involving expulsion from the party, if it comes from his declared supporters. He is hostile, also, to notions of equality. Though Fascism was, in its first phases, republican, since its accession to power it has found reasons to believe in monarchical government. It is avowedly favorable to a régime of classes; and it regards the hierarchical structure of society as the natural reward of ability in an order where the weaker must go to the wall. It is opposed to public enterprise at a period when the increasing control of basis monopolies is more and more regarded as a vital part of social policy. It is imperialistic in foreign affairs. It regards the League of Nations as the ill-begotten child of Anglo-Saxon plutocracy. It is determined to expel England and France from the domination of the Mediterranean. It regards Jugoslavia with suspicion. Wherever Italians dwell in foreign lands, it proposes to create *enclaves* of Fascismo that they may "be brought to live the Italian life more intimately" and be protected "legally and extra-legally" where they are dependent upon foreign employers. It seeks the domination, in particular, of the Adriatic, which involves the economic penetration of Albania. It demands a sympathetic policy towards Turkey in its new form.

The student of Fascismo who desires to glean from its literature any definite system of ideas will be astonished at its incoherent naïveté. The Italian mind has always been prolific of eloquence; but Cavour and Mazzini, whatever their limitations, had always in view a tangible ideal. Mussolini has offered no such hostages to fortune. His writings and speeches have been sedulously kept within the realm of the impalpable. He emphasizes the importance of patriotism and the duty of upholding the national interest, as at Fiume, at all costs. He denies the validity of class-warfare. Capital must be protected; but labor must be given a due coöperation in its management. He believes, particularly, in the promotion of peasant proprietorship. It is at once a safeguard against Bolshevism and a means of giving individualism the opportunity of active expression. He believes in law, but, so to say, in a lawless sense. When government is weak it must be made strong; and direct action is the path to strength. For the subversive tyranny of Lenin there is substituted the creative tyranny of Mussolini. He has a ruthless will to power; and the extreme situation in which he found himself seemed to demand heroic remedies. The will to power justifies the assumption of power. Its victory means the close of the period of internal trouble and foreign disappointment. Production is to be intensified; all political and economic deficiencies are to be repaired. When life "has resumed its peaceful rhythm" violence may be discarded; but it is an essential method until the national reconstruction is complete.

No one who has seen a political party constructing its electoral program can fail to recognize phrases of this kind. The promise of a new heaven and a new earth are part of the common stock-in-trade of those who traffic in the art of government. Wherein, perhaps, Mussolini differs from his predecessors is in the passionate conviction by which his activity is inspired. He literally regards opposition to his views as a crime. He literally insists that all Italian history since the time of Virgil finds its consummation in the movement he leads. Any party, of course, which regards its dogmas as a religion is bound to derive strength from its fanaticism. It is too early yet to pronounce a judgment upon the meaning of this victory. Declarations of truth are inevitably easier than their realization in the event. Insistence that violence must give place to order is more easily announced than applied. Expectations that one's opponents will start from the acceptance of the condition one has established are often doomed to disappointment. Mussolini has used all the weapons at the disposal of force to hew his way to power. He has trampled down all opposition. He has cowed his critics into silence. He may have yielded a little here, as in his support of England's policy to Germany, or his conciliatory attitude to the Vatican; in general, he holds office without conditions or limitations of any kind. He has made a revolution as vital as any in the history of the last decade by methods which Machiavelli would have understood and admired. If he establishes at length the rule of reason, it will be in terms of the rejection of its essential instruments. For there is no connection between conviction that is won by persuasion, and acceptance that is extorted by force. The victories of the former are enduring; but the conquests of violence produce a reaction conceived in the tragic terms of the model they create.

IV

The historian of the next generation cannot fail to be impressed by the different reception accorded to the changes of which Lenin and Mussolini have been the chief authors. Where Lenin's system has won for itself international ostracism and armed intervention, that of Mussolini has been the subject of widespread enthusiasm. He himself has been decorated by the governments of foreign powers; ambassadors have exhausted the language of eulogy at official banquets; and great men of business have not hesitated to say that only the emulation of his methods can reduce the working classes to a proper state of mind. Yet, save in intensity, there has been no difference in the method pursued by the two men; and it is difficult to avoid the conclusion that the different reception of their effort is the outcome of their antithetic attitudes to property.

Yet the danger implicit in each philosophy is a similar one. We have spent so many years in war that we have grown accustomed to a code of conduct peculiar to times of disorder, and we have even erected laws of behavior which are special to periods of rebellion. In Greece, in Turkey, in Bulgaria, the writ of violence alone receives allegiance; and the news of murder and pillage is accepted without a sense of outrage. We are training to the thought of seizing power numbers of desperate men who are careless of the historic tradition and contemptuous of the morality upon which our civilization has been built. The same temper may be found in America and Ireland; and evidence of its existence in England and France can be found on every hand. Mussolini and Lenin are merely the last term in a series which pervades the circumference of western civilization.

The attitude they represent is the simple one that they serve a great end, and that barriers in the way of their goal must be removed at any cost. Yet it is obvious that if any group of men may, because of ardent belief, ignore the tested constitution of society, there is no prospect of peaceful development. For it is the plain lesson of experience that the only permanent basis of power is action built upon the wills and desires of the mass of men; and those who govern must be humble enough to be so skeptical of their conclusions as to be willing continuously to submit them to the judgment of their fellows.

Since, at least, the Renaissance, what improvement we have made in matters of social organization has been built upon the maintenance of this temper. The willingness to abide by free enquiry is the one certain avenue of progress. We may dislike the result; and we may seek to persuade men by further investigation to reject decisions that have been made. What is above all important is the notion that toleration is the persistent atmosphere of experiment. Once we are willing to be aggressively dogmatic about what are, after all, the most difficult of all questions, we invite the abandonment of reason. For every system of government which fails to rely upon persuasion and argument will always attract to itself men who are capable of neither. They may begin by asserting that they have seized power for a great end; they are bound to continue by holding power for its own sake. And they are certain to hold power by penalizing dissent from their views.

Such systems have been tried before in history, most notably in the case of religion. They have always failed for the final reason that the bonds which unite the social fabric are too fragile to survive a constant assault. Medieval dogmatism did not produce conviction; it involved the wars of religion. The price we pay for militant certitude in social affairs is always the establishment of a despotism. From despotism to conflict the step is near and logical.

Lenin and Mussolini alike have established a government not of laws but of men. They have degraded public morality by refusing to admit the terms upon which civilized intercourse alone becomes possible. By treating their opponents as criminals, they have made thought itself a disastrous adventure; and that at a time when what is needed, above all, is inventiveness in social affairs. They have penalized sincerity in politics. They have given rein to passions which are incompatible with the security of life. They have insisted on the indispensability of themselves and their dogmas even though we cannot afford to pay the price incurred in the enforcement of that notion. If, as with both men, the problem of social change is to be restricted to a struggle between property and poverty, we shall end either by the establishment of an iron industrial feudalism or an anarchy in which our intellectual heritage will perish.

It may well be that the time has come for a revolution in the temper of human affairs; certainly no modern state can at once widely distribute political power and seek to maintain great disparities of fortune. But the only revolution that can hope for permanence is that which wins by slow persuasion the organized conviction of men. To endanger that process by exalting violence will not merely destroy a law here and a government there. It will, in the end, disrupt the foundations of the social fabric. Great events are not produced by the mechanisms of law or the efforts of single men. They depend, in the last analysis, upon the spirit which surrounds the circumstances of government. If that spirit is habituated to methods of violence, we cannot maintain the traditions of civilization.❷

Lenin

Victor Chernov

Foreign Affairs, March 1924

Lenin is dead—this time dead physically, for spiritually and politically he has been dead a year at least. We have got in the habit of speaking of him as a thing of the past; and for that very reason it will not be difficult now to write of him dispassionately.

Lenin was a great man. He was not merely the greatest man in his party; he was its uncrowned king, and deservedly. He was its head, its will, I should even say he was its heart were it not that both the man and the party implied in themselves heartlessness as a duty. Lenin's intellect was energetic but cold. It was above all an ironic, sarcastic, and cynical intellect. Nothing to him was worse than sentimentality, a name he was ready to apply to all moral and ethical considerations in politics. Such things were to him trifles, hypocrisy, "parson's talk." Politics to him meant strategy, pure and simple. Victory was the only commandment to observe; the will to rule and to carry through a political program without compromise, that was the only virtue; hesitation, that was the only crime.

It has been said that war is a continuation of politics, though employing different means. Lenin would undoubtedly have reversed this dictum and said that politics is the continuation of war under another guise. The essential effect of war on a citizen's conscience is nothing but a legalization and glorification of things that in times of peace constitute crime. In war the turning of a flourishing country into a desert is a mere tactical move; robbery is a "requisition," deceit a stratagem, readiness to shed the blood of one's brother military

---

VICTOR CHERNOV, Russian Social-Revolutionary writer; Minister of Agriculture in the Kerensky Government.

zeal; heartlessness towards one's victims is laudable self-command; pitilessness and inhumanity are one's duty. In war all means are good, and the best ones are precisely the things most condemned in normal human intercourse. And as politics is disguised war, the rules of war constitute its principles.

Lenin was often accused of not being and of not wanting to be an "honest adversary." But then the very idea of an "honest adversary" was to him an absurdity, a smug citizen's prejudice, something that might be made use of now and then jesuitically in one's own interest; but to take it seriously was silly. A defender of the proletariat is under an obligation to put aside all scruples in dealings with the foe. To deceive him intentionally, to calumniate him, to blacken his name, all this Lenin considered as normal. In fact, it would be hard to exceed the cynical brutality with which he proclaimed all this. Lenin's conscience consisted in putting himself outside the boundaries of human conscience in all dealings with his foes; and in thus rejecting all principles of honesty he remained honest with himself.

Being a Marxist, he was a believer in "class struggle." As an individual contribution to this theory he used to confess his belief that civil war was the unavoidable climax of class struggle. We may even say that to him class struggle was but the embryo of civil war. Dissent in the party, whether serious or merely trifling, he often tried to explain as an echo of class antagonisms. He would then proceed to eliminate the undesirable by cutting them off from the party, and in doing this he "honestly" resorted to the lowest means. After all, is not a non-homogeneous party an illegitimate conglomeration of antagonistic class-elements? And all antago- nistic class-elements should be treated according to the precept "war is war."

His whole life was passed in schisms and factional fights within the party. From this resulted his incomparable perfection as a gladiator, as a professional fighter, in training every day of his life and constantly devising new tricks to trip up or knock out his adversary. It was this lifelong training that gave him his amazing cool-headedness, his presence of mind in any conceivable situation, his unflinching hope "to get out of it" somehow or other. By nature a man of single purpose and possessed of a powerful instinct of self-preservation, he had no difficulty in proclaiming *credo quia absurdum* and was much like that favorite Russian toy, the Van'ka-Vstan'ka boy, who has a piece of lead in his rounded bottom and bobs up again as fast as you knock him down. After every failure, no matter how shameful or humiliating, Lenin would instantly bob up and begin again from the beginning. His will was like a good steel spring which recoils the more powerfully the harder it is pressed. He was a hardy party leader of just the kind necessary to inspire and keep up the courage of his fellow fighters and to forestall panic by his personal example of unlimited self-confidence, as well as to bring them to their senses in periods of high exaltation when it would be extremely easy for them to become "a conceited party," as he used to say, resting on their laurels and overlooking the perils of the future.

This singleness of purpose was the thing that most imposed respect among his followers. Many a time when Lenin managed to survive, thanks only to some blunder of his foes, the credit for his survival was attributed to his unflinching optimism. Often it used to be mere blind luck—but then blind luck mostly comes to those who know how to hold out through a period of desperate ill-luck. Most persons soon give up. They do not care to sacrifice their strength in evidently futile attempts; they are sensible—and it is this good sense that precludes good luck. There is some supreme common sense, on the other hand, in a man who will spend his last ounce of energy in spite of all odds—in spite of logic, destiny and circumstance. And with such "unreasonable common sense" nature endowed Lenin to excess. Thanks to this tenacity he more than once salvaged his party from apparently inextricable straits, but to the masses at large such occurrences were miracles and were ascribed to his genius of foresight. Foresight on a large scale, however, was the very thing he lacked. He was a fencing master first of all, and a fencer needs only a little foresight and no complicated ideas. In fact, he must not think too much; he must concentrate on every movement of his adversary and master his own reflexes with the quickness of inborn instinct, so as to counter every hostile move without a trace of delay.

Lenin's intellect was penetrating but not broad, resourceful but not creative. A past master in estimating any political situation, he would become instantly at home with it, quickly perceive all that was new in it and exhibit great political and practical sagacity in forestalling its immediate political consequences. This perfect and immediate tactical sense formed a complete contrast to the absolutely unfounded and fantastic character of any more extensive historical prognosis he ever attempted—of any program that comprised more than today and tomorrow. The agrarian plan worked out by him in the nineties for the Social-Democratic Party, something he had been toiling over and digesting for ten years, met with complete failure, an accident which never prevented him subsequently from hastily borrowing from the Social-Revolutionaries agrarian slogans which he previously had spent much effort in combating. His concrete plans of attack were superbly practical; but his grandiose program of action after victory, which was to cover a whole historical period, went to pieces at the first touch of reality. His "nearer political outlook" was unexcelled; his "further political outlook" went permanently bankrupt.

As a man who already had the truth in his pocket he attached no value to the creative efforts of other seekers after truth. He had no respect for the convictions of anyone else, he had none of the enthusiastic love of liberty which marks the independent creative spirit. On the contrary, he was dominated by the purely Asiatic conception of a monopoly of press, speech, justice, and thought by a single ruling caste, agreeing therein with the alleged Moslem saying that if the library of Alexandria contained the same things as the Koran it was useless, and if it contained things contrary it was harmful.

Granting that Lenin was absolutely lacking in creative genius, that he was merely a skillful, forcible and indefatigable expounder of other thinkers' theories, that he was a man of such narrowness of mind that it could almost be called limited intelligence, nevertheless he was capable of greatness and originality within those limitations. His power lay in the extraordinary, absolute lucidity—one might almost say the transparency—of his propositions. He followed his logic unflinchingly even to an absurd conclusion, and left nothing diffuse and unexplained unless it were necessary to do so for tactical considerations. Ideas were made as concrete and simple as possible. This was most evident in Lenin's rhetoric. He never was a brilliant orator, an artist of beautiful speech. He would often be coarse and clumsy, especially in polemics, and he repeated himself continually. But these repetitions were his very system and his strength. Through the endless re-digesting, uncouth pounding and clumsy jokes there throbbed a live, indomitable will that would not be deviated by an inch from the appointed path; it was a steady, elemental pressure whose monotony hypnotized the audience. One and the same thought was expressed many times in many different shapes till finally in one way or another it penetrated each individual brain; then, as a drop of water perforates the rock, constant repetition was applied to implant the idea into the very essence of the hearer's intelligence. Few orators have known how to achieve such admirable results by dint of repetition. Besides, Lenin always *felt* his audience. He never rose too high above its level, nor did he ever omit to descend to it at just the necessary moment, in order not to break the continuity of the hypnosis which dominated the will of his flock; and more than any one he realized that a mob is like a horse that wants to be firmly bestrode and spurred, that wants to feel the hand of a master. When needed he spoke as a ruler, he denounced and whipped his audience. "He's not an orator—he's more than an orator," someone remarked about him, and the remark was a shrewd one.

The will of Lenin was stronger than his intellect, and the latter was everlastingly the servant of the former. Thus when victory was finally won after years of clandestine toil he did not embark upon the task of embodying his ideas as would a constructive socialist who had pondered over his creative work in advance; he merely applied to the new, creative phase of his life's program the same methods which had been used in his destructive struggle for power, "On s'engage et puis on voit"—he was very fond of these words of Napoleon's.

Lenin has often been painted as a blind dogmatist, but he never was such by nature. He was not the kind to become attached for better or worse to a symmetrically finished system, he merely set his mind on succeeding in his political and revolutionary gamble, where to catch the proper moment meant everything. This is how he often became a quack, an experimenter, a gambler; this is why he was an opportunist, which is something diametrically opposed to a dogmatist.

Many critics have thought Lenin greedy for power and honors. The fact is he was organically made to rule and simply could not help imposing his will on others, not because he longed for this but because it was as natural for him to do so as it is for a large astral body to influence the planets. As for honors, he disliked them. His heart never rejoiced in pomp. Plebeian in his tastes and by his inmost nature, he remained just as simple in his habits after the October revolution as he had been before. He has often been represented, too, as a heartless, dry fanatic. This heartlessness of his was purely intellectual and therefore directed against his enemies, that is, against the enemies of his party. To his friends he was amiable, good-natured, cheerful, and polite, as a good comrade should be; so it was that the affectionate, familiar "Iliich" became his universally accepted name among his followers.

Yes, Lenin was good-natured. But good-natured does not mean good-hearted. It has been observed that physically strong people are usually good-natured, and the good nature of Lenin was of exactly the same description as the amiability of a huge Saint Bernard dog toward surrounding pups and mongrels. So far as we can guess, real good-heartedness most probably was considered by him one of the pettiest of human weaknesses. At least it is a fact that whenever he wanted to annihilate some Socialist adversary he never omitted to bestow upon him the epithet of "a good fellow."

He devoted his whole life to the interests of the working class. Did he love those working people? Apparently he did, although his love of the real, living workman was undoubtedly less intense than his hatred of the workman's oppressor. His love of the proletariat was the same despotic, exacting, and merciless love with which, centuries ago, Torquemada burned people for their salvation.

To note another trait: Lenin, after his own manner, loved those whom he valued as useful assistants. He readily forgave them mistakes, even disloyalty, though once in a while calling them sternly to task. Rancor or vengefulness were alien to him. Even his foes were not live, personal enemies but certain abstract factors to be eliminated. They could not possibly excite his human interest, being simply mathematically determined points where destructive force was to be applied. Mere passive opposition to his party at a critical moment was a sufficient reason for him to have scores and hundreds of persons shot without a moment's consideration; and with all this he was fond of playing and laughing heartily with children, kittens and dogs.

It has been said that what the style is the man is. It would be even truer to say that what the thought is the man is. If it has been given to Lenin to leave any imprint of himself upon the doctrine of class struggle it is to be found in his interpretation of the dictatorship of the proletariat, an interpretation permeated with the conception of that will which was the essence of his own personality. Socialism means the enfranchisement of labor; and the proletariat is the warp and woof of the working mass. In the proletariat itself, however, there are purer and less pure strains of proletarians. Now if a dictatorship of the proletariat over the working masses is required there must be, on the same principles, within the proletariat itself a vanguard-dictatorship over the proletarian rank and file. This must be a kind of quintessence, a true Proletarian Party. Within this Proletarian Party there must likewise be an inner dictatorship of the sterner elements over the more yielding ones. We have thus an ascending system of dictatorships, which culminates and could not help culminating in a personal dictator. Such Lenin came to be.

His theory of concentric dictatorships, which reminds one of the concentric circles of Dante's Inferno, thus developed into a universally applicable theory of Socialist dictatorial guardianship over the people, that is, into the very antithesis of true Socialism as a system of economic democracy. This favorite and most intimate conception of Lenin—and the only one really his own—was a *contradictio in adjecto*. Such an inner contradiction could not help but become, ultimately, a source of disintegration inside the party he had created.

He is dead. His party is now headed by men whom for a long period of years he moulded after his own image, who found it easy to imitate him but who are finding it extremely difficult to continue his policy. That party as a whole is now beginning to experience the fate of its supreme leader: gradually it is becoming a living corpse. Lenin is no longer there to galvanize it with his surplus energy; he spent himself to the dregs—spent himself on a party which is now, in its turn, exhausted. Over his freshly made grave it may for a moment draw closer together and pronounce vows of fidelity to the revered teacher who has told it so much in the past, but who today is telling it no more, and who will tell it no more in the future. Then it will fall back into everyday life and again be subject to the law of disintegration and dissolution.

Stalin's Power

Paul Scheffer

Foreign Affairs, July 1930

The official handbooks of the Soviets do not give Stalin's family name or the date of his birth. He was born in the year 1879, and is supposed to have come from a peasant family. Between 1892 and 1898 he attended a seminary for priests at Tiflis, whence, as the official "Communist's Calendar" states, he was expelled. Thereafter Stalin's life revolved within the monotonous triangle of secret revolutionary conspiracies, banishments and flights. This was the case with many other Russians, for Russia has always been a great producer of professional revolutionists.

But Stalin's ups and downs, or rather ins and outs, were more drastic than those of the average rebel. After he had reached his nineteenth year he was sent to Siberia four times. Thrice he escaped. He was sentenced to his fourth deportation in 1913, and this time stayed in Siberia till the February Revolution. Returning to Petrograd he was advanced to the organizing committee of the Bolshevik Party. The "Calendar" makes bare mention of the fact that he fought in the field in the Civil War between 1918 and 1921. He became People's Commissar for the Control by Workers and Peasants, then People's Commissar for Nationalities, and then secretary of the party. Since 1917, he has been a member of the Politbureau. The "Calendar" says nothing of his exploit as organizer and leader of the daylight robbery on a main street in Tiflis of a money transport of the Russian Bank (the party treasury was empty after the unlucky revolution of 1905!). It says nothing of a subsequent short

PAUL SCHEFFER, for some years correspondent of the *Berliner Tageblatt* in Moscow, now stationed in Washington.

trip abroad—Stalin's only contact with foreign countries. It says nothing of the activities whereby he put Lenin on the defensive during the latter's last year, closed Trotsky's mouth after Lenin's death, bested his partners, Kamenev and Zinoviev, in the all-powerful triumvirate which succeeded to Lenin's inheritance, and finally dethroned the new associates with whom he replaced them—Rykov, Bukharin, Tomsky. Stalin must have known that this insignificant *curriculum vitæ* would fall under the eyes of a million or more Communists. He certainly saw it before it was published. He may even have revised it himself. Inconspicuousness is part of his policy. Stalin may be boundlessly ruthless; he is, nevertheless, shy and shrewd.

Stalin seems to have conceived his hatreds as a young man. They were strong enough to survive his many imprisonments under the Tsars. They endure to this day. One may say that they derive from an inferiority complex. Stalin is the homely, unattractive offspring of a handsome race: a bony, over-large nose; a deeply furrowed, uncommonly low but very broad forehead; small eyes under heavy lids and bushy brows; bristly upstanding hair; strongly marked cheek-bones; formidable jaws; a correspondingly strong chin; a puny, slender, apparently underfed figure, which, to judge by the way he carries himself, must in reality be wiry and muscular. Such things play their part in history. Stalin cannot derive his poise from his physical appearance. The latter, rather, must be counted among the deeper causes which make him one of those men whose whole life evolves around a struggle for self-assertion.

On one occasion, in 1928—it was a beautiful day in springtime—a parade of Communist athletic organizations was to be held in the Red Square at Moscow. The square easily accommodates fifty thousand people. The exercises had been scheduled for half-past eleven, but in accord with army customs everybody was on hand by eleven. The boys began killing time with one of the sports young people in Russia most enjoy—"girl-tossing" (a number of young men throw a girl high in the air and catch her as she comes down). All over the square one could see bright-colored shirts, skirts and bloomers sailing skyward and falling again. Stalin was to review the parade. As usual he came late. When he appeared, neither fanfares from the bands, nor a verse of the "International," nor the warnings of messengers sent hither and thither, could put an end to the "girl-tossing." In the peacolored raincoat which he wears even on sunny days, and with his cap pulled as usual far down over his face, Stalin stood on the balustrade of Lenin's tomb. Nobody noticed. Nobody was interested in him. An hour later "retreat" was sounded. The crowd quietly dispersed.

Stalin is not a man who appeals to the sympathies of crowds or stirs their imaginations. He is not an electric person. Let us be more blunt: he is frankly unattractive, and all the more so since he knows he is, and shows by his demeanor that he does not care! Even his voice, a voice as hard and brittle as glass, lacks the undertones, the rhythm, that work so powerfully upon the music-loving populace of Russia. Zinoviev dazzles a crowd, but take him in his personal contacts, and the celebrated *tribunus populi* is surly, repellant. Without sharing Zinoviev's advantages in his public appearances, Stalin has his disadvantages in private contacts. He is a very impressive person, but works as man to man only by giving an impression of concentrated and unbending willfulness. You feel at once that he is "dangerous."

Shortly after the bloody conquest of Turkestan, a delegation from that country appeared in the Kremlin, and a number of Soviet notables assembled to receive the visitors. The hosts were seated around the table. Stalin came in, looked about, and began dragging up chairs, that the guests also might sit down. The trait did not exactly fit in with what people knew of him. Someone asked him why he did it. He answered: "What else, except our politeness, have we Asiatics to meet you Europeans with?" A significant remark! The seminary student from the Caucasus, the man who early in life had writhed under the contempt of European Russia, now speaks through his lips with an Asiatic's pride, with a sense of belonging to those vast regions of the Orient where conceptions of life are so much simpler and, in their forms, surer, colder, clearer than in sophisticated, spiritually distracted Europe, a Europe intellectually so pretentious, so arrogant, so sentimental, so full of fine phrases which, in most cases, deceive the people who use them.

Stalin never belonged to the brilliant group which gathered in Russia from all lands after the February Revolution and to which history has ascribed the triumph of the Revolution of October 1917. They were men who had drawn on all the resources of Western civilization as they lingered safe and snug (buried in many-sided troubles, perhaps, but also in newspapers) in the cafés of Munich, Geneva, Paris and London. That was the way they sharpened *their* weapons for the revolution! They had, to be sure, kept in close touch with the active fighters on Russian soil, and had even returned to the homeland at one time or another, such as during the Revolution of 1905. But they had not, or at least not entirely, led dangerously exposed lives as had Stalin. He saw himself as the one to whom the "dirty work" had been left. He liked to refer to himself as the "hall sweeper" of the Revolution. And now, in the hour of victory, he was being admitted to the inner councils of the leaders grudgingly if at all. The eyes of the aroused populace stubbornly looked past him to men who had the knack of holding the immense followings who came trooping to "the Cause" that year, men who knew how to make ringing speeches, mouth big ideas, rattle off fine theories—the Lenins and the Trotskys, the Zinovievs, the Radeks, and the Bukharins. For Stalin, all such were "Europeans," "émigrés." He had been the one, after the grievous failure of 1905, to keep the fires of revolution glimmering in Russia. In the first year of the new régime, he felt that they regarded him as necessary but did not take him at full value. In their eyes, he was still the "savage from the Caucasus," the man with more fist than brain, more nerve than intelligence—a fanatic. All the more keenly, therefore, did he feel the slight that was never uttered. (It is not difficult to understand that a man so inured to hardship should have very few personal needs, be indifferent to material advantages and dumb to æsthetic values.)

It is evident, now, that all along he felt that his hour would come. He had at his disposal, in a way no one else could have, an immense acquaintance with the 150 million inhabitants of Old Russia. In those swarming masses he knew just which individuals were the men to realize and sustain a proletarian revolution such as he conceived in that still barbaric country. The hypnosis of crowds and the frenzy of words of the first year, then the inspired and inspiring civil crusade against the remnants of Tsardom and its allies, must some day come to an end. It would then be a question of governing people no longer hypnotized, of using ways and means for forcing the masses together independently of such ephemeral throngs. No one knew Russia as Stalin did. No one realized as he realized what it meant to set up a single class of people, the proletariat—3 millions of human beings in a land far from being industrialized—as the only class entitled to live, the only class entitled to rule, and then to drag 135 millions of peasants along in the same direction. Stalin also knew, as no one else knew, where to find the people who could be used in such a project: people of his mind and of his hardness, who were willing to look at the world only from below up; people of his origins, with undying animosities against everything "bourgeois" and against the arrogance and pretentiousness of the "intellectuals" who now claimed they had "made the Revolution!" They were instinctively certain that such educated individuals would, knowingly or unknowingly, be bound by a thousand spiritual ties to bourgeois ideas and ways and would never quite grasp the realities of a Communist revolution in Russia.

During the Civil War no one surpassed Stalin in self-sacrifice. Watching a parade at Tsarskoe Selo during the winter of 1918, he noticed a soldier who seemed dissatisfied, and asked him what the matter was. The man pointed to a pair of worn-out straw shoes. Stalin ordered him to take them off, put them on himself, and wore them all that winter. Trotsky devotes a brilliant chapter in his "Memoirs" to the railroad train in which he hurried from one dangerous point to another along the front over a year's time. Stalin never attained any such position of command. He has never forgiven Trotsky for that train, nor has he forgiven him for the wild enthusiasms he aroused in the Russian throngs by his speeches in Petrograd in the summer of 1917, calling for revolutionary action. It is characteristic of Stalin that he spent most of the period of the Civil War in the provinces, establishing himself with a few friends on the lower Volga, where they did very much as they pleased and were finally coaxed out by the people in the Kremlin—but only with the greatest difficulty—Trotsky acting as intermediary.

Stalin's special significance, which the other leaders could never refuse to recognize, lay, even during the first years, in his close contacts with the second, third, fourth and lowest ranks in the Bolshevik Party. While momentous political issues were being talked out in Moscow, the cohesion of the party rested largely on its "power on the spot," as the phrase went; in other words, on autonomous domination by the party's local representatives in each of the cities, large or small, of the vast territory of Russia. (Such, for that matter, is the situation today.) On the filling of these different posts, as well as on the ideas and conduct of the men who held them, Stalin came to have an enormous influence, even in Lenin's lifetime, as secretary of the party. He was by no means the only one who gave orders; but he did manage to organize among the local party chiefs a "guard" of " tough customers" whose ruthlessness in the exercise of their power could be taken for granted. They were not the people whom Trotsky, Lenin and Zinoviev were inclined to favor. They were men like Stalin—"non-intellectuals," "non-Europeans."

Some four months before his death, Lenin broke with Stalin. It is established that thereafter Lenin refused to have any further personal contacts with him, and stuck to that decision to the end. The idol of the Revolution was lying sick in a luxurious manor-house near Moscow. The letters he wrote to Trotsky and to the Central Committee of the party in regard to Stalin's rôle in party politics betray the utmost irritation at what the Caucasian had been doing. Lenin's intermediary, in the fight he made from his deathbed, was Trotsky.

No one, of course, can claim to have fully uncovered the secrets of Lenin's relations to Stalin. That Lenin feared for the party, for the state, for his whole achievement, there is not the slightest doubt. Max Eastman has reported a few characteristic details of the struggle Lenin had to wage against the "Moscow clique" in the party in order, for example, that his article on the fusion of the Soviet Control by Workers and Peasants with the powerful Central Committee might be even published. At that time Lenin refers to the existence of a "bureaucracy within the party" and expresses a determination that it shall not become all-powerful; this was one of the causes of the proposal of fusion. He was unmistakably alluding to Stalin.

Undoubtedly this was the ignition point of all the later conflict with Trotsky. By the phrase "party bureaucracy" Lenin meant to convey, with caution as to possible effects on the public and on the party at large, that a "ring" of party officials was forming within the party, that it had worked upward from deep down, that it was already making its influence felt in the Central Committee, in the Secretariat, in the Politbureau—and "on the spot" held the party agents and committees in the hollow of its hand. The ring in question seemed to Lenin and his intimates likely to eclipse the spontaneous coöperation of the whole party in the realization of Bolshevik ideals. And this, in the eyes of Lenin, was actually being done in an underhanded manner quite incompatible with Communist comradeship. It is an utterly unhistorical idea that Lenin ever ruled over his party with fatherly omnipotence. From the beginning to the very end he was called upon to fight vigorous battles on many subjects, battles in which blows were struck straight from the shoulder. Many a time Lenin knocked his opponents "cold;" but he seldom dropped them.

With Stalin he acted differently.

What worried Lenin in Stalin's case was the latter's secret, slinking, anonymous expansion of his personal power in the party and his preference for the backstairs to more conspicuous routes. The tactics which Stalin was later to use with such success against Trotsky, first to silence him and then to reduce him to complete helplessness, he used against Lenin, the moment the latter fell sick. This enraged Lenin. It is an interesting fact that Kubischev (the present chairman of the Supreme Economic Council), already Stalin's man at any decisive moment, was in a position to suggest that the article by Lenin which was in dispute should be laid before him in a single copy of the *Pravda* to be printed for his personal benefit! This sort of person from Stalin's following was already in evidence in the high councils of the party. It is an unanswerable,

though far from idle question whether Stalin might no
ceeded in unseating Lenin, if Lenin had remained in
of his powers. It must be recognized as at least possible. ...
tics which enabled him to triumph over all rivals he was already
turning against Lenin with success, in spite of the latter's immense
popularity. Nobody, nothing, has so far been able to resist him—
no prestige, no merit, no reputation.

When Lenin died, Trotsky's fate, as we may easily see after the
fact, was already sealed. Trotsky was the most significant, the most
influential, among the men whom the world at large regarded as
masters at the Kremlin. Nothing better illustrates the antithesis
between the two groups than the opposition which soon after
Lenin's death (as Eastman relates) Trotsky set up to an order of
Stalin's that all members of the party should be in duty bound to
report all "intrigues directed against the party" which appeared in
their groups or classifications. The order was in effect a death blow
to the free play of opinion, indeed to any exchange of opinions, on
the part of individuals within the party—a death blow to the spontaneous development of policies within party ranks. It was also a
death blow to Trotsky's personal position, which, like Lenin's, had
rested on his personal popularity and on the confidence which not
only the party but widely scattered elements in the population,
even a part of the bourgeoisie, reposed in him. Trotsky adopted
Lenin's phrase "party bureaucracy" and balanced it with one of his
own, "party democracy." The latter too, in Stalin's eyes, was just
another "European" and "liberal" idea. It connoted belief in a free
consensus omnium arising from a competition of opinions.

His answer was to consolidate the rigid system of party officials
he had long been quietly perfecting, a system resting on the local
agents who wielded power "on the spot," but with its peak entering
the party secretariat. The latter was composed of five secretaries; one
of them was Lenin (the leader until his death), another was Stalin.
Stalin now made himself General Secretary (a title not existing until
he brought it into use), with complete control over the routine of
organization. Was he not the best-informed on all local questions,
all questions of personnel? He spun his threads. The belief that the

cohesion and strength of the party was guaranteed by common convictions lay very far from his mind. Everything he had ever done bespoke contempt for any such thing. He used men who had an active understanding of absolute power and possessed the means of using force with which alone, as he knew, absolute power may be sustained in a hostile and not very responsive environment. He used these means no less readily against followers of his own, bearing heavily upon any form of resistance, even verbal; but leaving officials far-reaching freedom of action in all matters (especially personal matters) which did not seem directly to concern the interests of the Bolshevik régime.

People on the outside long regarded the fight on Trotsky as the work of the "triumvirate:" Kamenev, Zinoviev and Stalin. Kamenev was Trotsky's brother-in-law. He and Zinoviev had been close comrades of Lenin. That distracted attention from the fact that Stalin was pulling the wires. But how was it possible that the Central Committee of the party, which with the Council of People's Commissars had been in Lenin's time the decisive factor in guiding the party, could in any sense share or tolerate a baiting of Trotsky which—another impossibility—had been carried on for years within the very innermost circle of the party? Lenin's "Testament"—that great document in which carefully, judiciously, and with great self-control he reviews the capacities of his associates—contains two scathing words on Stalin: "Stalin is crude and narrow-minded." (Both words are there, not just "narrow-minded" as more often quoted.) Lenin said very positively that through these outstanding traits of character Stalin would ruin the party if ever he attained to leadership. In the past six years, by utilizing the very qualities for which Lenin coined his adjectives, Stalin has ascended to greater and greater power, and with him, if you like, the party. History has yet to judge whether Lenin was right.

In the Central Committee of the party Stalin found plenty of people available for the purposes of his tactics, people who had risen from the dark depths of revolutionary activity and whose intellectual horizons were as different from those of the "Europeans" as his own. He had worked tirelessly among them ever since 1917, while the "Europeans" held the spotlight. He worked with astounding shrewdness and foresight, with a keen instinct for the tempo at which his aims could mature. There was a group of "old Bolsheviks" (a discovery, it would seem, of Stalin himself), made up mostly of revolutionists who had passed their lives in agitation at home, and not in ease abroad. They were loyal to the Lenin group for the most part, but they were far removed, in the whole circle of their experience, from the sophisticated, cultivated intellectuals at the head of the government and were always full of honest anxiety lest the Revolution "go bourgeois." Their personal connections, like Stalin's, led toward the country, where Stalin had—and has—his "guard." The heirs of Lenin knew that they had to reckon with these gruff and bluff forces; but they thought they could easily do so, relying on the magic they had always used. But Stalin had come to the top precisely because he understood the organization of power from the bottom up better than anybody else.

"Old Bolsheviks," men of 1905 and earlier, had found their way into the Central Committee in great numbers. Stalin influenced them directly and indirectly. He played them against the lower orders of the active party membership, and the latter, to a much greater extent, against them. This net, woven strand by strand, artfully, with tireless energy, with brutal threats against the wavering and with well-calculated thrusts at Trotsky and Trotsky's followers, was the "party democracy" which Stalin aimed at. While he was quietly making these manœuvres, he was hacking in a thousand different ways at the tender roots of the "European." Fickle, jealous, and ambitious Kamenev and Zinoviev, whose nerves were not made of iron, he turned with great subtlety against Trotsky and toward himself. He reminded them that the European varnish on the party was very thin—that they had to look out for their own hides.

Meantime public opinion was worked as vigorously as possible. A short time after Lenin's letter became known (Stalin resisted its reading before the Central Committee as long as he could) there appeared in hundreds of thousands of copies, distributed all over Russia, a colored print which showed Lenin and Stalin sitting comfortable and smiling side by side on a bench in a garden. Stalin's dead enemy had become a friend! Lenin's apotheosis was launched the day of his death—just to keep Trotsky out of the public eye. No one worked for it more zealously than Stalin. No one sought more assiduously for the immediate falsifying of the version which the public, and even the party, would receive of Lenin's relationship to Trotsky and the latter's group.

When, next, he succeeded in preventing discussions and rectifications before the country and the rank and file of the party the battle was won. By that time Stalin had solidly established (in the minds of many people of good faith) his opinion that governing is the affair of those who govern, and of nobody else—a strictly "Asiatic" conception. He had already drawn all power from the circumference to the centre of the party. Observers of Soviet politics must have remarked with astonishment that Trotsky had to close his mouth. The Kremlin was with Stalin. That Trotsky was a poor politician, everybody, his friends and his enemies alike, are now agreed. When his newspaper articles began to be refused or censored he had the unlucky thought of exposing the Triumvirate in a history of October 1917. The book reached only an insignificant portion of the public when it appeared in the autumn of 1924. By its publication Trotsky, the would-be man of strenuous action, showed that he was at bottom a "literary fellow," full of superstitions as to the power of the word and of logic. Had not Stalin been right in his judgment of the "European?" Stalin had already so consolidated his position that neither anything Lenin may have said of him, nor any little episodes away back in 1917, could drag him from the saddle. He knew much better than Trotsky how the piles are driven to support a permanent edifice of power.

The history of the Bolshevik Party in Russia after Lenin's death (and, in many respects, even before) may be read today only with numerous lacunæ, which may never be filled. But looking back over these past years, one can remark only with astonishment how every one of Lenin's close associates, and later of Stalin's own associates, was shortly treated as a rival and a climber. Toward the end of 1925 he had driven Kamenev and Zinoviev from high position to secondary prominence; the competent and brilliant Sokolnikov had fallen even earlier. Kamenev and Zinoviev, with Trotsky, had been Lenin's closest comrades, and the former were Stalin's helpers against Trotsky after Lenin's death. Bukharin and Rykov come forward in 1926. Combining with these, Stalin drove the others, along with Trotsky and his followers (among them Radek, who had twice sacrificed himself for Stalin), first out of the party and then (in January 1928, four years after Lenin's death) definitely into exile. In the autumn of 1929, twenty-one months later, came the turn of Rykov and Bukharin and many other high dignitaries who had joined forces with Stalin against Trotsky. Toward the end of 1929 Stalin forced Bukharin and Rykov (who succeeded Lenin as President of the Council of People's Commissars) publicly to declare that they would no longer stray from "the general policies of the party" or lend their aid "to any further errors." There is something worse than banishment!

If anything shows the road which the spirit of the Bolshevik Party has traveled since Lenin's death, it is surely this declaration. Never for an instant would Lenin have thought of allowing such a degrading note-in-blank to be made in his name on the convictions of a political antagonist who was a comrade in his party. At that moment Stalin's strategy attained its highest triumph. From that point his star has been declining.

The foregoing survey would not reflect the facts, unless these were defined somewhat more precisely. Stalin got control of power in the state by withdrawing all important decisions and debates in the party from public view, and even from the view of the party at large. He shrouded the Kremlin in a thicker and thicker cloud of secrecy. Anyone who tried to work toward the outside or sought support in the majority sentiments of the party (to say nothing of publicity among the Soviets) was immediately and successfully dealt with as a traitor. Stalin had thoroughly convinced the Central Committee that the exclusion of the public from all controversies was the fundamental principle of self-preservation. By cutting off the danger of interference "from outside" Stalin was able to make use of the forces he held at his disposal inside his close and stuffy inner circle. Nobody had such a well-knit organization of henchmen to depend on. His opponents could rely on little more than the feelings and sympathies of people "outside." These for the most part they surely possessed; but by narrowing their contacts with such forces, Stalin progressively deprived them of their points of support.

Furthermore, it is important to observe that, in his war on Trotsky, Stalin did not proceed in such a way as to kill the man politically. He merely paralyzed him. Trotsky was already helpless in 1924. The end did not come till four years later. In the same way Kamenev and Zinoviev (an idol of the masses), all those individuals whose portraits were to be seen everywhere, who had had no end of buildings and institutions named after them, who received thunderous applause in public meetings even a day or two before their fall, were quietly paralyzed as a prelude to being eliminated. Only when sufficient poison had been administered in increasing doses in a thousand, ten thousand, party meetings, in pamphlets, and in resolutions from all over Russia, were they removed. Stalin never saw himself as replacing them with his own figure. He was all the more anxious, therefore, that they should disappear. He was resolved to be the darkest spot in the darkness at the Kremlin! The imponderables of popular administration and party devotion he valued highly as political assets of his antagonists, however much he may have despised affections which he could never hope to enjoy himself. But he was convinced that he could let mere popularities gradually fade away, be slowly strangled, by his own methods. Then would come the time to upset so many living corpses. He attacked his opponents or rivals on the ebbing tide of their reputations and always used the weaker against the stronger: first Trotsky, then Radek, and then Zinoviev, Kamenev and the dashing Sokolnikov.

The finish was not altogether easy. When he had herded all the people he thought dangerous together and saw that the opposition was struggling desperately in its death agony, he drew back for his blow in the open.

It was in July 1927 that for the first time he asked for their expulsion from the party. The blow missed. His motion was defeated.

However much Trotsky and former opponents of Trotsky's who had joined him with gnashing of teeth may have lost prestige before the Central Committee of the party, the Committee thought that to expel them would be going a bit too far.

The story of how, unobserved by the world at large and by Soviet Russia itself, this crisis was solved, is very instructive. Stalin's request for the expulsion of Trotsky and Trotsky's friends for the first time fully betrayed his power, his ruthlessness, his hatred for the men who had stood godfather to the Revolution. For the first time all members of the Central Committee could clearly see how far they had allowed themselves to be carried and just where they had arrived. Even Stalin's immediate henchmen must have wondered whether the shock would not prove too great for the party, the country, the world.

Just before the meeting of the full Committee, Stalin had been in the Caucasus. On his return he found keen opposition and determined faces. Immediately he changed his tactics, as his method was. He got out of his hole by introducing and forcing through an almost friendly resolution on the sins of Trotsky and his friends, provided of course with a clause of "probation." Then he drew off again, took another "vacation;" but he was back within a fortnight. The opposition had been lead by Uglanov. It came from Moscow—a typical trait, for Stalin's stronghold has always been in the provinces. Uglanov and the little Bukharin (always enthusiastic, always hypnotized by someone) now had to betake themselves to Achilles in his tent. Since Stalin's defeat and "vacation," serious confusion and disorganization had arisen in the party. The effort to establish power on a broader basis, in the Politbureau and in the Central Committee, was not enjoying a very encouraging success. The incident showed what the party would be without Stalin. Not a few people had regarded Uglanov as the coming man. Those few days were the end of him. In December the expulsion of the Opposition of the Left ensued without any difficulties.

In this case too, at a time when Stalin had reached the summit of his power, he followed his old tactics. We see him avoid letting his conflict with the party come to a head, yield apparently, gather his forces, again lead them forward and—win!

In spite of all his successes, Stalin could not possibly have been cherishing any illusions as to the extent and intensity of his personal unpopularity, as to the general and growing doubt of his right to impose his will on everybody, and, above all, as to the soundness of his practical policy, a corollary to his fundamental conviction that the economic welfare of the country must be subordinated to the exigencies of power (which is shown most clearly by his agricultural policy). This man who strides restlessly back and forth in his office as he listens to his visitors (who usually come all a-tremble into his presence), seldom looks at them, and then only to glare with fierce disdain—this man who derides anyone who incurs his displeasure with unprintable epithets—cannot count on sympathies. It is said that at the Politbureau of the party he always tries to speak last, avoids expressing any view of his own till he has fully grasped the tactical situation, and often gives the other fellow the impression that he agrees with him only to attack him from the rear later. Slow-moving, cautious, he more and more came to play against the men who were powerful at a given moment the men who felt they were being overshadowed by them. His choice of persons for such purposes was extraordinarily happy. It was not merely that he replaced the important Jews and Russians whom Lenin used with many Caucasians. He managed, by a process of systematic selection during these years, to develop all over the country petty bosses of a special type, individuals of his naturally quick intelligence and, like him, of ruthless self-assertion untempered by any influence of culture, men destined either to ruin Soviet Russia or else some day to give the capitalist world a real nightmare.

Let us push this characterization of his policy a little further. While progressively restricting the circle of individuals who participated in power at the top, he progressively transformed the whole public organization of the Soviet Union into the executive of the party and made the party itself the instrument of the few on top. The Politbureau, the highest executive body in the party, he made the supreme source of power as against the Council of People's

Commissars and the Central Committee. The G. P. U. had already packed these bodies with their henchmen. He did the same. He brought now this, now that, Commissariat under his personal influence: in 1928, the Commissariat on Agriculture, whose personnel, partly taken over from the Tsar's régime, had hitherto been regarded as the most "conservative;" and, in 1929, the Foreign Commissariat, as shown by the incidents with Germany, the straining of relations with Great Britain, and the form of the reply to the American Government on intervention in Manchuria. Despite the fact that, since 1921, Stalin has not held any official post, he has been busy not only personally deciding, but during the last two years personally reviewing and supervising—in addition to many other things—the whole Five Year Plan; and he has had entire personal charge of the problem of collectivization. In these connections he has so managed that all important questions are considered concurrently by the party secretariat and the public departments. In 1930 he saw fit to propose that the Central Committee should be divided into sections corresponding to the various Soviet departments. He has a private code for communicating with his subordinates in the Soviet delegations. All nominations to posts of any importance pass through the Politbureau. These are all developments which Lenin sought to avoid.

Certainly Lenin would have objected strongly to the measures taken by Stalin against the trade unions in order to render them wholly dependent on the will of the party. The trade unions had been a serious rival to the party in influencing the general trend of the economic policy and they had procured special material privileges for their members. During the past two years they have been reduced to purely technical institutions, and by the same methods which Stalin used elsewhere. Their leader, incontestably, was Tomsky. After a terrible scene in December 1928 (the explanation of which here would take us too far afield) Tomsky's fate was sealed. Nothing is more indicative of the balance of forces in Russia than the fact that his removal from office was not made public, that it took place illegally by the decision of a small group, and that many unions did not learn of it until several weeks after it had occurred.

And the party itself? As early as 1924, Trotsky tried to prevent Stalin from naming party secretaries. By the beginning of 1928 that had actually become an official arrangement. During the same year complicated proclamations were published. In connection with the question as to just how far, in view of the supremacy of the party, it was in point to speak of a "dictatorship of the proletariat," Stalin put forward the formula that the party dictated in the name of the proletariat. But there is a dictatorship over the party also—the dictatorship of the party secretaries, to whom Stalin in turn dictates. The formula of "party discipline" has proved useful again and again in this connection. Groupings and mass organizations are not tolerated. The union of the "old Bolsheviks," for example, has become meaningless. Stalin has driven its members, for the greater part, into Trotsky's camp.

All this has been taking place, it is true, under a zodiacal sign of self-hypnosis on the part of individual party members, under the sign of the "collective will" of the party, which speaks at all times, that no one else may have a chance to speak. But it has also been taking place under a sharp and uninterrupted "listening-in" on party and country, an accurate calculation of what is possible and not possible, and, further, with ever-present readiness to make detours if necessary. It has been taking place under constant warfare on the concept of party democracy. Was not Stalin obliged, in 1929, in order to deal with certain stirrings in the party, to put forward the ingenious formula of "central democracy?" Nevertheless, the concept of "party discipline" as the highest duty of a member had been playing an enormous rôle—practically, as regards the general trend of the policy, the decisive rôle.

I cannot describe in detail the last stages in the process of concentrating the power of the Politbureau in Stalin's hands, but I should like to touch upon the fate of such of his allies in the war on Trotsky as sat with him on the Politbureau—Stalin's treatment, in other words, of such prominent party members (and at the same time leaders in the Government) as Rykov, Bukharin, War Commissar Voroschilov, Tomsky, and the aged Kalinin, president of the Soviet Union.

At the moment when Trotsky's Opposition of the Left was expelled, the economic situation in Russia was the chief issue, especially the falling-off in agricultural production. Either there had to be a slowing-up in the tempo of industrialization and the available facilities supplied to the peasants; or else agriculture had to be brought to forced production by some method of socialization, so that its production could be assured independently of the willingness or unwillingness of the peasants, and the process of rapid industrialization continued as designed. Stalin chose the second course. The Five Year Plan became law during that same critical year, 1929. Its application had already begun in October 1928. The world may have observed the tremendous increase in inner worries and tensions in the economic sphere into which the Soviet Union was plunged by this decision. Looking backward now, one must say that in this phase of his policy also Stalin steered to his goal by keeping the latter as carefully concealed as possible from his collaborators. The destruction of the wealthy peasants, which had begun in earnest by July 1928, was protected from any interference on the part of the elements grouped about Rykov and Bukharin, which considered such a policy disastrous. Party resolutions had spoken against it as late as June. What was going on in the country was for months kept secret from party members in the great cities.

Nevertheless, directly after Trotsky's banishment serious personal friction arose in regard to agricultural policy among those who were then comrades in power. As early as March 1928, Kalinin said to a deserving civil employee who had been tossed into the gutter for differences of opinion in the domain of statistics, and had appealed to him for help: "My dear fellow, I am not sure I shall not be on the sidewalk myself tomorrow morning!" Rykov, Kalinin, Bukharin and even the insignificant Voroschilov felt growing around them the same creepy isolation which had spelled the finish of Trotsky and so many others. All through the year 1928, as one or another tried to assert themselves, there were bitter quarrels. In the secret meetings of the Central Committee Stalin was forced to allow his opponents to have their say. He even pretended to give in to them. In the Politbureau, however, he answered with short, sharp words, or with threats now veiled, now open; and in the mean-time, making full use of his organization, he forced things to the point he wished to arrive at. It is characteristic of him that, later on, in October 1928, he admitted with undisguised cynicism that unfortunately, by some mistake, 12 percent instead of 3 percent of the rural population had been treated as "Kulaks"—that is to say, more or less ruined. But Frumkin, who had courageously attacked him on this point, had to go. It was perfectly apparent now to everybody that Stalin had not only built up a state within a state, but also a party within a party.

In 1929, Bukharin, desperate, and in agreement with his com-rades in misfortune, wrote a letter to Kamenev, who had succeeded in getting back to Moscow from the exile into which he had been sent with Trotsky. In this highly imprudent document, Bukharin stated that the Soviet Union would be ruined by Stalin's high-handedness and his disastrous policies. He urged that Kamenev take over the leadership against Stalin in the party, the majority of which, as well as the majority of the highest Soviet councils (as Bukharin very well knew) shared his opinion of Stalin and of the consequences of his policy. This letter was "stolen" from Kamenev. The Opposition of the Right was therefore obliged precipitately to come out into the open (always within the four walls of the Kremlin, I hardly need say). A majority vote in the Politbureau that Stalin should resign was supported by a similar resolution, based on four "whereases," which carried in the Soviet Executive Committee by 16 votes to 9. About the middle of March came an answer from Stalin: he would retire! But meanwhile he had been manœuvring. He was certain at that moment that no one would dare accept his resignation. He had again eluded the grasp of his antagonists; he was again playing the bottom against the top in the party, promising, threatening, browbeating, winning. During this period he cynically went so far as to telephone Bukharin in an ef-fort to detach him from the enemy. He used the same argument he had put forward in the summer of 1928: "You and I, compared with others, are Schimborasso (Mount Everest)." Not a very coura-geous man as a rule, and standing with the stronger cohorts this time, Bukharin rang off. He had come to know his some-time partner too well!

In this proposal to Bukharin, Stalin clearly suggested the actual status of power in the Soviet Union. With or without allies, Stalin is Mount Everest. He is the dictator of dictators. Only, he prefers not to look the part. He is not Mussolini. Yet he has one trait in common with Mussolini—an extraordinary suppleness and pliancy—and he demonstrates it under a more difficult test. He has acted in full cognizance of the danger that lies in the usurpation of power by a small minority over a vast majority whose interests do not coincide with those of three million (or less) factory workers. He has not taken much stock in the myth of unity between workers and peasants, however much he may have supported the notion for propaganda purposes so long as it worked. He realized, with courageous insight, the futility of Lenin's conception of the NEP. He understood, without shirking any responsibilities, that active socialism and private initiative were incompatible in the same economic area, and he acted resolutely on the perception that the only salvation for the Soviet power lay in the ruthless socialization of the entire country, irrespective of the immediate consequences. These became very evident at once through the crisis in agriculture and through hunger in the towns. These consequences frightened his associates into desperate resistance (at the same time they evidently did not see fit to do without him). The fact that he reckoned with all these factors more accurately, more resolutely, with less disposition to compromise than his opponents and even than his some-time associates, has enabled him to achieve what he has achieved. His success is closely bound up with his perception of these factors. At the same time his success seems to be inseparably bound up with Lenin's characterization of him: "crude and narrowminded."

The same factors which have operated in the past will, in the last resort, determine the future of Sovietism. Stalin's course is not yet run, nor is that of the Soviet State assured. The test will most probably come when Stalin disappears. It is not yet settled whether his policy of centralizing all decisions in a small group can be maintained. A year ago he was constrained, as I have said, to put forward the complicated formula of "centralized democracy" as exemplified in the Soviet Union. The fact is that the Union is ruled by a dictating minority which is dictated to by another minority to which a dictator dictates. These minorities are in constant change. Their only stable nucleus so far has been Stalin. The more exclusively he has become this, the greater the danger to the situation which his energy has created. For there has been a corresponding growth in the number of people whom Stalin has used and exalted, only to ostracize and deprive of their power at the first sign of independence or resistance. It may be that in the same proportion the number of people capable of assuming responsibility has decreased.

It may be that Stalin has gradually exhausted the reserves required by his tactics. Whereas formerly Stalin allowed his opponents to vanish, he no longer dares to do so. What does the top of the party look like today? Rykov and Tomsky, who have been threatened officially with expulsion from the party if they are caught in any further "deviations," have nevertheless been retained in the Politbureau, as have Kalinin and Voroschilov. The place of Bukharin has never been filled. This is the most astonishing manifestation of Stalin's tactics. Evidently he does not dare for the moment to give the party a spectacle calculated to prove that he discards everybody who has ever been anywhere near him in power. He is afraid of another and greater test of strength, of the danger which might reside in the appearance of new and not yet discredited people in the Politbureau, whose unworthiness he would soon be called upon to demonstrate to the Central Committee, the party, and the Soviets. He prefers to be surrounded by persons so weakened in their political prestige that he can hold them down without too great difficulty, even when inside the party distrust and suspicion of the wisdom of his policy grows apace. As a matter of fact, Stalin has created a vacuum between himself and the party at large. He has reduced the Politbureau very much to a farce. Of its eight members four are altogether in his hands. Three are dependent on him. He holds the Politbureau and the Central Committee of the party as in a pair of tongs, between himself and the rank and file of the "active" portion of the party—the party bureaucracy. The majority of the party as a whole is against him, or at least has become very critical. His precipitate retreat from forced socialization of the Russian peasants has added to the doubts which already existed. But there is no substitute for Stalin! Nobody would fit into the armor he has forged for himself during recent years.

But this personal security of Stalin's hides, implicitly, a very serious question as to the permanence of his system. The whole organism of the Soviet State and of the party that controls it has been adapted to Stalin's methods. In this sense it has ceased to be self-supporting. There seems to be nobody capable of taking over his inheritance and directing the state along new lines. The men who might have done so have been eliminated from political consideration. After Stalin men will come to the front who will try to be Stalin. They will eat each other in his name and in his manner. It is characteristic that his nearest helpers, at present Molotov and Saroslavsky, are regarded as third-rate men in every respect, even by the party. The artificiality of this whole structure of power is obvious. The danger for Soviet Russia comes first of all from the top of the party—a danger of partition and decomposition; and this may happen even in Stalin's lifetime. The event depends mostly on future economic developments. Or perhaps the younger generation of Communists may hasten the end. Stalin and his ring have educated young Russia along demagogical lines—certainly they have taught them to be "crude" and "narrow-minded." These young people may demand the fulfillment of the gigantic promises of power in the country—nay, of power in Europe and in the whole world—which have been held out to them. They have been taught to believe in imminent revolution. As young people, they are terribly young and terribly eager. They are by no means certain that they could not do what older people have not dared, replace Stalin.☯

Making the Collective Man in Soviet Russia

William Henry Chamberlin

Foreign Affairs, January 1932

The individual human personality is fighting a losing battle against heavy odds in Russia today. When one hears of state planning in the Soviet Union one usually thinks of factories, steel plants, large grain farms and cotton plantations, tractors and other accessories of industrialization. What is perhaps not generally realized is that man himself is the first and most important objective of Soviet planning and that the tendency to replace man, the individual, by collective man, the product of social groups and forces, is one of the most important and interesting currents in Soviet life.

Indeed the success which has been achieved in shaping the individual and placing a definite stamp upon him is perhaps greater up to the present time than the success in standardizing types of tractors or railroad equipment. The Soviet Union has certainly gone further than any other country has ever gone in building up a gigantic mechanism of social, economic, educational and propaganda forces which tend to repress many old aspects of human personality and to remold it in the image of Marx and Lenin. Of course even the strongest individuality does not exist in a vacuum, but is modified to a greater or lesser extent by the political, economic, social and intellectual atmosphere surrounding it. In the Soviet Union the balance

WILLIAM HENRY CHAMBERLIN, for some years correspondent of the *Christian Science Monitor* in Soviet Russia; author of "Soviet Russia."

which exists elsewhere between the claims of society and the autonomy of the individual has been heavily weighted in society's favor.

From the cradle to the grave the life and thought of the Soviet citizen are mapped out for him so far as external influences can be mobilized to achieve this end. The Soviet child about the age of eight is apt to join the Young Pioneers, an organization which numbers more than four million members and is steadily growing. From the moment when young Vasya and Sonya put on the red scarf that is the distinguishing sign of the Young Pioneer a process of intensive propaganda begins, of which a part consists in giving them definite tasks to do. Thus Young Pioneers are not only taught to disbelieve religion; they are encouraged at Christmas time to go around and convert those "backward" children who may still want to have Christmas trees and celebrate the holiday in the traditional manner. When harvest time comes one is apt to answer a knock on the door and find two or three children in red scarves, asking for grain sacks which somehow never seem to be furnished in sufficient quantity through ordinary channels.

No meeting of workers or employees for the election of delegates to the Soviet is complete unless a troop of Young Pioneers marches in and, through its leader, gravely announces its "nakaz," or set of instructions for the future Soviet delegates. The "nakaz" usually includes a point about closing more churches and turning them into Pioneer clubs or schools. When a "chistka," or purge, of Soviet institutions and offices is in progress it is not uncommon for a ten-year-old Pioneer to stand up, after some preliminary coaching, and solemnly denounce some middle-aged official or professor as a bureaucrat or a saboteur.

Fairy stories and even pictures of genuine animals, accompanied by jingling rhymes, are now frowned on; and children from an early age are supposed to concentrate on the problems of the Five Year Plan. Even toys are made with a view to turning children's ideas along definite lines; the following excerpt from a symposium on the proper kind of Soviet toys is quite typical: "Show the children malignant caricatures of tsars, capitalists, policemen, priests. Show them the faces of saboteurs, bureaucrats, private traders. Show them proletarians of Europe, America, Asia and Africa. And instead of carriages and phaetons we need toys that reflect our technical revolution: cranes, machines, tractors, motorcycles, automats."

That the intensive political training of the Young Pioneers tends to make them quite different both from pre-war Russian children and from children in other countries is quite generally testified. Karl Radek recently pointed out that the authority alike of parents and of teachers is thoroughly undermined under present conditions. If parents are not communist their Young Pioneer children are apt to look on them rather condescendingly as "politically backward." Even when this issue does not arise there are other factors that make for the disintegration of normal family life: the frequency of divorce, for instance, and the absorption of many active communists in their work to such a degree that little time is left for their children. As for the teachers, few of them, especially of the older generation, are communists; and the children, as Radek observes, knowing that the Party is the highest authority in the country, cannot have full respect for a teacher who is not identified with the Party. Under these circumstances the Young Pioneer "otryad," or troop, tends to become an important force in regulating the lives of its members. The ten-year-old who is indifferent or rebellious to a rebuke by parent or teacher may be greatly affected if his comrades in the troop, in solemn imitation of their elders, bring him before a "social court," consisting of themselves, and pass a resolution condemning him for loafing, hooliganism or some violation of the rules of conduct for Young Pioneers.

Of course not all Russian children are Young Pioneers. But almost all children in Russia now attend primary school, at least for three or four years; and the present school is almost as much of a forcing-ground for the inculcation of communist ideas as the Young Pioneer organization itself. Every teacher is obligated to give anti-religious instruction, not only in the classroom but through such media as excursions to anti-religious museums and the organization of atheistic skits, plays and carnivals. Then too a good dose of the Five Year Plan is inserted into every course of study, and a bust or picture of Lenin is to be found in almost every schoolroom.

Children are politically propagandized in the schools from a very early age, even to the point of being pressed to vote approval for sentences of execution which are passed upon accused counter-revolutionaries and saboteurs.

From the Young Pioneers it is a natural upward step to membership in the Union of Communist Youth, an organization with a membership of more than four million young people between the ages of sixteen and twenty-three. Here the clay of human personality that has been given preliminary shape in the Pioneer stage is subjected to further and more vigorous psychological kneading. The khaki uniform and Sam Browne belt which Young Communists of both sexes wear are symbolic of the militantly active type of life which they are expected to lead. Not only is theoretical training in the teachings of Marx and Lenin intensified for the Young Communists; but they are given the most effective kind of propaganda, the propaganda of action, that finds expression in various ways. Sometimes groups of Young Communists, without their distinctive uniforms, will descend on a store, factory, office or public institution, take notes on any real or supposed cases of inefficiency or bureaucracy which they may discover and report their discoveries to higher authorities. This sort of informal inspection is called "a raid of the light cavalry." The Young Communist "yacheika," or local branch, is a power to be reckoned with in any higher school or university.

Young Communists are all bound to take military training; and anyone who fails to comply with this requirement is liable to expulsion from the organization. These four million fanatically ardent young people (for girls also take the military training) are a very important element in the huge trained civilian reserve which is steadily being built up for the regular Red Army. The Young Communist also has his duties on the so-called economic front. When a large new tractor plant was built at Stalingrad thousands of Young Communists were mobilized by their local organizations all over the country and sent there to work. One often reads of similar mobilizations for the "timber front" or the "coal front." Failure to comply with such an order, or unauthorized departure from the new place of work, are punishable with expulsion from the Union.

Now the passing of a large and increasing part of the Russian youth through the political school represented by the Young Pioneers and the Union of Communist Youth tends to shape, direct and repress the individual in various ways. First of all, the child from an early age is under collective or group influence. Then the whole channel of thought and action is marked out with a definitiveness and precision scarcely paralleled in any other country. There is short shrift for any kind of questioning or doubting. A Young Communist leader named Sten recently brought down a storm of criticism on his head by voicing the opinion that "every Young Communist must seriously work out all questions by his own experience and thus become convinced of the correctness of the general line of the Party." The official newspaper of the Union of Communist Youth read Sten a severe lecture and informed him that "his formula is at best the formula of a petty-bourgeois revolutionary individualist, not the formula of a Bolshevik. Sten's Young Communist is some sort of critically thinking personality, who has no concern with the collective experience of the Party." The sort of individuality that finds expression in a "critically thinking personality" is decidedly not in favor in the Soviet Union today. The human type which is wanted is a sort of gramophone which plays without a hitch the records that are placed on it.

The tremendous pressure of "obshestvennost," which might be loosely translated as organized public opinion, does not slacken when the Soviet citizen grows out of the Communist Youth age and takes up his regular work in life. True, the proportion of the adult population enrolled in the Communist Party and subject to its severe discipline is much smaller than the percentage of young people who wear the red scarf of the Young Pioneers or the khaki uniform of the Young Communist. But other agencies, such as the trade-unions, which were rather aptly described by Lenin as "schools of communism," continue the work of molding individuality and repressing it when it comes into conflict with the supposed interests of the social organism as a whole. Thus if our Soviet citizen goes to work in a factory he will be under strong pressure to join a "shock brigade," which may mean that he will be obligated to work over-time, to increase productivity without demanding higher wages, to remain at his post until the Five Year Plan is finished, even though he may hear of more attractive work elsewhere, and so on. If he is an engineer and is sent to an uncomfortable post he will have diffi-culty in declining the appointment. Some group organization, most probably his trade-union, will report and denounce him as "a deserter from the industrial front" and do its best to make him an outcast.

Moreover, it is difficult for anyone living outside of Russia to understand the tremendous machinery for the regimentation of the individual which exists when every agency of information and entertainment—the press, the radio, the drama, the motion-picture—is centrally controlled for the purpose of making people communistically minded. Compared with this gigantic state monopoly of all the main forces that contribute to the making of ideas the most elaborate schemes of governmental propaganda and private advertising in other countries seem very puny.

When the Soviet citizen picks up his newspaper, no matter which one it may be or whether it is published in Moscow, Kharkov, Tiflis or Vladivostok, and no matter whether it is printed in Russian, Ukrainian, German, Tatar or any one of the other numerous languages of the Soviet Union, he gets precisely the same picture of political and economic events, often expressed in virtually identical phraseology. The outside world is represented as writhing in the throes of a hopeless crisis, with widespread hunger and unemployment and communist revolution as the sole way of salvation, while the Soviet Union is depicted as living through an era of unprecedented prosperity, tempered perhaps by a few prosaic difficulties in such matters as supply with food and clothing, housing shortage, overcrowded trains and street-cars, all difficulties, however, of growth, which will soon be victoriously over-come by the creative energy of the proletariat under the direction of its leader, the Leninist Communist Party.

The Soviet press has a number of stock methods of suggestive reporting. Whenever a new state loan is issued (and subscriptions to such loans, while nominally free, actually are virtually compulsory for workers and employees, as a result of the social pressure which is placed on them by trade-unions) it is always "in response to the overwhelming demand of the workers." When an ardent shock brigade member, trying to speed up the other workers, is beaten or killed his assailant is almost always described as a drunkard, a hooligan and, as a final damning trait, of kulak origin. Any international dispute in which the Soviet Government may become involved or any trial of persons accused of treason or sabotage is always the occasion for a vast outpouring of very similarly worded resolutions from factories, institutions and organizations, all expressing their support of the government, their detestation of the persons on trial and pledging the signers to work harder as a response to the incident in question.

The radio, which is entirely under state or public control, broadcasts a vast amount of political agitation and economic exposition. The Soviet citizen cannot escape from the Five Year Plan by going to a new play, which in most cases will be a dramatized story of the building of some new enterprise, or by going to the motion-picture theater, where the newsreel certainly and the film quite probably will be full of excavators, cranes, pulleys and blast-furnaces. Even concerts are often accompanied by short explanatory lectures in which the class origin of the composer is analyzed and his music is discussed as reflecting both his origin, whatever it may be, and the general historical problems of his time. Amateur theatricals, of which the Russians are enormously fond, represent still another means of influencing sentiment. There are now 120,000 circles under the central direction of the so-called "Theater of Self-Activity." The members of these circles are not professional actors, but workers, employees and peasants, who put on plays and skits in the factory or village club in their spare time. The themes for these amateur plays and playlets are carefully worked out in the center and are, of course, designed to stimulate enthusiasm for Soviet policies.

So the individual personality is attacked from every side by forces which are all controlled from a common center and which are working in accordance with a prearranged plan to remake the traditional human individualist into a collective man, a citizen of the future communist society. Of course character in every country is shaped by a variety of institutions—home, school, church, books, radio, newspaper, and so on—and critics sometimes see in modern industrialism a potent and even sinister force for the standardization of tastes, habits and thoughts. But there can be no convincing analogy between the loose, jarring and sometimes conflicting influences which operate for the creation of personality in most countries and the closeknit, intense concentration of effort upon the production of a definite type of citizen which goes on today in the Soviet Union.

The idea given expression in the blunt phrase "None of your business" finds little toleration in the Soviet Union. There almost everything is almost everybody's business, as witness the numerous groups of people who go about inspecting, warning, reprimanding, purging institutions and organizations. A typical Soviet practice in this connection is the so-called "chistka," or purge, carried out periodically both among the members of the Communist Party and among employees of state institutions. The purging of a state institution is carried out under the supervision of a commission appointed by the Commissariat for Workers' and Peasants' Inspection, which is a sort of supreme state department of audit, inspection and control. The commission hears evidence from employees about the conduct and efficiency of their colleagues and holds public purges of those individuals whose behavior has given occasion for suspicion. The commission may inflict penalties ranging from complete debarment from state employment for serious offenders to dismissal from the particular post, without prejudice to future employment. So-called workers' brigades, usually recruited from the more active communists and members of the Union of Communist Youth sometimes inspect the work of libraries, hospitals, museums and other institutions. The wall newspaper which is typewritten or written out by hand and posted up in every large factory or office is also a vehicle of criticizing individuals who are accused of not fulfilling their duties.

A little incident which I recently witnessed on a Moscow street-car illustrates the difference between the Russian and the foreign attitude toward personal criticism. An American woman was getting on the car with her little daughter and a Russian work-man, who had perhaps participated in a commission which told some professor or physician how his library or hospital ought to be run, offered criticism of the way in which the child had been lifted onto the car. The American woman knew enough Russian to tell him rather tartly that it was none of his business. An expression of sheer blank and hurt incomprehension came over the Russian proletarian's face. "How? None of my business?" he stammered.

Still another important way in which old individualist ideas of possession and privacy are being designedly supplanted is seen in the architectural blueprints for the new "socialist cities" which are growing up in various parts of Russia as the building of huge new plants creates new centers of population. Some of these socialist cities, like Stalingrad and Cheliabinsk, are additions to old towns; others, like Magnitogorsk and the new town which is growing up in the neighborhood of the great hydro-electric power plant on the River Dneiper, are built almost to order. In the apartment-houses which are constructed in these cities comparatively little space is reserved for individual dwelling quarters; and the cottage type of house, designed for one or two families, is frowned on. On the other hand, lavish appropriation is made for communal buildings: common dining-rooms, mechanized laundries, clubs, reading-rooms, nurseries, kindergartens. Soviet city planners are projecting not only new houses but new people whose group in-terests will predominate over their individual interests as a direct result of the living quarters in which they will be placed.

In the field of economic enterprise the individual has received blow after blow. The big prizes which the capitalist system offers to a restricted number of people, ownership or part ownership of a bank, a railroad, a big industrial or commercial corporation, have been abolished in Russia ever since the revolution, which transferred to the state the title to the large industries, the transportation and banking systems, along with monopolistic control of foreign trade. And during recent years the smaller individual prizes which in most countries are vouchsafed to the doctor or lawyer who builds up a large practice, to the farmer who adds steadily to his acres and his stock, to the mechanic who develops into a small businessman, have been all but entirely swept away. The wages of thrift, industry and commercial shrewdness for the more prosperous peasants, the so-called kulaks, have been "liquidation as a class," *i. e.*, expulsion from their homes and confiscation of their property; and the absorption of over half the peasant homesteads into collective farms during the last two years heralds the disappearance in Russia of a world-wide bulwark of economic individualism: the independent peasant-proprietor.

"The butcher, the baker, the candlestickmaker" of the nursery rhyme, such craftsmen as shoemakers, tailors, barbers and locksmiths are also being pulled into the collectivist net. They are under strong economic pressure to give up their little separate businesses and to band together in so-called cartels, or coöperative groups, where each member receives a definite wage. Private legal practice has almost completely ceased; lawyers, as a general rule, are enrolled in associations and are assigned in rotation to such cases as arise in the courts. The same tendency is visible in medical practice, although some of the older doctors and dentists with established reputations still carry on private practice, usually combining it with work in some state hospital. The younger doctor is almost invariably a state employee, with a definite salary, attached to a hospital or assigned in rotation to treat cases which may arise in homes. A further curtailment of the economic enterprise of the individual may be seen in the regulations which, combined with social pressure, make it difficult if not impossible for a worker or employee to move from one place of employment to another without the consent of the director of his enterprise. Workers in factories are urged to sign pledges not to leave until the end of the Five Year Plan; and an engineer or specialist of any kind who leaves a post without permission may be blacklisted and barred from further employment.

Communists, of course, would contend that their present system is not merely one of restrictions and deprivations. It may be true, they say, that wealth, even very modest wealth, is not attainable for the individual under present Soviet conditions; but the specter of unemployment is also banished. While the present standard of living is low for everyone, lower in proportion for the professional classes than for manual workers, there is the hope that it will rise steadily after the first rough construction jobs of the Five Year Plan are finished. As a substitute for the acquisition of individual wealth there is an effort to find socialist stimuli for productivity in the shape of public honoring of the best "shock brigade workers" through publication of their names and pictures in the newspapers and by giving them the title of Heroes of Labor.

Moreover, it is important to bear in mind that the communists themselves realize that the time is still far off when people will give their best services merely in return for the satisfaction of benefiting the community. Curious and even paradoxical as it may seem, during the very period when the wiping out of the individual *entrepreneur* even of the smallest type—the peasant with three horses and a farm of a hundred acres, the corner barber, the trader with a small shop—has gone ahead most rigorously, the insistence upon the necessity for piecework methods of payment in state enterprises and collective farms has increased.

I recently remarked jokingly to a communist acquaintance that the whole process of liquidating the kulaks as a class would have been in vain if, under piecework methods of payment, new classes would spring up among the peasants in the collective farms ranging from those who would be relatively well-to-do as a result of earning high piecework rates to those who would be poor because they would receive little pay for slovenly and indifferent work. "Ah," he replied, "but differences of wealth in such cases will not grow out of the exploitation of one man by another. The peasant who earns more money in the collective farm will not be able to buy land and machinery and to increase his wealth by utilizing the labor of others." This reflects the present dominant communist view that original economic sin is expressed not in varying wage and salary scales and standards of living but in the use of capital by one man to employ, or in communist phraseology to exploit, others.

One last sanctuary of the individual personality, artistic creation, has recently been ruthlessly invaded in Soviet Russia. Pegasus has been firmly hitched to the chariot of the Five Year Plan. The present tendency is not to encourage free flights of individual creative fancy, but to regiment art in all its forms and to place before it definitely propagandist objectives. The contrast with the situation of a few years ago is very marked. There has always been a strict political censorship in the Soviet Union; but from 1922 until 1928 or 1929 authors and playwrights were given a fairly wide scope in their choice of themes. There was a school of so-called proletarian writers who wrote the slogans of class war, but there was also a group of "poputchiki," or "traveling companions," who often stood aloof from political and economic questions, eschewed moralizing along communist lines, and concerned themselves with problems of individual character and psychology.

Now there has been a great shift of emphasis. It is perhaps most clearly reflected in drama, where an extraordinarily high percentage of the new plays of the last two seasons conform to a rather narrow and simple pattern, something as follows. An effort is being made to build a new factory, or to step up production in one which already exists. There are difficulties in the path; some of the newly recruited workers grumble about physical hardships; a counter-revolutionary engineer usually is cast for the villain's rôle and plots sabotage. But in the end the enthusiasm of the workers, under communist leadership, sweeps all before it; the program is carried out in record time; the "internationale" blares out as the symbol of the invariably happy ending. There are probably a score of new plays which would conform to this formula with minor variations, while new Russian dramas based on historical or personal psychological themes have been extremely uncommon in the last two seasons. Even the Kamerny Theater, long a stronghold of æstheticism in dramatic art, has fallen in line with the new tendencies, and its director, Alexander Tairov, quite correctly described one of the Theater's new plays, "The Line of Fire," as "the victorious building of socialism, the industrialization of the Soviet land, the electrification of the Soviet Union, cultural revolution and socialist reconstruction of human psychology." This transformation of the Soviet theater is partly but by no means entirely explained by a tightening of the censorship, which has found perhaps its most visible expression in the banishing from the stage of the satirical comedies of Mikhail Bulgakov, whose mordant wit at its best had a suggestion of Gogol. Bulgakov disappeared from the stage just about the time, early in 1929, when the clamor for "art in the service of the Five Year Plan" became very insistent.

More important probably than the negative influence of the censorship is the direct and intensive effort to mold the temperament and forms of expression both of authors and producers. The *VAPP*, or All-Union Association of Proletarian Writers, is perhaps the most active of several organizations which are quick to pounce on any taint of heresy in a new book or play. The subordination of the autonomy of the theatrical producer to social control, and of aesthetic to political considerations, is vividly reflected in the following instructions which one of the Moscow district committees of the Communist Party gave to the communists engaged in the Vakhtangov Theater: "Decisively and consistently to turn the theater in the direction of artistic reflection of the problems of socialist construction, struggle of the proletariat for the Five Year Plan in four years, cultural revolution, problems of struggle for the mastery of technique, questions of the international struggle of the proletariat and of the defense of the Soviet Union."

The same sort of regimentation affects painters and sculptors. With the disappearance of the well-to-do private purchaser these artists have become dependent on state, trade-union and other public patronage, and many, especially of the younger painters, sculptors and engravers, are attached to institutions which pay them salaries and instruct them as to just what subjects they shall depict. Last year 347 artists were sent into industrial regions and large state and collective farms, and commissioned to paint scenes of new Soviet life. Employing the economic phraseology is habitual in Russia in discussing literature, art and drama, the newspaper *Soviet Art* complains that "the artists did not receive from their organizations definite production assignments," with the result that "we had unsatisfactory production." The *Rabis*, the artists' trade-union, has now decreed that "the sending of artists must be carried out in strict accordance with production plans, and every artist must receive a definite concrete assignment as regards production and theme, linked up with proposed exhibitions, as for instance, 'For the strengthening of the defensive capacity of the Soviet Union,' 'The Storm of the Second Five Year Plan,' etc." It would not seem that under this system much scope is left for caprices of the artistic temperament.

"Art organizes thought. And, as it formerly served the priesthood, the feudal classes and the bourgeoisie, so in the Soviet Union it must serve the proletariat." This statement, made to the author by Mr. Felix Kon, head of the Arts Department of the Commissariat for Education, sums up concisely the communist view of the function of art.

A parallel process is to be observed in the field of science. There is now no toleration for the idea that science should be divorced from politics. Classes in Marxian theory and dialectic materialism are instituted for greybearded professors. There is a strong tendency to give preference to utilitarian and applied as against pure science. Quite typical of the effort to bring into the field of scientific research the element of class struggle that communists see in every branch of intellectual life was a recent decision of the Leningrad Academy of Sciences to study not "remnants of patriarchal life," but "remnants of patriarchal life as a weapon of class struggle and an obstacle to socialist construction."

The Tsarist censorship was probably the strictest in Europe. Yet it is doubtful whether anyone who reads the Russian classics— Dostoevsky, Tolstoy, Turgeniev, Gogol—would derive from them any idea that the Tsarist régime was a desirable or admirable one. On the other hand, emphasis on the desirability of the communist social order, on the necessity for struggling for its ideals, certainly permeates a considerable portion of contemporary Soviet literature. The Tsarist censorship was purely negative in its operation. So long as an author did not advocate "dangerous thoughts" he could be neutral or indifferent in his attitude toward politics. Neutrality or indifference is not enough today.

So the machinery for the forging of the new type of collective man is functioning at full speed. It includes almost every external influence that may touch or affect the development of a human personality, from the song taught to an eight-year-old Young Pioneer to the book or play or newspaper that attracts the attention of an adult man. Of course human clay is malleable in varying degrees. The most finished standardized type of collective man is perhaps the young factory worker who has grown up since the revolution and who has felt most strongly the concentrated propaganda force of the new régime. The most resistant types are probably the pre-war intellectual, who may have travelled abroad and whose world outlook was formed before the communist mechanism began to operate, and the old peasant, whose struggle with the soil and the elements has cultivated in him an incurably individualist psychology. But the new Soviet intelligentsia is, on the whole, very cocksure and dogmatic, very different from the eternally doubting Hamlet type of the pre-war Russian student; and the collective farm may be as big a factor in remolding the individualist psychology of the peasants as the Soviet factory has been in producing a new type of worker, shot through and through with new political and social ideas.❧

The Philosophic Basis of Fascism

Giovanni Gentile

Foreign Affairs, January 1928

For the Italian nation the World War was the solution of a deep spiritual crisis. They willed and fought it long before they felt and evaluated it. But they willed, fought, felt and evaluated it in a certain spirit which Italy's generals and statesmen exploited, but which also worked on them, conditioning their policies and their action. The spirit in question was not altogether clear and self-consistent. That it lacked unanimity was particularly apparent just before and again just after the war when feelings were not subject to war discipline. It was as though the Italian character were crossed by two different currents which divided it into two irreconcilable sections. One need think only of the days of Italian neutrality and of the debates that raged between Interventionists and Neutralists. The ease with which the most inconsistent ideas were pressed into service by both parties showed that the issue was not between two opposing political opinions, two conflicting concepts of history, but actually between two different temperaments, two different souls.

For one kind of person the important point was to fight the war, either on the side of Germany or against Germany: but in either event to fight the war, without regard to specific advantages—to

---

GIOVANNI GENTILE, philosopher and member of the Italian Senate; Minister of Public Instruction in the first Cabinet of Premier Mussolini, during which time he put into effect the so-called "Gentile Reform" of Italian education.

fight the war in order that at last the Italian nation, created rather by favoring conditions than by the will of its people to be a nation, might receive its test in blood, such a test as only war can bring by uniting all citizens in a single thought, a single passion, a single hope, emphasizing to each individual that all have something in common, something transcending private interests.

This was the very thing that frightened the other kind of person, the prudent man, the realist, who had a clear view of the mortal risks a young, inexperienced, badly prepared nation would be running in such a war, and who also saw—a most significant point—that, all things considered, a bargaining neutrality would surely win the country tangible rewards, as great as victorious participation itself.

The point at issue was just that: the Italian Neutralists stood for material advantages, advantages tangible, ponderable, palpable; the Interventionists stood for moral advantages, intangible, impalpable, imponderable—imponderable at least on the scales used by their antagonists. On the eve of the war these two Italian characters stood facing each other, scowling and irreconcilable—the one on the aggressive, asserting itself ever more forcefully through the various organs of public opinion; the other on the defensive, offering resistance through the Parliament which in those days still seemed to be the basic repository of State sovereignty. Civil conflict seemed inevitable in Italy, and civil war was in fact averted only because the King took advantage of one of his prerogatives and declared war against the Central Powers.

This act of the King was the first decisive step toward the solution of the crisis.

II

The crisis had ancient origins. Its roots sank deep into the inner spirit of the Italian people.

What were the creative forces of the *Risorgimento*? The "Italian people," to which some historians are now tending to attribute an important if not a decisive rôle in our struggle for national unity and independence, was hardly on the scene at all. The active agency was always an idea become a person—it was one or several determined wills which were fixed on determined goals. There can be no question that the birth of modern Italy was the work of the few. And it could not be otherwise. It is always the few who represent the self-consciousness and the will of an epoch and determine what its history shall be; for it is they who see the forces at their disposal and through those forces actuate the one truly active and productive force—their own will.

That will we find in the song of the poets and the ideas of the political writers, who know how to use a language harmonious with a universal sentiment or with a sentiment capable of becoming universal. In the case of Italy, in all our bards, philosophers and leaders, from Alfieri to Foscolo, from Leopardi to Manzoni, from Mazzini to Gioberti, we are able to pick up the threads of a new fabric, which is a new kind of thought, a new kind of soul, a new kind of Italy. This new Italy differed from the old Italy in something that was very simple but yet was of the greatest importance: this new Italy took life seriously, while the old one did not. People in every age had dreamed of an Italy and talked of an Italy. The notion of Italy had been sung in all kinds of music, propounded in all kinds of philosophy. But it was always an Italy that existed in the brain of some scholar whose learning was more or less divorced from reality. Now reality demands that convictions be taken seriously, that ideas become actions. Accordingly it was necessary that this Italy, which was an affair of brains only, become also an affair of hearts, become, that is, something serious, something alive. This, and no other, was the meaning of Mazzini's great slogan: "Thought and Action." It was the essence of the great revolution which he preached and which he accomplished by instilling his doctrine into the hearts of others. Not many others—a small minority! But they were numerous enough and powerful enough to raise the question where it could be answered—in Italian public opinion (taken in conjunction with the political situation prevailing in the rest of Europe). They were able to establish the doctrine that life is not a game, but a mission; that, therefore, the individual has a law and a purpose in obedience to which and in fulfillment of which he alone attains his true value; that, accordingly, he must make sacrifices, now of personal comfort, now of private interest, now of life itself.

No revolution ever possessed more markedly than did the Italian *Risorgimento* this characteristic of ideality, of thought preceding action. Our revolt was not concerned with the material needs of life, nor did it spring from elementary and widely diffused sentiments breaking out in popular uprisings and mass disturbances. The movements of 1847 and 1848 were demonstrations, as we would say today, of "intellectuals;" they were efforts toward a goal on the part of a minority of patriots who were standard bearers of an ideal and were driving governments and peoples toward its attainment. Idealism— understood as faith in the advent of an ideal reality, as a manner of conceiving life not as fixed within the limits of existing fact, but as incessant progress and transformation toward the level of a higher law which controls men with the very force of the idea—was the sum and substance of Mazzini's teaching; and it supplied the most conspicuous characteristic of our great Italian revolution. In this sense all the patriots who worked for the foundation of the new kingdom were Mazzinians—Gioberti, Cavour, Victor Emmanuel, Garibaldi. To be sure, our writers of the first rank, such as Manzoni and Rosmini, had no historical connection with Mazzini; but they had the same general tendency as Mazzini. Working along diverging lines, they all came together on the essential point: that true life is not the life which is, but also the life which ought to be. It was a conviction essentially religious in character, essentially anti-materialistic.

III

This religious and idealistic manner of looking at life, so characteristic of the *Risorgimento*, prevails even beyond the heroic age of the revolution and the establishment of the Kingdom. It survives down through Ricasoli, Lanza, Sella and Minghetti, down, that is, to the occupation of Rome and the systemization of our national finances. The parliamentary overturn of 1876, indeed, marks not the end, but rather an interruption, on the road that Italy had been following since the beginning of the century. The outlook then changed, and not by the capriciousness or weakness of men, but by a necessity of history which it would be idiotic in our day to deplore. At that time the fall of the Right, which had ruled continuously between 1861 and 1876, seemed to most people the real conquest of freedom.

To be sure the Right cannot be accused of too great scruple in respecting the liberties guaranteed by our Constitution; but the real truth was that the Right conceived liberty in a sense directly opposite to the notions of the Left. The Left moved from the individual to the State: the Right moved from the State to the individual. The men of the Left thought of "the people" as merely the agglomerate of the citizens composing it. They therefore made the individual the center and the point of departure of all the rights and prerogatives which a régime of freedom was bound to respect.

The men of the Right, on the contrary, were firmly set in the notion that no freedom can be conceived except within the State, that freedom can have no important content apart from a solid régime of law indisputably sovereign over the activities and the interests of individuals. For the Right there could be no individual freedom not reconcilable with the authority of the State. In their eyes the general interest was always paramount over private interests. The law, therefore, should have absolute efficacy and embrace the whole life of the people.

This conception of the Right was evidently sound; but it involved great dangers when applied without regard to the motives which provoked it. Unless we are careful, too much law leads to stasis and therefore to the annihilation of the life which it is the State's function to regulate but which the State cannot suppress. The State may easily become a form indifferent to its content— something extraneous to the substance it would regulate. If the law comes upon the individual from without, if the individual is not absorbed in the life of the State, the individual feels the law and the State as limitations on his activity, as chains which will eventually strangle him unless he can break them down.

This was just the feeling of the men of '76. The country needed a breath of air. Its moral, economic, and social forces demanded the

right to develop without interference from a law which took no account of them. This was the historical reason for the overturn of that
year; and with the transference of power from Right to Left begins
the period of growth and development in our nation: economic
growth in industry, commerce, railroads, agriculture; intellectual
growth in science, education. The nation had received its form
from above. It had now to struggle to its new level, giving to a State
which already had its constitution, its administrative and political
organization, its army and its finance, a living content of forces
springing from individual initiative prompted by interests which
the *Risorgimento*, absorbed in its great ideals, had either neglected
or altogether disregarded.

The accomplishment of this constitutes the credit side of the
balance sheet of King Humbert I. It was the error of King Humbert's
greatest minister, Francesco Crispi, not to have understood his
age. Crispi strove vigorously to restore the authority and the prestige
of the State as against an individualism gone rampant, to reassert
religious ideals as against triumphant materialism. He fell, therefore, before the assaults of so-called democracy.

Crispi was wrong. That was not the moment for re-hoisting the
time-honored banner of idealism. At that time there could be no
talk of wars, of national dignity, of competition with the Great
Powers; no talk of setting limits to personal liberties in the interests
of the abstract entity called "State." The word "God," which Crispi
sometimes used, was singularly out of place. It was a question rather
of bringing the popular classes to prosperity, self-consciousness,
participation in political life. Campaigns against illiteracy, all kinds
of social legislation, the elimination of the clergy from the public
schools, which must be secular and anti-clerical! During this period
Freemasonry became solidly established in the bureaucracy, the
army, the judiciary. The central power of the State was weakened
and made subservient to the fleeting variations of popular will as
reflected in a suffrage absolved from all control from above. The
growth of big industry favored the rise of a socialism of Marxian
stamp as a new kind of moral and political education for our proletariat. The conception of humanity was not indeed lost from view:

but such moral restraints as were placed on the free individual were all based on the feeling that each man must instinctively seek his own well-being and defend it. This was the very conception which Mazzini had fought in socialism, though he rightly saw that it was not peculiar to socialism alone, but belonged to any political theory, whether liberal, democratic, or anti-socialistic, which urges men toward the exaction of rights rather than to the fulfillment of duties.

From 1876 till the Great War, accordingly, we had an Italy that was materialistic and anti-Mazzinian, though an Italy far superior to the Italy of and before Mazzini's time. All our culture, whether in the natural or the moral sciences, in letters or in the arts, was dominated by a crude positivism, which conceived of the reality in which we live as something given, something ready-made, and which therefore limits and conditions human activity quite apart from so-called arbitrary and illusory demands of morality. Everybody wanted "facts," "positive facts." Everybody laughed at "metaphysical dreams," at impalpable realities. The truth was there before the eyes of men. They had only to open their eyes to see it. The Beautiful itself could only be the mirror of the Truth present before us in Nature. Patriotism, like all the other virtues based on a religious attitude of mind, and which can be mentioned only when people have the courage to talk in earnest, became a rhetorical theme on which it was rather bad taste to touch.

This period, which anyone born during the last half of the past century can well remember, might be called the demo-socialistic phase of the modern Italian State. It was the period which elaborated the characteristically democratic attitude of mind on a basis of personal freedom, and which resulted in the establishment of socialism as the primary and controlling force in the State. It was a period of growth and of prosperity during which the moral forces developed during the *Risorgimento* were crowded into the background or off the stage.

IV

But toward the end of the Nineteenth Century and in the first years of the Twentieth a vigorous spirit of reaction began to manifest itself in the young men of Italy against the preceding generation's ideas in politics, literature, science and philosophy. It was as though they were weary of the prosaic bourgeois life which they had inherited from their fathers and were eager to return to the lofty moral enthusiasms of their grandfathers. Rosmini and Gioberti had been long forgotten. They were now exhumed, read, discussed. As for Mazzini, an edition of his writings was financed by the State itself. Vico, the great Vico, a formidable preacher of idealistic philosophy and a great anti-Cartesian and anti-rationalist, became the object of a new cult.

Positivism began forthwith to be attacked by neo-idealism. Materialistic approaches to the study of literature and art were refuted and discredited. Within the Church itself modernism came to rouse the Italian clergy to the need of a deeper and more modern culture. Even socialism was brought under the philosophical probe and criticized like other doctrines for its weaknesses and errors; and when, in France, George Sorel went beyond the fallacies of the materialistic theories of the Marxist social-democracy to his theory of syndicalism, our young Italian socialists turned to him. In Sorel's ideas they saw two things: first, the end of a hypocritical "collaborationism" which betrayed both proletariat and nation; and second, faith in a moral and ideal reality for which it was the individual's duty to sacrifice himself, and to defend which, even violence was justified. The anti-parliamentarian spirit and the moral spirit of syndicalism brought Italian socialists back within the Mazzinian orbit.

Of great importance, too, was nationalism, a new movement then just coming to the fore. Our Italian nationalism was less literary and more political in character than the similar movement in France, because with us it was attached to the old historic Right which had a long political tradition. The new nationalism differed from the old Right in the stress it laid on the idea of "nation;" but it was at one with the Right in regarding the State as the necessary premise to the individual rights and values. It was the special achievement of nationalism to rekindle faith in the nation in Italian hearts, to arouse the country against parliamentary socialism, and to lead an open attack on Freemasonry, before which the Italian bourgeoisie was terrifiedly prostrating itself. Syndicalists, nationalists, idealists succeeded, between them, in bringing the great majority of Italian youth back to the spirit of Mazzini.

Official, legal, parliamentary Italy, the Italy that was anti-Mazzinian and anti-idealistic, stood against all this, finding its leader in a man of unfailing political intuition, and master as well of the political mechanism of the country, a man skeptical of all high-sounding words, impatient of complicated concepts, ironical, cold, hard-headed, practical—what Mazzini would have called a "shrewd materialist." In the persons, indeed, of Mazzini and Giolitti, we may find a picture of the two aspects of prewar Italy, of that irreconcilable duality which paralyzed the vitality of the country and which the Great War was to solve.

v

The effect of the war seemed at first to be quite in an opposite sense—to mark the beginning of a general *débâcle* of the Italian State and of the moral forces that must underlie any State. If entrance into the war had been a triumph of ideal Italy over materialistic Italy, the advent of peace seemed to give ample justification to the Neutralists who had represented the latter. After the Armistice our Allies turned their backs upon us. Our victory assumed all the aspects of a defeat. A defeatist psychology, as they say, took possession of the Italian people and expressed itself in hatred of the war, of those responsible for the war, even of our army which had won our war. An anarchical spirit of dissolution rose against all authority. The ganglia of our economic life seemed struck with mortal disease. Labor ran riot in strike after strike. The very bureaucracy seemed to align itself against the State. The measure of our spiritual dispersion was the return to power of Giolitti—the execrated Neutralist—who for five years had been held up as the exponent of an Italy which had died with the war.

—But, curiously enough, it was under Giolitti that things suddenly changed in aspect, that against the Giolittian State a new State arose. Our soldiers, our genuine soldiers, men who had willed our war and fought it in full consciousness of what they were doing, had the good fortune to find as their leader a man who could express in words things that were in all their hearts and who could make those words audible above the tumult.

Mussolini had left Italian socialism in 1915 in order to be a more faithful interpreter of "the Italian People" (the name he chose for his new paper). He was one of those who saw the necessity of our war, one of those mainly responsible for our entering the war. Already as a socialist he had fought Freemasonry; and, drawing his inspiration from Sorel's syndicalism, he had assailed the parliamentary corruption of Reformist Socialism with the idealistic postulates of revolution and violence. Then, later, on leaving the party and in defending the cause of intervention, he had come to oppose the illusory fancies of proletarian internationalism with an assertion of the infrangible integrity, not only moral but economic as well, of the national organism, affirming therefore the sanctity of country for the working classes as for other classes. Mussolini was a Mazzinian of that pure-blooded breed which Mazzini seemed somehow always to find in the province of Romagna. First by instinct, later by reflection, Mussolini had come to despise the futility of the socialists who kept preaching a revolution which they had neither the power nor the will to bring to pass even under the most favorable circumstances. More keenly than anyone else he had come to feel the necessity of a State which would be a State, of a law which would be respected as law, of an authority capable of exacting obedience but at the same time able to give indisputable evidence of its worthiness so to act. It seemed incredible to Mussolini that a country capable of fighting and winning such a war as Italy had fought and won should be thrown into disorder and held at the mercy of a handful of faithless politicians.

When Mussolini founded his Fasci in Milan in March, 1919, the movement toward dissolution and negation that featured the post-war period in Italy had virtually ceased. The Fasci made their appeal to Italians who, in spite of the disappointments of the peace, continued to believe in the war, and who, in order to validate the victory which was the proof of the war's value, were bent on recovering for Italy that control over her own destinies which

could come only through a restoration of discipline and a reorga-
nization of social and political forces. From the first, the Fascist
Party was not one of believers but of action. What it needed was
not a platform of principles, but an idea which would indicate a
goal and a road by which the goal could be reached.

The four years between 1919 and 1923 inclusive were characterized by the development of the Fascist revolution through the
action of "the squads." The Fascist "squads" were really the force
of a State not yet born but on the way to being. In its first period,
Fascist "squadrism" transgressed the law of the old régime because
it was determined to suppress that régime as incompatible with
the national State to which Fascism was aspiring. The March on
Rome was not the beginning, it was the end of that phase of the
revolution; because, with Mussolini's advent to power, Fascism
entered the sphere of legality. After October 28, 1922, Fascism was
no longer at war with the State; it *was* the State, looking about for
the organization which would realize Fascism as a concept of State.
Fascism already had control of all the instruments necessary for
the upbuilding of a new State. The Italy of Giolitti had been
superseded, at least so far as militant politics were concerned.
Between Giolitti's Italy and the new Italy there flowed, as an
imaginative orator once said in the Chamber, "a torrent of blood"
that would prevent any return to the past. The century-old crisis
had been solved. The war at last had begun to bear fruit for Italy.

VI

Now to understand the distinctive essence of Fascism, nothing is
more instructive than a comparison of it with the point of view of
Mazzini to which I have so often referred.

Mazzini did have a political conception, but his politic was a
sort of integral politic, which cannot be so sharply distinguished
from morals, religion, and ideas of life as a whole, as to be considered apart from these other fundamental interests of the human
spirit. If one tries to separate what is purely political from his religious beliefs, his ethical consciousness and his metaphysical con-

cepts, it becomes impossible to understand the vast influence which his credo and his propaganda exerted. Unless we assume the unity of the whole man, we arrive not at the clarification but at the destruction of those ideas of his which proved so powerful.

In the definition of Fascism, the first point to grasp is the comprehensive, or as Fascists say, the "totalitarian" scope of its doctrine, which concerns itself not only with political organization and political tendency, but with the whole will and thought and feeling of the nation.

There is a second and equally important point. Fascism is not a philosophy. Much less is it a religion. It is not even a political theory which may be stated in a series of formulæ. The significance of Fascism is not to be grasped in the special theses which it from time to time assumes. When on occasion it has announced a program, a goal, a concept to be realized in action, Fascism has not hesitated to abandon them when in practice these were found to be inadequate or inconsistent with the principle of Fascism. Fascism has never been willing to compromise its future. Mussolini has boasted that he is a *tempista*, that his real pride is in "good timing." He makes decisions and acts on them at the precise moment when all the conditions and considerations which make them feasible and opportune are properly matured. This is a way of saying that Fascism returns to the most rigorous meaning of Mazzini's "Thought and Action," whereby the two terms are so perfectly coincident that no thought has value which is not already expressed in action. The real "views" of the *Duce* are those which he formulates and executes at one and the same time.

Is Fascism therefore "anti-intellectual," as has been so often charged? It is eminently anti-intellectual, eminently Mazzinian, that is, if by intellectualism we mean the divorce of thought from action, of knowledge from life, of brain from heart, of theory from practice. Fascism is hostile to all Utopian systems which are destined never to face the test of reality. It is hostile to all science and all philosophy which remain matters of mere fancy or intelligence. It is not that Fascism denies value to culture, to the higher intellectual pursuits by which thought is invigorated as a source of action. Fascist anti-intellectualism holds in scorn a product peculiarly typical of the educated classes in Italy: the *leterato*—the man who plays with knowledge and with thought without any sense of responsibility for the practical world. It is hostile not so much to culture as to bad culture, the culture which does not educate, which does not make men, but rather creates pedants and aesthetes, egotists in a word, men morally and politically indifferent. It has no use, for instance, for the man who is "above the conflict" when his country or its important interests are at stake.

By virtue of its repugnance for "intellectualism," Fascism prefers not to waste time constructing abstract theories about itself. But when we say that it is not a system or a doctrine we must not conclude that it is a blind praxis or a purely instinctive method. If by system or philosophy we mean a living thought, a principle of universal character daily revealing its inner fertility and significance, then Fascism is a perfect system, with a solidly established foundation and with a rigorous logic in its development; and all who feel the truth and the vitality of the principle work day by day for its development, now doing, now undoing, now going forward, now retracing their steps, according as the things they do prove to be in harmony with the principle or to deviate from it.

And we come finally to a third point.

The Fascist system is not a political system, but it has its center of gravity in politics. Fascism came into being to meet serious problems of politics in post-war Italy. And it presents itself as a political method. But in confronting and solving political problems it is carried by its very nature, that is to say by its method, to consider moral, religious, and philosophical questions and to unfold and demonstrate the comprehensive totalitarian character peculiar to it. It is only after we have grasped the political character of the Fascist principle that we are able adequately to appreciate the deeper concept of life which underlies that principle and from which the principle springs. The political doctrine of Fascism is not the whole of Fascism. It is rather its more prominent aspect and in general its most interesting one.

VII

The politic of Fascism revolves wholly about the concept of the national State; and accordingly it has points of contact with nationalist doctrines, along with distinctions from the latter which it is important to bear in mind.

Both Fascism and nationalism regard the State as the foundation of all rights and the source of all values in the individuals composing it. For the one as for the other the State is not a consequence—it is a principle. But in the case of nationalism, the relation which individualistic liberalism, and for that matter socialism also, assumed between individual and State is inverted. Since the State is a principle, the individual becomes a consequence—he is something which finds an antecedent in the State: the State limits him and determines his manner of existence, restricting his freedom, binding him to a piece of ground whereon he was born, whereon he must live and will die. In the case of Fascism, State and individual are one and the same things, or rather, they are inseparable terms of a necessary synthesis.

Nationalism, in fact, founds the State on the concept of nation, the nation being an entity which transcends the will and the life of the individual because it is conceived as objectively existing apart from the consciousness of individuals, existing even if the individual does nothing to bring it into being. For the nationalist, the nation exists not by virtue of the citizen's will, but as datum, a fact, of nature.

For Fascism, on the contrary, the State is a wholly spiritual creation. It is a national State, because, from the Fascist point of view, the nation itself is a creation of the mind and is not a material presupposition, is not a datum of nature. The nation, says the Fascist, is never really made; neither, therefore, can the State attain an absolute form, since it is merely the nation in the latter's concrete, political manifestation. For the Fascist, the State is always *in fieri*. It is in our hands, wholly; whence our very serious responsibility towards it.

But this State of the Fascists which is created by the consciousness and the will of the citizen, and is not a force descending on the citizen from above or from without, cannot have toward the mass of the population the relationship which was presumed by nationalism.

Nationalism identified State with Nation, and made of the nation an entity preëxisting, which needed not to be created but merely to be recognized or known. The nationalists, therefore, required a ruling class of an intellectual character, which was conscious of the nation and could understand, appreciate and exalt it. The authority of the State, furthermore, was not a product but a presupposition. It could not depend on the people—rather the people depended on the State and on the State's authority as the source of the life which they lived and apart from which they could not live. The nationalistic State was, therefore, an aristocratic State, enforcing itself upon the masses through the power conferred upon it by its origins.

The Fascist State, on the contrary, is a people's state, and, as such, the democratic State *par excellence*. The relationship between State and citizen (not this or that citizen, but all citizens) is accordingly so intimate that the State exists only as, and in so far as, the citizen causes it to exist. Its formation therefore is the formation of a consciousness of it in individuals, in the masses. Hence the need of the Party, and of all the instruments of propaganda and education which Fascism uses to make the thought and will of the *Duce* the thought and will of the masses. Hence the enormous task which Fascism sets itself in trying to bring the whole mass of the people, beginning with the little children, inside the fold of the Party.

On the popular character of the Fascist State likewise depends its greatest social and constitutional reform—the foundation of the Corporations of Syndicates. In this reform Fascism took over from syndicalism the notion of the moral and educational function of the syndicate. But the Corporations of Syndicates were necessary in order to reduce the syndicates to State discipline and make them an expression of the State's organism from within. The Corporation of Syndicates are a device through which the Fascist State goes looking for the individual in order to create itself through the individual's will. But the individual it seeks is not the abstract political individual whom the old liberalism took for granted. He is the only individual who can ever be found, the individual who exists as a specialized productive force, and who, by the fact of his specialization, is brought to unite with other individuals of his same category and comes to belong with them to the one great economic unit which is none other than the nation.

This great reform is already well under way. Toward it nationalism, syndicalism, and even liberalism itself, were already tending in the past. For even liberalism was beginning to criticize the older forms of political representation, seeking some system of organic representation which would correspond to the structural reality of the State.

The Fascist conception of liberty merits passing notice. The *Duce* of Fascism once chose to discuss the theme of "Force or Consent?;" and he concluded that the two terms are inseparable, that the one implies the other and cannot exist apart from the other; that, in other words, the authority of the State and the freedom of the citizen constitute a continuous circle wherein authority presupposes liberty and liberty authority. For freedom can exist only within the State, and the State means authority. But the State is not an entity hovering in the air over the heads of its citizens. It is one with the personality of the citizen. Fascism, indeed, envisages the contrast not as between liberty and authority, but as between a true, a concrete liberty which exists, and an abstract, illusory liberty which cannot exist.

Liberalism broke the circle above referred to, setting the individual against the State and liberty against authority. What the liberal desired was liberty as against the State, a liberty which was a limitation of the State; though the liberal had to resign himself, as the lesser of the evils, to a State which was a limitation on liberty. The absurdities inherent in the liberal concept of freedom were apparent to liberals themselves early in the Nineteenth Century. It is no merit of Fascism to have again indicated them. Fascism has its own solution of the paradox of liberty and authority. The authority of the State is absolute. It does not compromise, it does not bargain, it does not surrender any portion of its field to other moral or religious principles which may interfere with the individual conscience. But on the other hand, the State becomes a reality only in the consciousness of its individuals. And the Fascist corporative State supplies a representative system more sincere and more in touch with realities than any other previously devised and is therefore freer than the old liberal State.✿

Radical Forces in Germany

Erich Koch-Weser

Foreign Affairs, April 1931

Economic depression and political radicalism go hand in hand. When economic distress reaches a certain point, the individual citizen no longer uses his political power to serve the public weal, but only to help himself. His ideal of political liberty pales before his ideal of economic equality.

Once this sentiment has eaten its way into the hearts of the majority of a nation, any political system is doomed to failure. It is useless to tell the embittered masses that their political and economic rulers are not responsible for their misfortunes. It is equally useless to point out to them that a revolution with its attendant disorders would not improve their situation, but would hopelessly compromise it. The world is not ruled by reason, but by passion, and when a man is driven to despair he is ready to smash everything in the vague hope that a better world may arise out of the ruins.

Intelligent and orderly as the German people are, patiently as they have borne the sufferings of war and of inflation, they are in danger today of falling into this reckless state of mind. It would seem that the economic crisis, the reduction of large classes of the German population to the level of the proletariat, and the unemployment of nearly five million persons, cannot go on for many more years without ruining the German nation as a whole. Here is a population, well-equipped from the point of view of health and intellect, which in general is forced to be satisfied with an income barely sufficient for a minimum existence. One-eighth

ERIC KOCH-WESER, former Minister of Justice of the German Republic, recently leader of the Democratic Party.

of those who are able and eager to work are unable to find any opportunity to do so. And those who are employed see no possibility of little by little rising to positions where their abilities will have fuller scope. Above all—and this is perhaps the worst aspect of the situation—not only are great numbers of persons forced to abandon any hope of advancement themselves but they must also relinquish the idea of giving their children an adequate education and thus opening up a way for them to better their situation. About 30 percent of the German people have received an education higher than that acquired in the ordinary public schools. But only about 12 percent of all positions available in Germany are of a nature to require this higher education or make it advisable. Thus vast sections of the people feel oppressed and bitterly discontented.

The consequence is a pronounced and inclusive dissatisfaction with the prevailing economic system. All the blame for every ill is laid on the shoulders of the capitalistic system, despite the fact that it has been hampered and weakened to a considerable degree by governmental interference. The number of people who feel confident that they can get on by their own abilities is steadily declining. You will recall the saying that Napoleon's soldiers were inspired by the belief that each of them carried a marshal's baton in his knapsack. Perhaps this was not really the case. But certainly it is one of the secrets of success of any efficient régime not to allow the feelings of self-reliance and self-help which exist in a nation to go to waste. America has managed things better in this respect than have the nations of the old world. In Germany, the self-made man is no longer the ideal of the people. This marks the end of the "bourgeois" way of thinking in the best sense of that word. The number of those who are beginning to think in terms of socialism is increasing. The adherents of the middle parties, who oppose this development, are dwindling in the same proportion that the number of independent, progressive and self-reliant citizens is being diminished through the increasing pauperization.

Of the non-bourgeois parties, the Social Democratic Party, notwithstanding its general socialistic attitude, is the one that cares least about remodeling the state in the socialistic sense. This is not so strange as it sounds. This party, which is still by far the strongest political group in Germany, consists of brain and manual workers, employees, foremen, small officials and peasants. It is proletarian in name, but actually the individuals who compose it have attained a greater degree of lower-middle-class security than have many of those in the ranks of the old bourgeoisie. This is partly the result of extensive social legislation, but in the main it is due to the protection offered by the trade-unionist organization. In these times of economic distress it has been unable to hold its own in open economic strife with the capitalists, but thanks to its power at the polls it nevertheless has been almost completely successful in averting the reductions of wages which would otherwise have accompanied increasing unemployment.

In consequence, this whole social group has become as conservative as any other class which has something to lose. Their economic and political phraseology is radical, but as a matter of fact they are concerned to preserve the present economic order because they see that their own existence and that of their children is tied up with it. Radical as this party is apt to be when there is a question of limiting capitalistic profits, it nevertheless turns resolutely away from any sort of revolutionary violence which would ruin the basis of their livelihood. For the time being, then, it is almost completely absorbed in the ungrateful but historically significant task of keeping alive, in wide circles of the population, a sense of order and an appreciation of the value of the state. Nor does it allow itself to be diverted from this attitude by the evidences of unfounded or exaggerated dislike which many well-to-do and well-educated citizens frequently exhibit against it. It has in the end become a party standing for the preservation of the state.

The attitude of the Communist Party is totally different. It constitutes a reservoir for all those proletarians who—either without fault or by their own fault—have failed to find suitable employment or adequate wages. Of the great altruistic idea of communism there is not a trace to be found in this party. The watchword is not the Christian one, "What is mine shall be thine," but rather one of envy, "What is thine shall be mine." The blind submission shown by the leaders of the party towards edicts issued by Soviet Russia increases its danger to Germany, as does also their financial dependence on Moscow. But—leaving out of account some disgruntled writers who are not in touch with world currents—the party members are recruited from the lower strata of the working classes. Unless the distress among the German people should become insupportable, any sudden advance movement on their part that relied on force would be doomed to failure without armed support and assistance from outside.

Greater danger is threatening at the present time from the National Socialists, popularly called the Nazis. This movement comprises the large ranks of the disinherited and the *déclassés*— middle-class citizens, officials, officers and landowners. All of these deserve our sympathy and pity. Enormous numbers of them have been uprooted from a satisfactory social position by war, revolution and inflation, and thrust out to seek an uncertain and penurious existence. In supporting and voting for the National Socialist Party they are generally influenced to only an inconsiderable degree by its rhetoric. For Germany's foreign policy in its main features is compulsory, not a matter of conviction, but of diplomatic and geographic fate. The success of the party lies principally in the fact that those who belong to it despair of ever again being able to win a substantial share of the goods of this world or to secure a higher post than the one they fill today.

The National Socialist Party offers the advantage that one may indulge in cheap socialism, or rather in a socialism of envy, without having at the same time to forego class-consciousness or a sense of superiority over the proletariat. Both the membership and the political aims of the party show extraordinary variations. Some of its members condemn the present Republic on account of its ruthlessness in breaking loose from the old traditions of the German people. Others blame it for being lukewarm about the necessity for a new social order. That is why nobody knows exactly what their "third empire" would be like. They call themselves socialists, and probably really mean to be. But they use the word

"Marxists" as a term of opprobrium and reserve it for their adversaries. Their "socialism" is hatred of capitalism; their "Marxism" is hatred of social democracy. Whether this party will ever make up its mind to take the leap and try an assault upon the Republic is extremely doubtful. And after all, it comprises at present not more than one-fifth of the population. Moreover, it is animated by a club or fraternity spirit more than by the sort of will which resorts to revolutionary measures. But no matter whether its deeds remain undone or whether it succeeds in temporarily usurping power or a slice of power, the main danger in the long run will be that it has no goal to attain. It therefore is bound to lead the hosts of its disappointed adherents not to a victory of reason but to some sort of embittered union of forces with left-wing radicalism.

Is there any way of counteracting the dangers inherent in this whole situation? One must not forget what difficulties Germany had to overcome in her struggle for economic progress even before the war. History has no parallel to offer of the way in which, during the years 1871–1914, Germany achieved the gigantic feat of increasing her population of 40 millions to 70 millions and of providing them with tolerable conditions of existence within her same narrow frontiers. England maintains the standard of living of the English people only by means of the interest and dividends from her foreign investments, which are almost great enough to cover the cost of feeding the entire nation. The American workman has one-fourth of the raw materials of the whole world at his disposal for his work, so that, with every turn of his hand, he enriches America not only by the value of his work but also by the value of the raw materials thus turned to account. In Russia a host of slaves, consisting of 120 millions of peasants who live in a state of serfdom, with few needs and in a state of misery beyond that of the Middle Ages, is toiling for an oligarchy of 6 or 8 millions of industrial workers. Germany was unable to draw on any such resources even before the war.

Will Germany be able to continue along the line of her past achievements?

The energy and willingness of the German workman, the intelligence and enterprise of the German capitalist, the adaptability and versatility of the German merchant, the efficiency and technical training of the German man of science—these have not decreased, at least not to any considerable degree. It has been aptly said that Germany "starved herself to greatness" during the nineteenth century. She would be able to do the same thing again today if the conditions imposed on her from without were the same as they were then. But these conditions have become harder in two respects.

Germany is groaning under burdens arising out of the lost war. She has obligations at home and obligations abroad. The number of invalids, widows and orphans created by the war, all of whom have a claim to maintenance, is enormous. The cession of important territories has made it difficult for Germany to provide the needed raw materials, and the establishment of impossible frontier lines has mutilated her physical body to such an extent as to make it difficult to regulate economic exchange and the supply of goods. The fabulous reparations imposed on her people bleed her capital strength, notwithstanding that an increase in her exports has been made possible by cutting prices.

The second adverse factor is a general one, and consists in the increased isolation of the various countries of the world from one another. Germany by herself is too small to turn to account and develop the vital energies of her population. World commerce is a necessity for her. But the greater the need of the nations, the greater their dependence on coöperation in the field of international economics, the more obstinately they seem to set their mind on nationalism and protectionism. They shut themselves off from one another. Tariff walls rise higher and higher. Meanwhile emigration of the laborers and peasants for whom there is no longer room in Germany is coming to a standstill. Even German physicians, chemists, technicians and merchants, many of whom formerly put their abilities to work in different parts of the world and then brought home the fruits of their labor, are now excluded almost everywhere. Germany is thus confined to her own narrow limits, within which her people wear themselves out in fruitless competition.

From both the economic and the political point of view Germany's collapse would mark a long stage on the road leading to the decay of our modern culture. The German is easily satisfied and by nature is opposed to revolution. Only when he becomes a prey to despair does he lend his ear to agitation. With some good will, the world could prevent Germany's collapse. Germany was overwhelmed in the war because the world got the erroneous conception that she was an obstacle to the idea of democracy and liberty. Today the world ought to help Germany defend her democratic and liberal institutions by showing some understanding of her economic and political needs. In doing so, the world will be defending its own liberty and its own democratic institutions. ❧

Hitler

Phenomenon and Portent

Paul Scheffer

Foreign Affairs, April 1932

The National Socialist Party came into being in Germany eleven years ago, founded by a group of seven men. Adolf Hitler was the seventh to join. He was soon, however, "the man" in the group; and so he is today in the party numbering millions of adherents which is often designated by his name. There may be cleverer, better educated, more energetic individuals in the party than he. All the same, "the Nazis" and "Hitler's Party" are synonymous terms. The party, such as it is, exists because there has been a man like Hitler for it to gather around, a man of a definite driving force that is powerful and contagious; an electric person whose appeal is irresistible.

I have used the word party as the term readiest to hand. It is not, however, a case of Hitler's having added just one more parliamentary machine to the many—the far too many—which figure in German political life. Here is a movement nourished on a variety of social, moral and economic forces and which has hardly reached the political stage in its evolution. For this very reason Hitler's party is as intolerant as any young movement can be. It has as yet no definite program, nor as yet any definite support which it can use to bargain with other parties and measure

PAUL SCHEFFER, Washington correspondent of the *Berliner Tageblatt*, formerly correspondent in Soviet Russia, author of "Sieben Jahre Sowjet Union."

its pretensions with reference to what it can actually obtain. In a word, the Hitler movement has not yet assumed its rational physiognomy. The currents of feeling which it expresses lie deep down in German life. They have still to come to practical expression.

As always happens in such cases, there is no way of knowing whether the party can ever take on full status as a party. We do not know whether its leaders feel certain that it can. We are not even sure whether Hitler in his secret heart is free from doubts, whether, out of the inner aspirations, the chemically pure ideals, which his following shares with him—out of so much still fluid metal—he can forge a weapon of steel adapted to practical politics. We do not know whether at bottom he is a "strong man."

It is difficult for traditional democracies to picture embryonic political movements of the Hitler type in their beginnings. But no less idealistic, no less utopian, were the beginnings of the Communist movement in Russia. That movement, too, started with a few individuals of glowing convictions and extremist aims. Did not Italian Fascism likewise begin with a few persons of strong but vague aspirations—vague so far as any application of them to practical life was concerned? And did not those petty groups enlarge suddenly into big organizations? As late as 1927 the Fascist Minister of Justice, Signor Rocco, remarked to the author of this article that the theory and the general program of Fascism would have to evolve out of an actual struggle with realities; that the Fascist movement did not derive from a program, nor was it being guided by one; that the program would be supplied by the march of events. In Fascism, accordingly, the prime factor has been something altogether subjective, a driving force that does not know precisely where it is headed, but which, wherever it is, will be sure of itself. Mussolini has been a statesman and not merely a stirrer of emotions. The dynamic elements which he crystallized, he soon pressed into the service of very definite aims—and that was the case with Lenin, too. The leaders of the National Socialists in Germany admit, in thoughtful moments, that for "ten years or so" they will make mistakes, even bad ones. But the success of their Bolshevist and Fascist predecessors inclines them to view that prospect with calm. Those who consider the

Hitler movement from a detached standpoint—indifferently, maybe, or even with sympathy or hostility—should not beguile themselves with the consideration that it is "utopian," or that "it has no fixed program," or that its concrete demands are "nonsensical." In the party's present stage of development its demands are more safely to be regarded as symbols, as signboards indicating a general direction, but saying nothing as to what will be found at the end of the road. It is true, of course, that these symbols represent in large part real things, existing institutions, other facts, against which National Socialism is making radical protest. The danger lurking in the situation is therefore enormous. Irreparable havoc may be wrought in Germany if the movement grows in power without maturing correspondingly in its thought. Soviet Russia has been through just that experience—and its leaders as well. It is all the more important, therefore, to appraise the Hitler movement as the thing that it really is today, and to understand its true meaning.

Hitler is the most successful orator that Germany has ever possessed. It is a striking fact that the spoken word should be exerting such a strong influence at the present moment in German history. The Germans are a people of books, not of auditoriums. It is an interesting and a stirring experience to listen to Hitler—his bitterest enemies have often fallen under his spell. And it is very instructive to examine his audiences. The hall where he is to speak often closes its doors an hour before the meeting is scheduled to begin because it is already filled to overflowing. One always sees a clean, neatly-dressed crowd with faces that betray intellectual pursuits of one kind or another: clerks, professors, engineers, school teachers, students, civil service employees. These audiences are preoccupied, chary of words, quiet. Their faces are tense, often drawn. The only bustle in the room will come from the "hall guards," a typical product of these new times—rough young fellows—the *Sturm Abteilungen*, or "shock troops." The predominant element in the picture is what is so aptly described in Germany as the "de-classed" middle class: creatures visibly down at the heel, spiritually crushed in the struggle with everyday reality, distraught under a perpetual worry about the indispensable necessaries of life. One notes many young people among them. All in all, it is an exceedingly variegated mixture of types from the past, from the present, and one might almost say from the future of Germany: it is that famous "brew" into which Germany, once so stably articulated in her classes and callings, has dissolved during these past ten years as a result of economic disaster, unemployment and shifts in power. They are all people who have had conceptions of life, and conceptions of their personal rôles in life, with which their present situation stands in violent contrast. Often they are people who have been pushed aside, people who have not been admitted to German life under present-day conditions. The proletariat, the working man, has on the whole bettered his financial situation under the Republic; whereas the middle strata of society have had to lower their standard of living to an incredible minimum.

Even if the observer had never heard of Hitler's program he might guess what this depressing assemblage of people is waiting for. It is waiting for a gospel, a message, a Word that will release it from the pinch of want, something that will compensate for the unbearable limitations of its present mode of existence. It wants to get hold of an ideal that will guide it forth from the quagmire where it finds itself. It wants to hear an assurance that it is entitled to a place in this new world. The man who can lift these people from their depression of spirit even for the space of an hour can win them to himself and to the cause that he tells them represents the substance of "liberation." A situation for a great orator! A great situation for an orator!

Hitler's adversaries are right in charging that such an audience can easily be misused. Hitler's utterances on the subject of propaganda, both from the platform and in print, show in fact that he is willing to use any means which he judges serviceable in winning adherents to his cause. He fans the flames of hatred just as unscrupulously as he arouses the most exaggerated hopes.

However, let us keep to his audiences. What is it that stirs them? What keys can Hitler strike with such effect that he can drag millions of people whithersoever he chooses?

Fundamentally it is a question of the hard times which have settled over Germany ever since the war. Great fortunes have come into being, though they are probably more apparent than real. Meantime, statistics show that as regards the middle classes, which used to be Germany's backbone, the standard of living is far below the pre-war level. Since 1929 it has sunk to unprecedented depths. Hitler turns his guns against those people who have increased their fortunes disproportionately to the general average of wealth accumulation in Germany, and especially against the anonymous wealth of the trusts—"coupon slavery." He attacks reparations which are sapping the life-blood of Germany. All this is well known abroad.

Hitler berates "Marxism," denounces and vilifies it. In this lies a very instructive portion of his propaganda and of his fanaticism. Unquestionably it is his most emphatic theme. The people before him are Germans. Can they, as Germans, consent that a large number of their fellow-citizens, the industrial workers, should be taught that in the last analysis they are more closely bound up with the working classes in other lands than with their own countrymen who do not happen to be "proletarians?" The people who are sitting in front of Hitler have, for the most part, sunk below the standard of living of a German workingman with a job. As for some of the others, there is only a slight difference between their income and the wages of a workingman. For all that, they do not think of themselves as proletarians. That they do is one of Moscow's illusions. Quite the contrary! On that very account they insist that they prefer to live in a state that is not governed by workpeople, a state that knows no discriminations of class—not a state according to the ideals which Marx set up for his state of workingmen, where the proletariat hold the power and set the tone. On just such grounds they want to be "national." From just such feelings nationalism has taken on a new meaning and impetus, not only in Germany, but in Italy and other countries.

To the same extent these people feel strangers to the "forces of wealth." They have nothing—just as the working classes have nothing. Hence the surprising mixture of concepts apparent in the baroque expression, "National Socialism." The effects of the capitalist system also weigh down upon them. They hate "the plutocrats." Their battle cry is about what they call the "Jewish financial tyranny," an artificial scarecrow, devised *ad hoc*, and aimed at one individual or another. Propaganda requires such things.

Hitler proclaims that a German today cannot properly say "we Germans." The "we" has no meaning. Marxism says "we," but it knows a different kind of "we." And is not capitalism international, after its fashion? Germany must become one again. Germany needs to become one again in order to be "free" again. She will be "free" again when she is again respected abroad! All this, as is apparent, is held together by very simple stress on German homogeneity, on things that seem self-evident. But in the impoverished and "enslaved" Germany of the present "the program" must prevail absolutely, actively, as the highest expression of the country's life.

In this clamor for unity, for unification, there is something that is never put clearly into words but which is nevertheless playing an important part. It is a problem of German "culture." Hitler storms at the "intellectuals." He is forever crying alarm against their conception of the world. The best educated people in Germany are indifferent to the national interest—and the word for "interest"—"*belange*"—is a new German term taken over to replace the Latin word. They have an international outlook. They do not "think German."

In Germany, as everywhere else, there are great differences in degrees of popular education; but such differences have greater social significance in Germany than in other countries. They create sharper distinctions between one individual and another. Hitler is against all that. He is fighting for the right of the half-educated to their own picture of the world, to a culture which is illumined by love of country. He shouts at the university students that they are not worthy of pursuing their scholarly studies if they cannot find a common ground with the mechanic who is intent on serving his country. Hitler takes into account the reaction of the moderately educated but thinking person to the superiority of those who are highly educated, a reaction that is not without its resentments. Hitler himself is a self-educated person, a thorough-going "autodidact," and he has read in many directions. In his eyes the essential thing is not high intellectual finish, but active love of country and mutual understanding among all. Germany, with a huge intellectual proletariat, which in many cases does not come up to the older standards of education, really finds herself in an educational crisis. Hitler's idea is to give the people a common meeting ground of convictions which abolish all distinctions and in which all share. Cultural differences must yield to patriotic sentiments, not result in divisions between individuals and classes. This expresses itself in attacks on the intellectuals whom the plain man least understands.

What unites all of Hitler's listeners is a feeling of humiliation, of injured self-respect. This comes into play in many directions, economic, social, cultural. And even diplomatic! For it is a quite natural thing that all these feelings of hurt should gather and precipitate about the rôle which Germany has been playing in the world since Versailles. While, with some undulations, the international position of Germany has been improving, this relative increase in her prestige has made no great impression on the German masses. Discriminations against Germany within the world of nations have, on the other hand, been generally noticed by the plain people. By dint of careful nursing, the notion of reparations has been transmuted into the notion of "payments of tribute;" and economic distress has found in reparations an explanation that is clear and convincing to everybody. The same is true of social unrest. The people who sit before Hitler have in their minds a very clear picture of the forces that are determining their present situation, and it is not difficult to carry them on to the corollaries. Hitler can lay hold on them in their innermost sensibilities when he raises his cry for unity, promises them the "respect" of the world as the fruit of unity, and tells them that Germany can have no foreign policy—on this theme he harps in every conceivable connection—until she has made herself one. No party in Germany has a formula so simple. No party has gone to the trouble of understanding this particular class of people as Hitler has done. That is why he has succeeded in leading such an astonishing following whithersoever he will.

The foregoing will perhaps help one to understand the simple primitive impulses on which Hitler continually plays in order to draw the masses to him. One may find them understandable, and even see in them much that is constructive for the preservation of Germany. But a person may well be shocked at the expression which Hitler and his people have given to the forces which they have mobilized, and wince at the anti-Semitism and the chauvinism which he is ever stirring up with such reckless skill.

It is important here to distinguish between the propagandist aspect of the Hitler movement and its realistic political aspect. On the one side it is devoted wholly to the acquisition of power, and so drives unscrupulously ahead as all such movements do. On the other side it has to consider the exercise of power, or at least preparations for such exercise. What National Socialism, once in power, will become under the pressure of adverse conditions, under the influence of the German temperament which is by nature disinclined to extremes, is the real question—a question not answerable today, but which the student of foreign affairs must consider quite apart from watchwords of the moment.

It is evident that Hitler himself is impressed by the fact that his movement is predominantly of an emotional character and is held together by sentiment. His movement lives in opposition and on opposition. How will it act when it is called upon to deal with the tremendously difficult concrete problems which confront Germany both at home and abroad? Can the movement be carried over into practical politics?

It is striking, in this connection, that recently Hitler and his entourage have declared that members of the National Socialist Party are to occupy no public offices in "the Third Reich." In "the Third Reich," the party would be just a power station for driving the state machine. In "the Brown House" in Munich, the headquarters of the party, many specialists of varying political complexions are at work on ways and means for dealing with concrete economic problems, and other sorts of questions. Hitler, furthermore, has recently been making connections with individuals of importance in the business world. The cabinet in "the Third Reich" is to be a cabinet of experts. Inside the party, meantime, there is not a little quiet criticism of many deputies who were most unexpectedly swept into the Reichstag by the surprising triumph at the last elections. They now are not experienced, not competent, enough. They were good enough to run, but not good enough to be elected! The party leaders are well aware of all this. In Russia and Italy "the party" stands as a general directorate behind the administration, but it has also taken over high positions in the state. Hitler will have none of that. Efficiency is to be rewarded with tolerance. Even a Jewish minister of finance—the thing has actually been said—is not beyond the range of possibility. As regards anti-Semitism, there are proofs that in matters political Hitler recognizes not only the absolute, but also the relative! In practical terms, trouble will be made only for the "immigrant Jew" who has not "fitted himself in."

Little by little, too, it will be made clear to the masses standing behind Hitler that the movement cannot become active in foreign policy until it has attained its domestic goals. Hitler's emissaries went to Geneva with instructions to state to the French that Hitler "afterwards as now" will "regard a rapprochement between France and Germany as absolutely essential." That shows a point which this article set out to show: how plastic the notions of the National Socialist leadership can be. On January 26, behind closed doors but watched attentively by all the nation, Hitler made a speech before representatives of the Manufacturers' Club at Düsseldorf. The audience, made up of people who were eager for a glance at the dangerous demagogue, was in large part hostile. But he enjoyed a complete success. He was in a position to say things which worked just as effectively upon that select audience as upon the crowds of six thousand that flock to the Tennis Hall in Berlin. And that shows how elastic are the possibilities of the movement in its present stage of development. One may add, also, that it shows its political vagueness. But there is nothing vague about the millions of followers. They are formidably real; and it would hardly be sound statesmanship to ignore them.

Chancellor Brüning has had three interviews with Hitler since September 1930. The last took place in the full limelight of public attention and public curiosity. Dr. Brüning is one of the most significant statesmen that Germany has had in the last hundred years. He is no less a patriot than Hitler; and he has an iron nerve with which Hitler is far from being blessed. He has a crystal-clear picture of the German life about him. It is inconceivable that the significance of such a movement as Hitler's has escaped Dr. Brüning. The contacts with Hitler did not lead to any common understanding—on good grounds, so far as Brüning is concerned: he is responsible for the stability of a most complex Germany, a Germany that is rapidly nearing a new economic crisis and is holding her balance only with the greatest effort. National Socialism is not, as the French say, "ministrable." It has not worked itself up to the point where it can be given a diploma in politics. It is torn within by conflicting currents. It has a half-Communist wing; it is quarreling over the question of participation in parliament, and over the question of the national Presidency; its leaders are not sure of their following, nor are they in agreement among themselves— their common basis is propaganda, rather than anything else. Hitler and his associates are striving to give a body to this young and obstreperous soul. That is Hitler's problem in particular; and to such an extent that many say he is afraid to assume power.

But to get hold of the energies that are expressed in National Socialism, and to use them, is also the problem of the men who are keeping Germany alive today—business leaders, the Government, everyone, in short, who represents tradition in German achievement. The surprising triumph of National Socialism at the polls has slowly awakened the routine parties to the issue. It has revealed to them a grand political task, on the performance of which the very existence of Germany may depend.

Let us imagine that the millions of German citizens who are today following Hitler prove to be disappointed. In that case no patriotic movement could have any chance in Germany for a long time. Economic distress and social unrest would then destroy the foundations of present-day Germany. The bourgeois Germany of moderate views—and the Social Democracy must stand with that Germany—is confronted with a technical problem. It has a gasoline tank before it. The tank may explode, with disastrous effects upon the whole country. But the tank also contains riches which may be cleverly used to drive many a profitable machine. Such is the alternative which the patriotic movement, born of unprecedented conditions, sets before the German people.☯

Hitler's Reich

The First Phase

Hamilton Fish Armstrong

Foreign Affairs, July 1933

A people has disappeared. Almost every German whose name the world knew as a master of government or business in the Republic of the past fourteen years is gone. There are exceptions; but the waves are swiftly cutting the sand from beneath them, and day by day, one by one, these last specimens of another age, another folk, topple over into the Nazi sea. So completely has the Republic been wiped out that the Nazis find it difficult to believe that it ever existed, at any rate as more than a bad dream from which they were awakened by the sound of their own shouts of command, their own marching feet. To them it signifies nothing that this or that compatriot shouldered more than his share of the load in the long uphill struggle to establish Germany's prestige and means of existence in the black years after the military collapse, or that his German nationalism and patriotic devotion were, according to the lights of that day, beyond question. The measure of his right to any sort of present consideration is first of all whether or not he was a Nazi. If he was not, he is wiped out, usually even though he might now wish to swallow his past and accept Adolf Hitler's leadership.

Not merely is he wiped out, but the memory of him is wiped out. It is pretended that he never was. His name is not mentioned, even in scorn. If one asks about him, a vague answer is given: "Oh yes—but is he still alive? Maybe he is abroad. Or is he in a nursing home?"

HAMILTON FISH ARMSTRONG, Editor of *Foreign Affairs*.

This does not merely apply to Jews and Communists, fled or imprisoned or detained "for their own protection" in barbed-wire concentration camps. It applies to men like Otto Braun, leader of the great Social Democratic Party, perennial Premier of Prussia, the strong man of whom Germans used to say: "When Hindenburg dies, we have him." Ill and broken, he escaped to Switzerland the day before the election. It applies to the series of Chancellors furnished by the once-powerful Center Party, traditional provider of Chancellors; Dr. Brüning alone has managed to keep a few slender lines of communication with the present, but at a sacrifice of reputation among such of his friends as are not thorough expedientists. The generals who were talked about as embryo dictators—von Seeckt, Groener, even the powerful von Schleicher—are no more heard of or seen. It is said that when General von Schleicher leaves the confines of his country place at Glienicke two of the *Sturm Abteilung* (generally referred to as the *S.A.*) attend him. Stresemann is not merely dead, but has been dead as long as the last Pharaoh. The men who ruled Germany in these fourteen years have been swept away, out of sight, out of mind, out (according to the program of Dr. Goebbels, propagandist-in-chief) of history. Hindenburg himself is a legend, a fable. His picture is on the walls of the coffee houses, for he played his rôle for the Nazis; their need for him is finished, and to all intents and purposes he is also.

The Stahlhelm, the organization of front-line veterans, credited with having saved the country from anarchy and communism in several post-war crises, but feared by the Nazis as a possible rival to their *S.A.*, has been broken and subjected. Its second in command, Colonel Düsterberg, a few short months ago candidate for President of the Reich, but with Jewish blood in his veins, was turned out in a manner which was no less humiliating because President Hindenburg wrote him a letter of condolence. The other Stahlhelm leader, Herr Seldte, followed with the announcement that he had gone over to the Nazis and had put the organization at Hitler's orders. The rank and file, disciplined ex-soldiers, who looked upon the *S.A.* as a rabble of mercenaries and looters, were left gasping. They had not been ready to shoot when they had the chance; the chance is theirs no longer.

The Reichswehr, on which General von Schleicher counted and which as recently as last December could and would have supported him in a determined move to establish authority in the name of the flickering Republic, now stands glumly aside. Its barracks are the sole government buildings to fly only the black-white-red flag of the Reich; over all the others (except the President's residence, which has a special flag) floats the Nazi swastika. But despite this last symbol of independence, the Reichswehr knows its day for action has slipped by. All that its leaders can do is wait (as the Royal Italian Army has waited without result) to see whether there will ever come a moment of chaos when they might step in to reëstablish the state they were enlisted to serve. It is a forlorn hope.

One by one continue to fall the last possible citadels of defense against uncontradicted Nazi dictatorship.

Federal Germany is gone. The *Gleichschaltung* law disposes of the prerogatives of the separate States, and Nazi leaders have been named *Statthalter*, with power from Berlin to dismiss State governments should they not prove fully amenable. Eminent Lutheran and Reformist theologians are hastily forming a new and unified *Reichskirche* to meet the fear of the Nazis that opposition or weakness might develop in the former 28 autonomous churches in the various States, and to simplify their drive against religious organizations which are not two parts blood and iron and only one part milk of human kindness. The Socialist trade unions, already dead as a political power and presumably resigned to the abolition of the strike as a weapon in wage bargaining, were finally seized outright on May 2, the day after the celebration of the "Festival of National Labor." Their buildings were occupied by storm troops, their officers were jailed, and their funds were appropriated to the new Nazi union which is now organizing all labor as an instrument of party will. They had hoped to be allowed to continue their social insurance and banking activities for their 3,500,000 members, preserving at least their identity after fifty years of activity in German life. The answer was the raid, and the simultaneous Nazi proclamation attacking the union leaders as "Red criminals" and announcing to German labor that "Adolf Hitler is your friend, Adolf Hitler is fighting for your freedom, Adolf

Hitler will give you bread!" The smaller Catholic and other trade unions promptly "submitted themselves unconditionally and without reserve," and the agricultural organizations and coöperatives followed suit. Freemasonry has been abolished; the Grand Lodge of Prussia has abjured its origins, dissolved its ties with other Masonic lodges, and is now the exclusively Aryan "German Christian Order of Friendship."

The judiciary has been weeded over with minute care, and as a result many judges (beginning with Dr. Tigges, President of the Supreme Court of Prussia) have either resigned or been dismissed. Henceforth, says a circular of the Prussian Ministry of Justice, judges will be tested for their patriotism and social principles and will be put through periods of service in military camps to school them in "martial sports." In Nazi eyes the conception of abstract justice is outworn. The essential justice is that which serves the higher ends of the state.

Even the great Nationalist Party, co-partner with the Nazis in the March election which followed the fall of von Schleicher, and supported by all the clans of Junkers, monarchists, landed proprietors, former army officers and officials, is left hanging in the air, its toes barely touching the ground, slowly strangling in the noose of its own devising. When on the night of January 30 von Papen persuaded Hitler to join him in making the election, he thought that he had prepared the way for his own conservative forces to swallow up the Nazis. But it was the reverse which happened. Since the elections, the strength of the Nationalist Party has been sapped in every direction. Most strikingly, perhaps, has this been true in the Junker stronghold of East Prussia, where on one excuse or another (the latest Nazi method is simply to say that an unregenerate official has been recreant to his trust, but without proffering specific charges) the key men of the Nationalist Party organization have been removed from controlling places in the government and banks and agricultural organizations. Throughout the Reich, chambers of commerce and other public organizations in which Nationalist elements were strong are being "assimilated," while private associations and even important industrial organizations are experiencing the novelty of having Nazi commissars appear at board meetings, announce the expulsion of Jewish, "liberal" or otherwise undesirable members, and constitute new boards amenable to party orders.

In answer to this smashing of his strongholds, and in effect replying to frequent prophecies that he would have to resign, Dr. Hugenberg, Chairman of the Nationalist Party and Minister of Industry in the present government, began at the end of April to issue appeals, sometimes plaintive, sometimes threatening, calling on everyone to remember that he and his non-Nazi colleagues were in the cabinet by agreement with Hitler and that the Enabling Act which had put the power in Hitler's hands for four years was conditioned upon that agreement. But, in the cabinet or out, Hugenberg and his friends are condemned to becoming more and more helpless. Some non-Nazis may manage to cling to their posts for a time by adopting Nazi ways.[1] But they will be few. The smile is on the face of the bigger, more ruthless and cleverer tiger.

These new rulers of this new people have also a new vocabulary. In literature and art, in the professions and even in sport, new specifications replace taste and skill and experience. It is hard for a foreigner to learn this language. A work of art or a performance of any sort is not good unless the creator is an Aryan, preferably Teutonic to the last drop of his blood (if such a being exists), preferably a Nazi, and in any case not a liberal or a Jew. Music, the theatre, the cinema, all have been bent to Nazi propaganda aims. The universities are being "cleansed." Eminent professors who are of Jewish descent or who are known to entertain liberal ideas, as well as their colleagues who show regret at their fate or who are suspected of believing in academic freedom, are dismissed either by the government or more often simply by orders of the student committees.[2] Meanwhile their books are removed from

---

1 Cf. Vice-Chancellor von Papen's speech at Münster on May 13, glorifying the Mediæval Teutonic love of death on the battlefield. "Mothers," he said, "must exhaust themselves to give life to children. Fathers must fight on the battle-field to secure the future for their sons." And he added that Germany had struck the word pacifism from its vocabulary.

2 So far the studenthoods have not been definitely given the right to dismiss professors; but they have terrorized the university administrations by their power to turn suspicion on anyone who opposes them, and as a result of their demonstrations, boycotts and proclamations have succeeded in forcing out even the Jewish or liberal professors for whom the government had proposed making exceptions because of service at the front.

the university and public libraries and suffer the same fate in the bookshops which is now being meted out to the works of a long list of writers headed by Thomas Mann—namely, confiscation and burning, sometimes officially, sometimes by Nazi groups who cannot be held accountable for their actions with the police or in any court or in any department of the official government.3 The press has also been "assimilated," unfriendly or lukewarm or liberal or pacifist or "internationalist" or Jewish proprietors, editors and correspondents have been expelled, and Nazi commissars put at the side of the writers who remain. Attention is centered almost exclusively upon news of the revolution—texts of proclamations, speeches of leaders, accounts of mass meetings and celebrations. Everything is reported in a feverish tempo, with what seems to a foreigner no sense of proportion, with scant reference to the facts of history, and with little notice of world opinion except to abuse or jeer at it.

II

How has it been possible thus to clip short all ties with the past—with the Kaiser's Germany as well as with the Republic? Because the young people who dominate the Third Reich care absolutely nothing at all about history before the beginnings of the Nazi movement in Munich in 1919. They live exclusively in the present, except for a little private history which they have created for themselves, consisting (apart from embellished and purified records of Nazi growth) of the glorification of certain martyrs to the cause of German awakening—for example, Horst Wessel, a Nazi labor organizer murdered by communist rivals, and Schlageter, a young German patriot of uncertain antecedents who was executed in

---

3 Outside the Hochschule on Invalidenstrasse in Berlin, and on the doors of similar institutions throughout the Reich, is nailed the red proclamation of "Die Deutsche Studentenschaft" proclaiming the Jew as the enemy of German thought and culture; a Jew's book must not be printed in German characters, or if it is the title page must be inscribed "translated from the Hebrew." This follows the Nazi program announced in Munich in February 1920, where among other things was written: "No Jew . . . may be a member of the nation." It remains to be seen whether the policy will be made retroactive; the works of Heinrich Heine are said to be still on the shelves.

May 1923 after conviction by a French court-martial on charges of espionage and sabotage in the Ruhr. The rest is for them the history of the Aztecs or the Trojans. They haven't the remotest interest in the politics or program of old Imperial Germany, or in the origins of the World War, or in the military victory of the Allies, or even in the Treaty of Versailles. Those are causes; they care only about consequences. What they do know about is the 1918 "stab in the back" by the communists (or was it socialists or republicans?—the labels are practically interchangeable); the weakness and treachery of the men who came to power by "giving away" parts of the fatherland to Germany's enemies; the failure of these same republicans to throw off more rapidly the servitudes which they had tamely accepted on Germany's behalf; the sufferings and indignities undergone by the German masses while Jewish bankers trafficked in currencies and Jewish businessmen profiteered. Against the materialism of Marx they set the self-sacrifice of Schlageter. It does not count that the old German Jews were among the most thoroughly respectable, industrious and patriotic of German citizens, that they fought in the Kaiser's armies, gave lives and fortunes for their country. It does not matter that out of Germany's post-war population of some 65,000,000 only 600,000 were Jews—*less than one percent*. Marx was a Jew. He curses the whole race, and even the families into which they have married, to such an extent that super-racist circles talk of sterilizing all women in Germany who are unable to bear exclusively Teutonic offspring and of forbidding Jewish men to have intercourse with Teutonic women under pain of capital punishment.[4]

The movement may hark back in some of its aspects to the Middle Ages, and in others to the régime of Wilhelm II, but plainly in its essence it is not reactionary. It is a revolt against the

---

4 Speech of Julius Streicher, leader of the Nuremberg Nazis, chief organizer of the April 1 boycott, reported in the London Times of April 24. Similar ideas recur in Nazi speeches, and are being translated into action in a preliminary way by the "Race Offices" now being set up with the task of separating the population into two groups which may not intermarry. The present article does not discuss Nazi "atrocities," nor the fate of the various categories of "un-German" emigrés, now estimated to total between 30,000 and 50,000.

men, methods and aims of the past fourteen years. It is not a return to any old Germany as such. It is a twentieth century revolution, as radical in its implications and potentialities as the Russian Revolution, but in the Prussian manner.

It is very Prussian because the people have had the desire, the will, to subordinate themselves to leaders with imperious voices and gestures, to obey them even when violence was involved, and individually to merge themselves in the *totalitätstat*. They felt Germany ready once again to command in the world; and because they were conscious of being part of a superior force they did not individually mind being commanded. Marching, singing, smashing windows, delighted to be in uniform though usually too young to have known the war first-hand, others of them never having had a chance of steady employment since they left the army, immunized from any knowledge of all but the most recent past, without sense of proportion about the events of the present, protected from all disturbing opinion, foreign or domestic, the Nazi rank and file have swept along, accepting the symbols and slogans and ideology which all the instruments of modern mechanized propaganda have blared out at them, forgetting everything else in the exaltation of accepting their new lot. Democracy to them had become tedious, intolerable. Without allowing ourselves to be drawn into too theoretical an analysis of this collective movement, we none the less can perceive in it a strong undercurrent of the twentieth century, to some phases of which the Spanish philosopher Ortega y Gasset has drawn attention. These young Nazis are proud to be ignorant, proud to despise the skill and attainments of the specialist. Like young Soviet workers a few years ago in Russia, they also are proud to be free of the burdens of possessions, proud to be hungry. Particles of the mass which is to rule the world, they are compelled forward by some cosmic urge which their leaders as well as their enemies say frankly no foreigner can possibly understand, much less—alas!—explain.

The mentality of the Nazi leaders is mainly an intensification of the instincts and feelings of the Nazi masses. Among them, as among those whom they lead, are elements of idealism, of romanticism, of enthusiasm, of naïveté. We find here, too, the same elements seeking adventure, power, revenge and profit at the expense of competitors and rivals. One suspects as one reads the calculated statements of certain Nazi chiefs that there also must be an element of sadism, the counterpart of what in the mob is bloodthirstiness. And of course there is in all classes and groups the reaction against what the chief financial adviser of the party characterized to the writer as "wild capitalism"—speculation, the cycle of giddy profits and fearful drops, corruption, the power of money and banks. Further, what in the bands roaming the streets often is merely intolerance and bull pride of ignorance has its parallel among the intellectual leaders (who, incidentally, are not many) in an impulse to abjure reason and cool classicism, to fly from Apollo. The impulse needs no special description here, because in many countries there have been manifestations of dissatisfaction with science and with classical rules, in art as well as in social politics.

Of a remaining characteristic noted in the talk of Nazi leaders somewhat more must be said, however dangerous the ground it offers for exaggeration and error—the characteristic, namely, of twentieth century Teutonic mysticism, what might be called Wotan second-hand. The current manifestation seems to stem from Houston Stewart Chamberlain, who preached race conflict and the invincibility of the blonde Teuton hero. But the German super-man was defeated in the war. Obviously here is a contradiction. Either he is not a super-man, or there is an alibi. The alibi is furnished by the Jew, the traitor within the gates. Let him be extirpated, along with the soft liberals who helped him betray Germany, and be-hold! the Nibelungen hero will once again know how to cope with his enemies. If we take with Chamberlain's racial teachings the contempt for democracy which exudes from Spengler, carrying as it does the suggestion to exploit the masses as a means to power, we have two principal keys to Nazi mental processes. The second conception has enabled Nazi leaders to sweep rivals aside and to bind the masses—for already they are bound, though they do not yet know it, as securely as are the masses in Soviet Russia—to the chariot of self-appointed dictatorship, helpless any more to find the instruments or arms to free themselves, helpless even to cry out. The first conception will enable them, they hope, to build up a pure and whole Teutonism, ready to move invincibly forward on its appointed mission throughout the world.

III

Given these origins, is there cause for surprise in the fact that the foreign policy of the Nazis was at the start a very primitive thing indeed? On the day they came to power there were few of them from top to bottom who had ever seen a foreign land, and probably there was not one whose conception of what the world is like corresponded to reality. Striding back and forth across platforms or cooped up with microphones, forever preaching in hoarse voices or planning the strategy of violent party warfare, they had had no time to turn their eyes across the frontiers long enough to see more than lowering masses of enemy troops, clouds of aeroplanes on the horizon. Wishes and words were their facts, force their measure of success. It was not to be expected that when suddenly the responsibility for directing the foreign policy of a great nation fell on their shoulders they would adopt a less impatient or less brash method than that which had just brought them success at home.

The method became apparent in the statements of German representatives at the Disarmament Conference in April and early in May, and in the statements of Chancellor Hitler and other Nazi notables, both public and private, during the same period. Thus, in a conversation with the writer on April 27, Chancellor Hitler said that the Allies would have been more honest had they denied Germany even the 100,000 soldiers allowed by the Versailles Treaty, for they were useless as protection and simply gave Germany's neighbors an excuse to call her chauvinistic; that to allot her so inadequate a number was obviously a "swindle;" that equality of armaments was a *sine qua non* of his policy; and that he doubted whether progressive disarmament of offensive weapons by Germany's neighbors, and her own progressive rearmament, *pari passu,* with forts and other means of defense, could possibly close the gap quickly enough to satisfy German needs. The plain implications in this line of argument were given substance by Foreign Minister von Neurath on May 11, when he announced Germany's intention, regardless of the results of the Disarmament Conference, to create a military and naval air force, to arm with big guns, and to increase her man-power. Vice-Chancellor von Papen's belligerent speech at Münster two days later seemed designed to strengthen the determination of the German public to be satisfied with no other course.

But on May 11, the same day that Baron von Neurath published his interpretation of Hitler's intentions, the British Secretary of State for War, Lord Hailsham, gave expression in the House of Lords to the world's rising fear that Germany would precipitate another armaments race while the Disarmament Conference was still sitting at Geneva, and to England's determination to prevent that result. In deliberate tones he pronounced the word "sanctions." The German press had brushed aside as "French propaganda" the warning given Germany by Sir Austen Chamberlain in his speech of April 13, and the plain implications of the Rosenberg incidents during the second week in May. But this was a different matter. Moreover, Signor Mussolini, who had been not a little shocked by the universal outcry against his ally, now sent strong admonitions to him, giving notice that Italian sympathies could not be stretched to the point of engaging in a struggle against the united forces of England and France. At the same time he intimated that the Nazi persecution of the Jews had misrepresented Fascist doctrine and had been a tactical error: "You put all the Jews of the world against you," he told Hitler, "and you put against you the Christians also!" In this, Hitler's first important test in foreign affairs, he showed himself more supple than his critics expected. Seizing upon President Roosevelt's message to the world, he adroitly used it as a shield to cover his retreat. As this is being written, the world is waiting for evidence whether the speech to the Reichstag on May 17 was a manœuver or whether it represents a change of heart which will lead Germany to postpone rearming.

What do the Nazis want in addition to rearmament or equality of armaments? They want the *Anschluss* with Austria. They want the Corridor and Silesia back from Poland, and Danzig back from its truancy as a Free City. Less immediately, they want Northern Schleswig back from Denmark,[5] Memel back from Lithuania, Eupen and Malmedy back from Belgium, and the former German colonies back from the present possessors. It goes without saying that they count on receiving back the Saar after the 1935 plebiscite.[6] Alsace is usually mentioned indirectly, as when the Nazi Premier of Bavaria on May 7 said that the Nazis would take an oath "never to rest or relax until the Rhine flows to the sea once more as Germany's river, not as Germany's frontier." If Nazi leaders think of the South Tyrol they say nothing about it—for the moment. As the Nazi textbooks proclaim the right and duty to use force to attain Nazi goals, and as the use of force to attain the very first of their territorial goals would entail war, and since France will necessarily be party to that war if she is not to wait passively to be dealt with singly later on, it cannot be claimed that a general European war is excluded from the Nazi program. Conscious that they are super-men, and having made sure that they will not again be stabbed in the back by pacifists and Jewish traitors, they do not doubt that when the time comes they could win such a war. It is not necessary, then, to speak definitely about Alsace or to breathe the words "South Tyrol." These will fall into Germany's lap by the logic of events and the law of gravity.

About the cancellation of the so-called war guilt clause in the Versailles Treaty the Nazis seem to care much less than did von Papen. He wanted that concession as a trophy to bring back from Lausanne, along with the end of reparations. The Nazis have so

---

5 In the 1920 plebiscite about 75 percent of the inhabitants of Northern Schleswig voted for union with Denmark. The campaign for re-annexation of this territory has been led in German Schleswig by the Schleswigsche Zeitung and by the Nazi organization in Flensburg.

6 Nazi threats as to what will happen to the administrative and judicial officials who have been serving the Saar international governing commission have had so demoralizing an effect that the League commissioner has appealed to the Council (in an official communication made public at Geneva on May 23) to secure some sort of guarantees from the German Government.

many real scalps hanging on their belt that at the moment they feel no need of trophies of sentimental value.

The annexation of Austria has figured first among territorial aims of the Nazis because until recently they thought it the goal most easily attained, as well as because of Austria's proximity to the home base in Bavaria and because of Hitler's Austrian origin. The situation in Austria has been so tense, the strife between the Christian Socialists and the Social Democrats so bitter, that the Nazis well might have considered that a sudden *putsch* would soon be feasible. And indeed in the first weeks after Hitler's victory the Nazi forces in Austria grew steadily. The Pan-German party of course went over to the Nazis en masse, and they were followed by many adherents of Chancellor Dollfuss and by younger Social Democrats who accused their leaders of inaction and of stupidity in having actually created the situation which allowed Dollfuss (head of a minority party) to function without parliamentary restraint. But the most important recruits to the Nazi banner came from the Heimwehr, which in Styria accepted the Nazi program entirely and in the Tyrol in large part.

To meet the Nazi menace Chancellor Dollfuss had a choice of two courses—to out-do the Nazis in an anti-Marxist drive, the while drawing support from Fascist Italy (which is far from anxious to see a greater Germany on the Brenner and looking down at the blue waters of the Adriatic from above Trieste); or to make some sort of armistice with the Social Democrats. The aim of the Social Democrats has been to avoid both *Anschluss* and Hapsburg restoration; to arrange a neutralized status for Austria like Switzerland's; and to bring her into some sort of Danubian confederation where she might fulfill her traditional rôle as middleman between east and west. With the benevolent neutrality of the Social Democrats, and supported from without by the League, Dollfuss would have had a fair chance of waiting successfully for Austrian public opinion—notoriously variable—to become disillusioned by Nazi performances in Germany. In choosing the first course he probably made his task more difficult. The risk, evidently, is that he may not be strong enough to keep on waging a battle on two fronts at once, and that either he will eventually find himself swallowed up by the Nazis, or, to avoid that, will follow Italy's wishes and throw himself into the arms of the legitimists who want Otto in the Hofburg. If the first of these eventualities occurs—if, that is to say, Dollfuss ends up by having played von Papen—the *Anschluss* will be consummated whenever Hitler finds it convenient. If the second occurs, Italy's will be the principal success. She will have prevented the *Anschluss*; she will have prevented the formation of a Danubian confederation; she will have nullified the strength of the Little Entente by isolating Jugoslavia and by setting up a focus of attraction (Hapsburg and Catholic) for the Croats who are discontented with the rule of Belgrade. Before Czechoslovakia and Jugoslavia accepted such a development Europe would certainly have had, if not war, then a war scare of the first order.

Meanwhile, all the radio stations of Germany continue to blare out their nightly messages across the Austrian frontier; arms and money have gone over to aid the Nazi cause, especially in the Tyrol; and care is taken that in every Nazi demonstration in Germany a prominent rôle shall be allotted to the representatives of the movement in Austria. As Herr Rosenberg said recently: "The first stage of the great German revolution will only be finished when National Socialism has become the foundation of the thought of 80,000,000 Germans." The population of the Reich is 65,000,000; of Austria 6,500,000; the balance is to be made up, presumably, in Danzig, parts of the present territory of Poland, and other lands not yet redeemed. Dr. Frick, Nazi Minister of the Interior, raised the ante to 100,000,000 in a speech on May 9 when he noted that "a full third of all Germans now live outside the Reich," thus adding the necessary specifications to the statement made by Hitler a week or so earlier to the effect that "the revolution will only be complete when the entire German world is inwardly and outwardly formed anew."

The German radios carry the voices of Hitler, Goebbels and the others over the eastern frontiers of Germany as well; and they have had a particular effect in the Free City of Danzig. This city, almost exclusively German in population, was given independent status in order that it might serve as a port for Poland.

From the first there were disputes between Poland and the city government. The Danzigers complained about unfair Polish competition, about Polish mismanagement of the railways, about Warsaw's alleged intention gradually to Polonize and absorb them. Poland complained of the obstacles put in the way of her merchants, bankers and shipping men who wished to establish themselves in Danzig. The continual wrangling, and the memory of the difficulties which she had encountered in importing arms through Danzig in July 1920 to carry on the war against Soviet Russia, led Poland in 1924 and 1925 to undertake the construction of an exclusively Polish port at Gdynia. The energy and success with which she pushed the undertaking were remarkable—so remarkable, in fact, that today the upstart port of Gdynia divides the sea-borne trade of Poland equally on a tonnage basis with her ancient rival, and takes an even larger share of the more profitable trade in non-bulk goods. As a result, Danzig is languishing, unemployment has reached about 40,000 out of a population of about 400,000, and there can no longer be any doubt in the minds of Danzigers that in their anxiety to monopolize the transit trade and show their resentment at Poland's high-handed ways they have over-reached the mark and now face gradual dry rot and in the end ruin. Their fate, they realize too late, is to be that of Riga, Libau, Fiume and other ports left without a hinterland to gaze out across stagnant seas.

For Danzig to rejoin East Prussia as the result of some desperate *coup d'état* which did not also bring the Polish Corridor and Gdynia within the German frontiers would merely hasten the eventual disaster, for all that Danzig could expect in those circumstances would be to divide with Königsberg the meagre local trade of East Prussia. The Nazi program of "Back to the Reich" offered, then, not a practical solution to the dilemma, but a development which appealed to the town's aroused German sentiment and feeling of desperation. The writer was in Danzig for a few days during the campaign which preceded the May 28 elections. Nazi flags were flying everywhere, motor cars were dashing about carrying brown-shirted couriers, and, in order to keep within the letter of the law forbidding political meetings, sports assemblies or concerts were being held daily, at which, after the necessary legal preliminaries of calisthenic exhibitions or patriotic music, the radio was tuned in on Berlin. The result of this intensive propaganda was that the Nazis swept the field, securing the right to organize the Diet and set up the city administration. In Nazi hands, the leader of the Danzig Nazis[7] told the writer, Danzig will be "safe for Germany," ready to be reincorporated in the Reich when and if Hitler gives the sign. In other words, here as in Austria, Hitler aims to secure the mastery, arouse or calm the populace as suits his plans, vex or pacify his foreign enemies as other aspects of his foreign policy make it seem expedient, and bide his time until Poland can be dealt with resolutely, the Corridor wiped out, and (in his own words) "once again it is all Germany."

I V

National Socialism will last in Germany, as the Soviet and Fascist dictatorships have lasted in Russia and Italy. So much can reasonably be said, even though its domestic program is still directed mainly toward a negative object—the extirpation of its enemies—and hence has not yet been tested for constructive statesmanship. Already, however, we can discern several possible sources of future weakness.

In the first place, the party has grown so rapidly, its final access to power was so sudden, that it is not homogeneous. The historical fact that divisions which occurred in the ranks of the Italian Fascists and the Russian Communists were overcome does not necessarily mean that similar divisions within the Nazi ranks will also be overcome. Among the seventeen millions who voted the Nazi ticket on March 5 must be many who already are uneasy over the new régime's treatment of its enemies and its violation of

---

7 An energetic young Bavarian named Foster, one of the "original seven" founders of the Nazi movement, whom Hitler despatched to Danzig about two years ago to organize the party there.

the old German standards of law and justice. The burning of the Reichstag enormously impressed the voters on the eve of going to the polls. But the proofs that it was done by communists (promised then for publication within a few days) were not forthcoming, and now some are asking themselves whether the whole communist menace was not a hoax. Up to the present time, however, individual waverings have been more than made up for by the general rush to the band-wagon.

More real at present than any likelihood of divisions in the Nazi masses is the possibility of divisions in the Nazi leadership. Two tendencies can already be distinguished. The conservative wing is represented by *der Führer* himself. Thus it was he who argued in the party councils against the Jewish boycott. But though he rejected the proposals of some of his colleagues for a protracted boycott he eventually was persuaded that a one-day boycott was indispensable as a means of letting off the accumulated hatred which Nazi propaganda machines had whipped up and to avoid "undisciplined" persecutions, plundering and very possibly a general pogrom. To say as much is to admit two important facts—that on this particular occasion the party masses were out of hand and had to be satisfied, regardless of consequences; and that there was a division of will among the leaders.[8] Again, it is no secret that Dr. Schacht's influence in the régime consists in large part of the weight his views carry with Hitler personally. This may prove of importance in party councils when the difficult economic and financial decisions of the next few months come to be taken. Again, at a private meeting of party leaders held in Munich the last week in April, Hitler gave notice that the first task was internal consolidation, and that talk about winning back lost territories should be postponed until Germany's internal position had become stronger, until not mere argument but positive action could be the order of the day. But the whole psychology of the intimate

---

8 It is instructive to note in this connection that apparently Hitler has never felt it wise publicly to disown or deprecate any act of violence committed by or attributed to members of his party.

circle of persons with whom he has worked in past years is contrary to moderation of this sort, even should the reasons for it be merely tactical.

Not exactly opposed to Hitler, for as yet no one dares to oppose him, but nevertheless suspected of pursuing more inflammatory and dangerous methods than his, are men like Captain Göring, head of the Prussian state government, Dr. Goebbels, head of the new propaganda ministry, some of the Bavarian ministers whose views have already been quoted, and the chiefs of the *S.A.* troops in various centers. The torrential but carefully phrased speech which Dr. Goebbels pronounced over the radio the evening before the boycott must be read to realize the extent of the man's will and ability subtly to incite to violence. There might well be a temptation for men like these to egg on the crowd, or to float with it should its demands grow more radical, even while pretending to accept the party decisions dictated by Hitler. After all, it is less a question of direction than of speed and intensity. Or they might elevate Hitler to the Presidency (or even, it is sometimes suggested, to some inaccessible religious height) and attempt to rule in his name. Or, should the program of the more moderate (i.e. less impatient) Nazis fail to fulfill popular expectations, the extremists might carry the party for a policy of immediate adventure and in one desperate stroke sweep away the whole underpinnings of European peace. To cross Hitler's will openly today is impossible; any disillusionment of the country about him personally would destroy the whole movement. But these are only the opening months of a long struggle to get and keep a monopoly of power. The possibilities of a division of wills later on in the very heart of the Nazi party are not to be excluded from an observer's calculations.

Among the economic effects of the Nazi accession to power have been a shrinking of the market for German goods in many parts of the world; a reluctance on the part of many people to travel by German boats, ship goods by German routes, patronize German films, or visit Germany as students or tourists; a retreat by foreign enterprises which were considering opening factories or branches in Germany, due to Nazi discrimination against concerns with foreign capital; a feeling of uncertainty and mistrust among domestic capitalists who might have started new enterprises; a general tendency of people to hoard money rather than spend it in such uncertain times; and to some extent an export of capital either because of the flight of Jews and others from the country or in preparation for such flight in the event that ways might later be found to cross the frontier.

Now these are all distressing developments in a country with some 6,000,000 men out of work, and which has managed to live in recent years because it had a favorable balance of trade. The trade figures for the two months following the election are now available. In March imports were valued at 362,000,000 gold marks, exports at 426,000,000 gold marks. In April imports had fallen to 321,000,000 gold marks, exports to 382,000,000 gold marks. Last year the figures were as follows: March, imports 364,000,000 gold marks, exports 516,000,000 gold marks; April, imports 427,000,000 gold marks, exports 472,000,000 gold marks. It will be noted that last year imports increased from March to April, a natural development (in a country which is a large importer of raw materials) in the spring of the year. This year, however, imports fell. The explanation undoubtedly is that in order to maintain a favorable balance of trade the Reichsbank had to restrict the import of raw materials. The result inevitably will be a subsequent further fall in exports. Dr. Schacht went to America in May in the hope of securing a loan to finance German exports. He failed. Germany's economy is obviously in a precarious situation.

Meanwhile, the position of the individual worker has not improved. Unemployment, so far as can be judged, has not decreased. The official figures show a fall in the number of unemployed from 6,000,958 in February, the last month before the Nazi victory, to 5,598,855 in March, representing an improvement from 33.0 to 30.7 in the percentage of workers who are without employment. It is doubtful whether this improvement is real. Part is seasonal, part is undoubtedly due to the transfer of numbers of men from the unemployed lists to service in the *S.A.*, while part is probably due to the elimination from the lists of those receiving help of many persons suspected of entertaining "un-German" political theories. While the government was issuing figures showing a decline in unemployment, the Trade Unions reported an increase in the percentage of unemployed from 47.4 percent in February to 52.7 percent in March. On the whole, it seems likely that the unemployment situation is really worse than it was in the winter. It is hard to see how the Hitler government is going to pay off its supporters, redeem its promise to improve the situation of agriculture as against industry, and in general bring better times, except by trying socialization schemes which may prove risky in a time when political tension is so high.

Another cause for apprehension in Berlin is furnished by American moves toward inflation. Germany has been through the mill of uncontrolled inflation, and knows its bitter ending as well as its pleasant first stages. The Reichsbank under Dr. Schacht, like German opinion in general, certainly is strongly set against another inflation, even if the United States proposes to join England in offering her goods to the world at lower prices due to a devaluation of the dollar. But could Germany long resist if the greater part of the world took that road? And what would happen to her export trade if she did resist? Inflation is one of the things which no German government, not even a Nazi government, could feel sure of coming through unscathed. In the decisions to be taken in this connection may lurk another threat to Nazi popularity and power.

As yet only a few Nazi leaders have had time or felt it necessary to look ahead at all these hurdles. They will reach some of them rapidly in the period of "trial and error" upon which they are now entering. But for the moment the revolution is still in course and fevers are high. A whole people has been given an inoculation. To all practical purposes it has taken universally.

v

Another of the new democratic states of Europe has retreated before the wave of dictatorship. Must we conclude that Western democracy as known in England, France and the United States has suffered a defeat? The truth is that it has only lost the semblance of a victory it had never won. In the lands of the Hohenzollerns, the Hapsburgs and the Romanoffs the soil was not yet ready for democracy. The old Germany, it is true, was a legal state. There was freedom of thought, a free press, confidence that one would secure justice if one kept within the law. But at the top was a stark force, militaristic and autocratic, which could command Germans to die, and which was ready to give the word when it thought its interests or prestige demanded.

The German Republic was a puny plant. Beneath the inch or so of top-soil in which its seeds were hastily placed were a dozen unyielding strata, packed down and solidified by tradition and usage. The servitudes of a punitive peace treaty, the galling pre-ponderance of France and her allies in Europe, the economic distress following the defeat and the inflation, all these hindered its growth. The cultivators, from Ebert and Scheidemann through Stresemann and Brüning down at last to von Papen and von Schleicher, cared less and less about saving it. Nor did the well-intentioned campaign of the liberal press abroad to rectify the extreme appraisal which the world had formed about Germany's part in causing the war, a campaign in which they white-washed the Imperial Government as uncritically as Lloyd George in an earlier incarnation had damned it, serve to make the task of sincere republican leaders any the more easy. But the final determining condition which caused the Republic's death was that it had no nourishment from below. As an eminent German said to the writer two or three years ago: "We made a republic; but there were no republicans."

The German people came to believe that their position was ignoble, intolerable, and could never be righted except by force. Even their best leaders (Stresemann included) were afraid of point-ing out how much better their position in Europe was becoming year by year. They hardly noticed that the hated treaty was grad-ually being revised in a whole series of vital respects (evacuation of the Rhineland, ending of military control, entry into the League, virtual cancellation of reparations), that France, the traditional enemy, was becoming perceptibly more pacific, that she had already recognized the necessity for taking the next great step in treaty revision—the accord of equal rights—and that progressive disarmament would come next.

Von Papen and von Schleicher prepared to break sharply with the method of appeasement and revision by stages which Stresemann, a man as thoroughly German as either of them, had pursued with concrete evidences of success. Hitler, going to the people with an eloquence and abandon of which none of the others were capable, actually made the break. Looking back at the position of the German people after the war, taking account of their psychological make-up, and remembering that ten years, though it is a short time in the life of a nation seems long in the life of individuals, we now see that the break was one day almost bound to be made.

Will Hitler, having given the German spirit an opportunity to purge itself of part of its store of resentment and hate and envy, and having counted from his new vantage point of supreme power and responsibility the cost of a desperate policy of revenge, decide to try gradually to return to the methods of piecemeal revision which some of his predecessors pursued? If he does, will it be possible for France, all of whose wartime fears have been revived by the events of recent weeks, to return to a conciliatory course promptly enough for the (hypothetical) moderate elements in the Nazi party to retain control? It will not be easy for France to assume good faith in a Germany which has been talking and acting as Nazi Germany has, to make concessions to a Hitler which she said she was not yet ready to make to a Stresemann and a Brüning. And if she refuses to be led rapidly into accepting German offers of collaboration (presuming they are forthcoming), will the German masses, "awakened" indeed, allow Hitler to delay rearming, no matter what has happened at Geneva? Then, feeling themselves stronger, will they refrain from producing *faits accomplis* in Austria and Danzig and the Saar and wherever else local conditions play into their hands?

One other question-mark cannot be ignored. National Socialism poses as a mighty bulwark against Bolshevism. But it fights with the enemy's own methods—repression, fear, propaganda, isolation from world thought and world opinion. The whole control of the state, mechanical and spiritual, is in the hands of an unchallengeable directorate. One turn of the knob, and the radio would play a German version of the Red International as unanimously as it now plays the Nazi marching songs. One order, and the *S.A.* would become a Red Army. A transformation like this would not be the result of chance. Germany is not a country of improvisations. It would happen because Hitler, or his colleagues, or his successors, planned it to happen as a way out of imminent failure, to avert the anger of a people which had been promised bread and given a stone.

It is with fears and questions such as these in mind that we watch each day's events in Germany. Three months after the Nazi revolution we cannot pretend that as yet there is any real evidence to cause our fears to diminish, or that our questions can as yet be given any conclusive answer.❸

Political Ideas in the Twentieth Century

Isaiah Berlin

Foreign Affairs, April 1950

Anyone desiring a quiet life
has done badly to be born
in the twentieth century.
—L. Trotsky.

Historians of ideas, however scrupulous and minute they may feel it necessary to be, cannot avoid perceiving their material in terms of some kind of pattern. To say this is not necessarily to subscribe to any form of Hegelian dogma about the dominant rôle of laws and metaphysical principles in history—a view increasingly influential in our time—according to which there is some single "explanation" of the order and attributes of persons, things and events. Usually this consists in the advocacy of some fundamental "category" or "principle" which claims to act as an infallible guide both to the past and to the future, a magic lens revealing "inner," inexorable, all-pervasive historical laws, invisible to the naked eye of the mere recorder of events, but capable, when understood, of giving the historian a unique sense of certainty—certainty not

ISAIAH BERLIN, Fellow of New College and University Lecturer in Philosophy at Oxford; attached to the British Embassy in Washington, 1942–45, and in Moscow, 1945–46, with rank of First Secretary; visiting professor at Harvard, 1949; author of "Karl Marx" and other works.

only of what in fact occurred, but of the reason why it could not have occurred otherwise, affording a secure knowledge which the mere empirical investigator, with his collections of data, his insecure structure of painstakingly accumulated evidence, his tentative approximations and perpetual liability to error and reassessment, can never hope to attain.

The notion of "laws" of this kind is rightly condemned as nothing but a metaphysical mystery; but the contrary notion of bare facts—facts which are nothing but facts, hard, inescapable, untainted by interpretation of arrangement in man-made patterns—is equally mythological. To comprehend and contrast and classify and arrange, to see in patterns of lesser or greater complexity, is not a peculiar kind of thinking, it is thinking itself. And we accuse historians of exaggeration, distortion, ignorance, bias or departure from the facts, not because they select, compare and set forth in a context and order which are in part, at least, of their own choosing, in part conditioned by the circumstances of their material and social environment or their character or purpose—we accuse them only when the result deviates too far, contrasts too harshly with the accepted canons of verification and interpretation which belong to their own time and place and society. These canons and methods and categories are those of the normal "common sense" outlook of a given period and culture, at their best a sharpened, highly-trained form of this outlook, which takes cognizance of all the relevant scientific techniques available, but is itself not one of them. All the criticisms directed against this or that writer for an excess of bias or fantasy, or too weak a sense of evidence, or too limited a perception of connections between events, are based not upon some absolute standard of truth, of strict "factuality," of a rigid adherence to a permanently fixed ideal method of "scientifically" discovering the past "*wie es eigentlicht gewesen ist,*" in contrast with mere theories about it, for there is in the last analysis no meaning in the notion of "objective" criticism in this timeless sense. They rest rather on the most refined concept of accuracy and objectivity and scrupulous "fidelity to the facts" which obtain in a given society at a given period, within the subject in question.

When the great Romantic revolution in the writing of history transferred emphasis from the achievements of individuals to the growth and influence of institutions conceived in much less personal terms, the degree of "fidelity to the facts" was not thereby automatically altered. The new kind of history, the account of the development, let us say, of public and private law, or government, or literature, or social habits during some given period of time, was not necessarily less or more accurate or "objective" than earlier accounts of the acts and fate of Alcibiades or Marcus Aurelius or Calvin or Louis XIV. Thucydides or Tacitus or Voltaire was subjective or vague or fanciful in a sense in which Ranke or Savigny or Michelet was not. The new history was merely written from what is nowadays called a "different angle." The kinds of fact the new history was intended to record were different, the emphasis was different, a shift of interest had occurred in the questions asked and consequently in the methods used. The concepts and terminology reflect an altered view of what constitutes evidence and therefore, in the end, of what are the "facts." When the "romances" of chroniclers were criticized by "scientific" historians, at least part of the implied reproach lay in the alleged discrepancies in the work of the older writers from the findings of the most admired and trusted sciences of a later period; and these were in their turn due to the change in the prevalent conceptions of the patterns of human development—to the change in the models in terms of which the past was perceived, those artistic, theological, mechanical, biological or psychological models which were reflected in the fields of inquiry, in the new questions asked and the new types of technique used, giving answers felt to be more interesting or important than those which had become outmoded.

The history of these changes of "models" is to a large degree the history of human thought. The "organic" or the Marxist methods of investigating history certainly owed part of their vogue to the prestige of the particular natural sciences, or the particular artistic techniques, upon whose model they were supposedly or genuinely constructed; the increased interest, for example, both in biology and in music from which many basic metaphors and analogies derived, is relevant to the historical writing of the nineteenth century, as the new interest in physics and mathematics is to the philosophy and history of the eighteenth; and the deflationary methods and ironical temper of the historians who wrote after the war of 1914–18 were conspicuously influenced by—and accepted in terms of—the new psychological and sociological techniques which had gained public confidence during this period. The relative proportions of, say, social, economic and political concepts in a once admired historical work throw more light upon the general characteristics of its time and for this reason are a more reliable index to the standards adopted, the questions asked, the respective rôles of "facts" to "interpretation," and, in effect, to the entire social and political outlook of an age, than the distance of the work in question from some imaginary, fixed, unaltering ideal of absolute truth, "factual" or "abstract." It is in terms of whether such shifts in the methods of treating the past or the present or the future, and of the idioms and the catchwords, the doubts and hopes, fears and exhortations which they expressed, that the development of political ideas—the conceptual apparatus of a society and of its most gifted and articulate representatives—can best be judged. No doubt the concepts in terms of which people speak and think are symptoms and effects of other processes, the discovery of which is the task of this or that empirical science. But this does not detract from their importance and paramount interest for those who wish to know what constitutes the conscious experience of the most characteristic men of an age or a society, whatever its causes and whatever its fate. And we are, of course, for obvious reasons of perspective, in a better situation to determine this in the case of past societies than for our own. But the very sense of contrast and dissimilarity with which the past affects us provides the only relevant background against which the features peculiar to our own experience stand out in sufficient relief to be adequately discerned and described.

The student of the political ideas of, for example, the mid-nineteenth century must indeed be blind if he does not, sooner or later, become aware of the profound differences in ideas and terminology, in the general view of things—the ways in which the elements of experience are conceived to be related to one another—which divide that not very distant age from our own. He understands neither that time nor his own if he does not perceive the contrast between what was common to Comte and Mill, Mazzini and Michelet, Herzen and Marx, on the one hand, and to Max Weber and William James, Tawney and Beard, Lytton Strachey and Wells, on the other; the continuity of the European intellectual tradition without which no historical understanding at all would be possible is, at shorter range, a succession of specific discontinuities and dissimilarities. Consequently, the remarks which follow deliberately ignore the similarities in favor of the specific differences in political outlook which characterize our own time, and as far as possible, solely our own.

I I

The two great liberating political movements of the nineteenth century were, as every history book informs us, humanitarian individualism and romantic nationalism. Whatever their differences—and they were notoriously profound enough to lead to a sharp divergence and ultimate collision of these two ideals—they had this in common: they believed that the problems both of individuals and of societies could be solved if only the forces of intelligence and of virtue could be made to prevail over ignorance and wickedness. They believed, as against the pessimists and fatalists, both religious and secular, whose voices, audible indeed a good deal earlier, began to sound loudly only toward the end of the century, that all clearly understood questions could be solved by human beings with the moral and intellectual resources at their disposal. No doubt different schools of thought returned different answers to these varying problems; utilitarians said one thing, and neo-feudal romantics—Tory democrats, Bonapartists, Pan-Germans, Slavophiles—another. Liberals believed in the unlimited power of education and the power of rational morality to overcome economic misery and inequality. Socialists, on the contrary, believed that without radical alterations in the distribution and control of economic resources no amount of change of heart or mind on the part of individuals could be adequate; or, for that matter, occur at all. Conservatives and Socialists believed in the power and influence of institutions and regarded them as a necessary safeguard against the chaos, injustice and cruelty caused by uncontrolled individualism; anarchists, radicals and liberals looked upon institutions as such with suspicion as being obstructive to the realization of that free (and, in the view of most such thinkers, rational) society which the will of man could both conceive and build, if it were not for the unliquidated residue of ancient abuses (or unreason) upon which the existing rulers of society—whether individuals or administrative machines— leaned so heavily, and of which so many of them indeed were typical expressions.

Arguments about the relative degree of the obligation of the individual to society and *vice versa* filled the air. It is scarcely necessary to rehearse these familiar questions, which to this day form the staple of discussion in the more conservative institutions of Western learning, to realize that however wide the disagreements about the proper answers to them, the questions themselves were common to liberals and conservatives alike. There were of course even at that time isolated irrationalists—Stirner, Kierkegaard, in certain moods Carlyle; but in the main all the parties to the great controversies, even Calvinists and ultramontane Catholics, accepted the notion of man as resembling in varying degrees one or the other of two idealized types. Either he is a creature free and naturally good, but hemmed in and frustrated by obsolete or corrupt or sinister institutions masquerading as saviors and protectors and repositories of sacred traditions; or he is a being largely, but not wholly, free, and to a high degree, but not entirely, good, and consequently unable to save himself by his own wholly unaided efforts; and therefore rightly seeking salvation within the great frameworks—states, churches, unions. For only these great edifices promote solidarity, security and sufficient strength to resist the shallow joys and dangerous, ultimately self-destructive liberties peddled by those conscienceless or self-deceived individualists who in the name of some bloodless intellectual dogma, or noble enthusiasm for an ideal unrelated to human lives, ignore or destroy the rich texture of social life, heavy with treasures from the past—blind, leaders of the blind, robbing men of their most precious resources, exposing them again to the perils of a life solitary, brutish, nasty and short. Yet there was at least one premise common to the controversy, namely the belief that the problems were real, that it took men of exceptional training and intelligence to formulate them properly, and men with exceptional grasp of the facts, will power and capacity for coherent thought to find and apply the correct solutions.

These two great currents finally ended in exaggerated and indeed distorted forms as Communism and Fascism—the first as the treacherous heir of the liberal internationalism of the previous century, the second as the culmination and bankruptcy of the mystical patriotism which animated the national movements of the time. All movements have origins, forerunners, imperceptible beginnings: nor does the twentieth century stand divided from the nineteenth by so universal an explosion as the French Revolution, even in our day the greatest of all historical landmarks. Yet it is a profound fallacy to regard Fascism and Communism as in the main more uncompromising and violent manifestations of an earlier crisis, the culmination of a struggle fully discernible long before. The differences between the political movements of the twentieth century and the nineteenth are very sharp, but they spring from factors whose full force was not properly realized until our century was well under way. For there is a barrier which divides what is unmistakably past and done with from that which most characteristically belongs to our day. The familiarity of this barrier must not blind us to its relative novelty. One of the elements of the new outlook is the notion of unconscious and irrational influences which outweigh the forces of reason; another the notion that answers to problems exist not in rational solutions, but in the removal of the problems themselves by means other than thought and argument. The interplay between the old tradition, which saw history as the battleground between the easily identifiable forces of light and darkness, reason and obscurantism, progress and reaction; or alternatively between spiritualism and empiricism, intuition and scientific method, institutionalism and individualism—the conflict between this order and, on the other hand, the new factors violently opposed to the humane psychology of "bourgeois" civilization— is to a large extent the history of political ideas of our time.

III

And yet to a casual observer of the politics and the thought of the twentieth century it might at first seem that every idea and movement typical of our time is best understood as a natural development of tendencies already prominent in the nineteenth century. In the case of the growth of international institutions, for instance, this seems a truism. What are the Hague Court, the old League of Nations and its modern successor, the numerous prewar and postwar international agencies and conventions for political, economic, social and humanitarian purposes—what are they, if not the direct descendants of that liberal internationalism— Tennyson's "Parliament of Man"—which was the staple of all progressive thought and action in the nineteenth century, and indeed of much in the century before it? The language of the great founders of European liberalism—Condorcet, for example, or Helvétius—does not differ greatly in substance, nor indeed in form, from the most characteristic moments in the speeches of Woodrow Wilson or Thomas Masaryk. European liberalism wears the appearance of a single coherent movement, little altered during almost three centuries, founded upon relatively simple intellectual foundations, laid by Locke or Grotius or even Spinoza; stretching back to Erasmus and Montaigne, the Italian Renaissance, Seneca and the Greeks. In this movement there is a rational answer to every question. Man is, in principle at least, everywhere and in every condition, able, if he wills it, to discover and apply rational solutions to his problems. And these solutions, because they are rational, cannot clash with one another, and will ultimately form a harmonious system in which the truth will prevail, and freedom, happiness and unlimited opportunity for untrammeled self-development will be open to all.

True, the consciousness of history which grew in the nineteenth century modified the severe and simple design of the classical theory as it was conceived in the eighteenth century. Human progress was presently seen to be conditioned by factors of greater complexity than had been conceived of in the springtime of rationalist individualism: education, rationalist propaganda, were perhaps not always, nor everywhere, quite enough. Such factors as the particular and special influences by which various societies were historically shaped—some due to physical conditions, others to more elusive emotional and what were vaguely classified as "cultural" factors— were presently allowed to have greater importance than they were accorded in the oversimple scheme of Diderot or Bentham. Education, and all forms of social action, must, it was now thought, be fitted to take account of historical needs which made men and their institutions somewhat less easy to mould into the required pattern than had been too optimistically assumed in earlier and more naïve times.

Nevertheless, the original program continued in its various forms to exercise an almost universal spell. This applied to the Right no less than to the Left. The thinkers of the Right, unless they were concerned solely with obstructing the liberals and their allies, believed and acted upon the belief that, provided no excessive violence was done to slow but certain processes of "natural" development, all might yet be well; the faster must be restricted from pushing aside the slower, and in this way all would arrive in the end. This was the doctrine preached by Bonald early in the century, and it expressed the optimism of even the stoutest believers in original sin. Provided that traditional differences of outlook and social structure were protected from what conservatives were fond of describing as the "unimaginative," "artificial," "mechanical" levelling processes favored by the liberals; provided that the infinity of "intangible" or "historic" or "natural" or "providential" distinctions (which to them seemed to constitute the essence of fruitful forms of life) were preserved from being transformed into a uniform collection of homogeneous units moving at a pace dictated by some "irrelevant" or "extraneous" authority, contemptuous of pre-scriptive or traditional rights and habits; provided that adequate safeguards were instituted against too reckless a trampling upon the sacred past—with these guarantees, rational reforms and changes were allowed to be feasible and even desirable. Given these guar-antees, conservatives no less than liberals were prepared to look upon the conscious direction of human affairs by qualified experts with a considerable degree of approval; and not merely by experts, but by a growing number of individuals and groups, drawn from, and representing, wider and wider sections of a society which was progressively becoming more and more enlightened.

This is a mood and attitude common to a wider section of opin-ion in the later nineteenth century in Europe, and not merely in the West but in the East too, than historians, affected by the political struggles of a later or earlier period, allow us to see. One of the results of it—in so far as it was a causal factor and not merely a symptom of the process—was the wide development of political representation in the West whereby in the end, in the succeeding century, all classes of the population began to attain to power, sooner or later, in one country or another. The nineteenth century was full of unrepresented groups engaged in the struggle for self-expression, and later for control. Its representatives counted among them heroes and martyrs, men of the moral and artistic genius whom a genuine struggle of this kind brings forth. The twentieth century, by satisfying much of the social and political hunger of the Victorian period, did indeed witness a striking improvement in the material condition of the majority of the peoples of Western Europe, due in large measure to the energetic social legislation which transformed the social order.

But one of the least predicted results of this trend (although isolated thinkers like Tocqueville, Burckhardt, Herzen, and, of course, Nietzsche, had more than an inkling of it) was a steep decline in the quality of moral idealism, and of romantic, artistic rebelliousness, which marked the early struggles of the dissatisfied social groups during their heroic period when, deeply divergent though they were, they fought together against tyrants, priests and militant philistines. Whatever the injustices and miseries of our time—and they are plainly no fewer than those of the immediate past—they are less likely to find expression in monuments of noble eloquence, because that kind of inspiration seems to spring only from the oppression or suppression of entire classes of society. There arrives a brief moment when the leaders of the most articulate, and socially and economically most developed, of these suppressed groups are lifted by the common mood and for a moment speak not for their own class or milieu alone, but in the name of all the oppressed; for a brief instant their utterance has a universal quality.

But a situation where all or nearly all the great sections of society have been, or are on the point of being, in at any rate the formal possession of power is unfavorable to that truly disinterested eloquence—disinterested partly at least because fulfillment is remote, because principles shine forth most clearly in the darkness and void, because the inner vision is still free from the confusions and obscurities, the compromises and blurred outlines of the external world inevitably forced upon it by the beginnings of practical action. No body of men which has tasted power, or is within a short distance of doing so, can avoid a certain degree of that cynicism which, like a chemical reaction, is generated by the sharp contact between the pure ideal nurtured in the wilderness and its realization in some unpredicted form which seldom conforms to the hopes or fears of earlier times. It therefore takes an exceptional effort of the imagination to discard the context of later years, to cast ourselves back into the period when the views and movements which have since triumphed and lost their glamor long ago were still capable of stirring so much vehement idealistic feeling: when, for example, nationalism was not in principle felt to be incompatible with a growing degree of internationalism, or civil liberties with a rational organization of society; when this was believed by conservatives almost as much as by their rivals, and the gap between the moderates of both sides was only that between the plea that reason must not be permitted to increase the pace of progress beyond the limits imposed by "history" and the counterplea that "*la raison a toujours raison,*" that memories and shadows were less important than the direct perception of the real world in the clear light of day. This was a time when liberals in their turn themselves began to feel the impact of historicism, and to admit the need for a certain degree of adjustment and even control of social life, perhaps by the hated state itself, if only to mitigate the inhumanity of unbridled private enterprise, to protect the liberties of the weak, to safeguard those basic human rights without which there could be neither happiness nor justice nor freedom to pursue the ends of life.

The philosophical foundations of these liberal beliefs in the mid–nineteenth century were somewhat obscure. Rights described as "natural," "inherent," absolute standards of truth and justice, were not compatible with tentative empiricism and utilitarianism; yet liberals believed in both. Nor was faith in democracy strictly consistent with belief in the inviolable rights of minorities or dissident individuals. But so long as the right-wing opposition set itself against all those principles, the contradictions could, on the whole, be allowed to lie dormant, or to form the subject of peaceful academic disputes, not exacerbated by urgent need for immediate factual application. Thus the contradictions further enhanced the rôle of rational criticism by which, in the end, all questions could and would one day be settled. The Socialists on their part resembled the conservatives in believing in the existence of inexorable laws of history, and, like them, accused the liberals of legislating "unhistorically" for timeless abstractions—an activity for which history would not neglect to take due revenge. But they also resembled the liberals in believing in the supreme value of rational analysis, in policies founded on theoretical considerations deduced from "scientific" premises, and with them accused the conservatives of misinterpreting "the facts" to justify the miserable status quo, of condoning misery and injustice; not indeed like the liberals by ignoring history, but by misreading it in a manner consciously or unconsciously calculated to preserve their own power upon a specious moral basis. But genuinely revolutionary as some among them were, and a thoroughly new phenomenon in the Western world, the majority of them shared with the parties which they attacked the common assumption that men must be spoken and appealed to in terms of the needs and interests and ideals of which they were, or could be made to be, conscious.

Conservatives, liberals, radicals, Socialists differed indeed in their interpretation of historical change. They disagreed about what were in fact the deepest needs and interests and ideals of human beings, and who held them, and how deeply or widely or for what length of time, or about their validity in this or that situation. They differed about the facts, they differed about ends and means, they seemed to themselves to agree on almost nothing. But what they had in common—too obviously to be clearly realized—was the belief that their age was ridden with social and political problems which could be solved only by the conscious application of truths upon which all men endowed with adequate mental powers could agree. The Marxists did indeed question this in theory, but not in practice: even they did not seriously attack the thesis that when ends were not yet attained, and the choice of means was limited, the proper way of setting about adapting the means to the ends was by the use of all the skill and energy and intellectual and moral insight available. And while some regarded these problems as akin to those of the natural sciences, some to those of ethics or religion, while others supposed that they were altogether *sui generis* and needed altogether unique methods, they were agreed—it seemed too obvious to need stating—that the problems themselves were genuine and urgent and intelligible in more or less similar terms to all clearheaded men, that all solutions were entitled to a hearing, and that nothing was gained by ignorance or the supposition that the problem did not exist.

This set of common assumptions—they are part of what the word "enlightenment" means—were, of course, deeply rationalistic. They were denied implicitly by the whole Romantic movement, and explicitly by isolated thinkers—Carlyle, Dostoevsky, Baudelaire, Tolstoy, Nietzsche. And there were obscurer prophets—Büchner, Kierkegaard, Bakunin, Leontiev—who protested against the prevailing orthodoxy with a depth and originality which became clear only in our own time. Not that these thinkers represent any one single movement, or even an easily identifiable "trend;" but in one relevant particular they display an affinity. They denied the importance of political action based on rational considerations, and to this extent they were rightly abhorred by the supporters of respectable conservatism. They said or implied that rationalism in any form was a fallacy derived from a false analysis of the character of human beings, because the springs of human action lay in regions unthought of by the sober thinkers whose views enjoyed prestige among the serious public. But their voices were few and discordant, and their eccentric views were ascribed to psychological aberrations. Liberals, however much they admired their artistic genius, were revolted by what they conceived as a perverted view of mankind, and either ignored it or rejected it violently. Conservatives looked upon them as allies against the exaggerated rationalism and infuriating optimism of both liberals and Socialists, but treated them nervously as queer visionaries, a little unhinged, not to be imitated or approached too closely. The Socialists looked on them as so many deranged reactionaries, scarcely worth their powder and shot. The main currents both on the Right and on the Left flowed round and over these immovable, isolated rocks with their absurd appearance of seeking to arrest or deflect the central current. What were they, after all, but survivals of a darker age, or interesting misfits, sad and at times fascinating casualties of the advance of history, worthy of sympathetic insight—men of talent or even genius born out of their time, gifted poets, remarkable artists, but surely not worthy of detailed attention on the part of serious students of social and political life?

There was (it is worth saying again) a somewhat sinister element dimly recognized from its very beginning in Marxism—in the main a highly rationalistic system—which seemed hostile to this entire outlook, denying the importance of reason in their choice of ends and in effective government alike on the part of individuals or groups. But the worship of the natural sciences which Marxism shared with its liberal antagonists was unpropitious to a clearer perception of its own true nature; and so this aspect of it lay largely unrecognized until Sorel brought it to life and combined it with the

Bergsonian anti-rationalism by which his thought is very strongly colored; and until Lenin, stemming from a very different tradition, translated it into an all too effective practice. But Lenin did not, and his followers to this day do not, seem aware of the degree to which it influenced their actions. Or, if aware, they did not and do not admit it. This was so when the twentieth century opened.

I V

Chronological frontiers are seldom landmarks in the history of ideas, and the current of the old century, to all appearances irresistible, seemed to flow peacefully into the new. Presently the picture began to alter. Humanitarian liberalism encountered more and more obstacles to its reforming zeal from the conscious or unconscious opposition both of governments and other centers of social power, as well as the passive resistance of established institutions and habits. It gradually found itself compelled to organize those classes of the population on whose behalf it fought into something sufficiently powerful to work effectively against the old establishment.

The history of the transformation of gradualist and Fabian tactics into the militant formations of Communism and Syndicalism, as well as the milder formations of Social Democracy and trade unionism, is a history not so much of principles as of their interplay with new material facts. In a sense Communism is doctrinaire humanitarianism driven to an extreme in the pursuit of effective offensive and defensive methods. No movement at first sight seems to differ more sharply from liberal reformism than does Marxism, yet the central doctrines—human perfectibility, the possibility of creating a perfect society by a natural means, the belief in the compatibility (indeed the inseparability) of liberty and equality—are common to both. The historical transformation may occur continuously, or in sudden revolutionary leaps, but it must proceed in accordance with an intelligible, logically connected pattern, abandonment of which is always foolish, always utopian. No one doubted that liberalism and Socialism were bitterly opposed both in ends and in methods: yet at their edges they shaded off into one another. Marxism is a doctrine which, however strongly it may stress the class-conditioned nature of action and thought, nevertheless in theory sets out to appeal to reason, at least among the class destined by history to triumph—the proletariat. In the Communist view the proletariat alone can face the future without flinching, because it need not be deterred into falsification of the facts by fear of what the future may bring. And, as a corollary, this applies also to those intellectuals who have liberated themselves from the prejudices and superstitions of their economic class, and have aligned themselves with the winning side in the social struggle. To them, since they are fully rational, the privileges of democracy and of free use of all their intellectual faculties may be accorded. They are to Marxists what the enlightened *philosophes* were to the Encyclopedists: their task is to transform all those who are historically capable of it into their own liberated and rational likeness.

But in 1903 there occurred an event which marked the culmination of a process which has altered the history of our world. At the conference of the Russian Social Democratic Party held in that year, which began in Brussels and ended in London, during the discussion of what seemed at first a purely technical question—how far centralization and hierarchical discipline should govern the behavior of the Party—a delegate named Posadovsky inquired whether the emphasis laid by the "hard" Socialists—Lenin and his friends—upon the need for the exercise of absolute authority by the revolutionary nucleus of the Party might not prove incompatible with those fundamental liberties to whose realization Socialism, no less than liberalism, was officially dedicated. He asked whether the basic, minimum civil liberties—"the sacrosanctity of the person"—could be infringed and even violated if the party leaders so decided. He was answered by Plekhanov, one of the founders of Russian Marxism, and its most venerated figure, a cultivated, fastidious and morally sensitive scholar of wide outlook, who had for 20 years lived in Western Europe and was much respected by the leaders of western Socialism, the very symbol of civilized "scientific" thinking among Russian revolutionaries. Plekhanov, speaking solemnly, and with a splendid disregard for grammar, pronounced the words, *Salus revolutiae suprema lex*. Certainly, if the revolution demanded it, everything—democracy, liberty, the rights of the individual— must be sacrificed to it. If the democratic assembly elected by the Russian people after the revolution proved amenable to Marxist tactics, it would be kept in being as a Long Parliament; if not, it would be disbanded as quickly as possible. A Marxist Revolution could not be carried through by men obsessed by scrupulous regard for the principles of bourgeois liberals. Doubtless whatever was valuable in these principles, like everything else good and desirable, would ultimately be realized by the victorious working class; but during the revolutionary period preoccupation with such ideals was evidence of a lack of seriousness.

Plekhanov, who was brought up in a humane and liberal tradi- tion, did, of course, later retreat from this position himself. The mixture of utopian faith and brutal disregard for civilized morality proved too repulsive to a man who had spent the greater part of his civilized and productive life among Western workers and their leaders. Like the vast majority of Social Democrats, like Marx and Engels themselves, he was too European to try to realize a policy which, in the words of Shigalev in Dostoevsky's "The Possessed," "starting from unlimited liberty ends in unlimited despotism." But Lenin accepted the premises, and being logically driven to conclu- sions repulsive to most of his colleagues, accepted them easily and without apparent qualms. His assumptions were, perhaps, in some sense, still those of the optimistic rationalists of the eighteenth and nineteenth centuries: the coercion, violence, executions, the total suppression of individual differences, the rule of a small, virtually self-appointed minority, were necessary only in the interim period, only so long as there was a powerful enemy to be destroyed. It was necessary only in order that the majority of mankind, once it was liberated from the exploitation of fools by knaves and of weak knaves by more powerful ones, could develop—trammeled no longer by ignorance or idleness or vice, free at last to realize to their fullest extent the infinitely rich potentialities of human nature. This dream may indeed have affinities with the dreams of Diderot or

St. Simon or Kropotkin, but what marked it as something relatively novel was the assumption about the means required to translate it into reality. And the assumption, although apparently concerned solely with methods, and derived from Babeuf or Blanqui or Marx or the French Communards, was very different from the practical program set forth by the most "activist" and least "evolutionary" Western Socialists towards the end of the nineteenth century. The difference was crucial and marked the birth of the new age.

What Lenin demanded was unlimited power for a small body of professional revolutionaries, trained exclusively for one purpose, and ceaselessly engaged in its pursuit by every means in their power. This was necessary because democratic methods, and the attempts to persuade and preach used by earlier reformers and rebels, were ineffective: and this in its turn was due to the fact that they rested on a false psychology, sociology and theory of history—namely the assumption that men acted as they did because of conscious beliefs which could be changed by argument. For if Marx had done anything, he had surely shown that such beliefs and ideals were mere "reflections" of the condition of the socially and eco- nomically determined classes of men, to some one of which every individual must belong. A man's beliefs, if Marx and Engels were right, flowed from the situation of his class, and could not alter—so far, at least, as the mass of men was concerned—without a change in that situation. The proper task of a revolutionary therefore was to change the "objective" situation, *i.e.* to prepare the class for its historical task in the overthrow of the hitherto dominant classes.

Lenin went further than this. He acted as if he believed not merely that it was useless to talk and reason with persons precluded by class interest from understanding and acting upon the truths of Marxism, but that the mass of the proletarians themselves were too benighted to grasp the rôle which history had called on them to play. He saw the choice as between, on the one hand, the gradual stimulation among the army of the dispossessed of a "critical spirit" (which would awaken them intellectually, but lead to a vast deal of discussion and controversy similar to that which divided and enfeebled the intellectuals), and on the other, the turning of them into a blindly obedient force held together by a military discipline and a set of perpetually ingeminated formulae (at least as powerful as the patriotic patter used by the Tsarist régime) to shut out independent thought. If the choice had to be made, then it was mere irresponsibility to stress the former in the name of some abstract principle such as democracy or enlightenment. The important thing was the creation of a state of affairs in which human resources were developed in accordance with a rational pattern. Men were moved more often by irrational than reasonable solutions. The masses were too stupid and too blind to be allowed to proceed in the direction of their own choosing. Tolstoy and the populists were profoundly mistaken; the simple agricultural laborer had no deep truths, no valuable way of life, to impart; he and the city worker and the simple soldier were fellow serfs in a condition of abject poverty and squalor, caught in a system which bred fratricidal strife among themselves; they could be saved only by being ruthlessly ordered by leaders who had acquired a capacity for knowing how to organize the liberated slaves into a rational planned system.

Lenin himself was in certain respects oddly utopian. He started with the belief that with sufficient education, and a rational economic organization, almost anyone could be brought in the end to perform almost any task efficiently. But his conclusion was in practice strangely like that of those reactionaries and Fascists who believed that man was everywhere wild, bad, stupid and unruly, and must be held in check and provided with objects of unreasoning worship. This must be done by a clear-sighted band of organizers, acting in accordance with the truths perceived by such men as Nietzsche, Pareto, or the French absolutist thinkers from De Maistre to Maurras, and indeed by Marx himself—men who by some process superior to scientific reasoning had grasped the true nature of social development, and in the light of their discovery saw the liberal theory of human progress as something unreal, thin, pathetic and absurd. Whatever his crudities and errors, on the central issue, Hobbes, not Locke, turned out to be right: men sought neither happiness nor liberty nor justice, but, above all and before all, security. Aristotle, too, was right: a great number of men were slaves by nature, and when liberated from their chains did not possess the moral and intellectual resources with which to face the prospect of responsibility, of too wide a choice between alternatives; and therefore, having lost one set of chains, inevitably searched for another or forged new chains themselves. It follows that the wise revolutionary legislator, so far from seeking to emancipate human beings from the framework without which they feel lost and desperate, will seek rather to erect a framework of his own, corresponding to the new needs of the new age brought about by natural or technological change. The value of the framework will depend upon the unquestioning faith with which its main features are accepted; otherwise it no longer possesses sufficient strength to support and contain the wayward, potentially anarchical and self-destructive creatures who seek salvation in it. The framework is that system of political, social, economic and religious institutions, those "myths," dogmas, ideals, conventional categories of thought and language, modes of feeling, scales of values, "socially approved" attitudes and habits (called by Marx "superstructure") representing "rationalizations," "sublimations" and symbolic representations which cause men to function in an organized way, prevent chaos, fulfill the function of the Hobbesian state. This is not so very remote from De Maistre's central and deliberately unprobed mystery— the supernatural authority whereby and in whose name rulers can rule and inhibit their subjects' unruly tendencies, above all the tendency to ask too many questions, to question too many established rules. Nothing can be permitted which might even a little weaken that sense of reliability and security which it is the business of the framework to provide. Only thus (in this view) can the founder of the new free society control whatever threatens to dissipate human energy or to slow down the relentless treadmill which alone prevents men from stopping to commit acts of suicidal folly, which alone protects them from too much freedom, from too little restraint, from the vacuum which mankind, no less than nature, abhors.

M. Bergson had, of course, been speaking of something not too unlike this when he had contrasted the flow of life with the forces of critical reason which cannot create or unite, but only divide, arrest, make dead, disintegrate. Freud, too, contributed to this; not in his work of genius as the greatest healer of our time, but as the originator, however innocent, of the misapplication of psychological and sociological methods by muddleheaded fools of good will and quacks and false prophets of every brand and hue. By giving currency to exaggerated versions of the view that the true reasons for a man's beliefs were most often very different from what they themselves thought them to be, being frequently caused by events and processes of which they were neither aware nor in the least anxious to be aware, these eminent thinkers helped, however unwittingly, to discredit the rationalist foundations upon which their own doctrines purported to rest. For it was but a short step from this to the view that what made men most permanently happy was not—as they themselves supposed—the discovery of solutions to the questions which perplexed them, but rather some process natural or artificial whereby the problems were made to vanish altogether. They vanished because their psychological "sources" had been diverted or dried up, leaving behind only those less exacting questions whose solutions did not demand resources beyond the patient's strength.

That this short way with the troubled and the perplexed, which underlay much right-wing thought, should be advocated from the left, was new indeed. It is this change of attitude to the function and value of the intellect that is perhaps the best indication of the great gap which divides the twentieth century from the nineteenth.

V

The central point which I wish to make is this: during all the centuries of recorded history the course of intellectual endeavor, the purpose of education, the substance of controversies about the truth or value of ideas, presupposed the existence of certain crucial questions, the answers to which were of paramount importance. How valid, it was asked, were the various claims to the best methods of discovering absolute knowledge and truth made by such great and famous disciplines as metaphysics, ethics, theology, and the sciences of nature and of man? What was the right life for men to lead, and how was it discovered? Did God exist, and could His purposes be known or even guessed at? Did the universe, and in particular human life, have a purpose? If so, whose purpose did it fulfill? How did one set about answering such questions? Were they or were they not analogous to the kind of questions to which the sciences or common sense provided satisfactory, generally accepted, replies? If not, did it make sense to ask them?

And as in metaphysics and ethics, so in politics too. The political problem was concerned with asking why any individual or individuals should obey other individuals or associations of individuals. All the classical doctrines which deal with the familiar topics of liberty and authority, sovereignty and natural rights, the ends of the state and the ends of the individual, the General Will and the rights of minorities, secularism and theocracy, functionalism and centralization—all these are but various ways of attempting to formulate methods in terms of which this fundamental question can be answered in a manner compatible with the other beliefs and the general outlook of the inquirer and his generation. Great and sometimes mortal conflicts have arisen over the proper techniques for the answering of such questions. Some sought answers in sacred books, others in direct personal revelation, some in metaphysical insight, others in the pronouncements of infallible sages or in speculative systems or in laborious empirical investigations. The questions were of vital importance for the conduct of life. There were, of course, skeptics in every generation who suggested that there were, perhaps, no final answers, that solutions hitherto provided depended on highly variable factors such as the climate in which the theorist's life was lived, or his social or economic or political condition, or those of his fellows, or his or their emotional disposition, or the kinds of intellectual interests which absorbed him or them. But such skeptics were usually treated as either frivolous and so not important, or else unduly disturbing and even dangerous; so that in times of instability they were liable to persecution. But even they—even Sextus Empiricus or Montaigne or Hume— did not actually doubt the importance of the questions themselves.

What they doubted was the possibility of obtaining final and absolute solutions.

It was left to the twentieth century to do something more drastic than this. For the first time it was now asserted that the way to answer questions, particularly those recurrent issues which had perplexed and often tormented original and honest minds in every generation, was not by employing the tools of reason, still less those of the more mysterious capacities called "insight" and "intuition," but by obliterating the questions themselves. And this method consists not in removing them by rational means—by proving, for example, that they are founded on intellectual confusion or verbal muddles or ignorance of the facts—for to prove this would in its turn presuppose the need for rational methods of logical or psychological argument. Rather it consists in so treating the questioner that problems which appeared at once overwhelmingly important and utterly insoluble vanish from the questioner's consciousness like evil dreams and trouble him no more. It consists, not in developing the logical implications and elucidating the meaning, the context, or the relevance and origin of a specific problem—in seeing what it "amounts to"—but in altering the outlook which gave rise to it in the first place. Questions for whose solution no ready-made technique could easily be produced are all too easily classified as obsessions from which the patient must be cured. Thus if a man is haunted by the suspicion that, for example, full individual liberty is not compatible with coercion by the majority in a democratic state, and yet continues to hanker after both democracy and individual liberty, it may be possible by appropriate treatment to rid him of his *idée fixe*, so that it will disappear to return no more. The worried questioner of political institutions is thereby relieved of his burden and freed to pursue socially useful tasks, unhampered by disturbing and distracting reflections which have been eliminated by the eradication of their cause.

The method has the bold simplicity of genius: it secures agreement on matters of political principle by removing the psychological possibility of alternatives, which itself depends, or is held to depend, on the older form of social organization, rendered obsolete by the revolution and the new social order. And this is how Communist and Fascist states—and all other quasi- and semi-totalitarian societies and secular and religious creeds—have in fact proceeded in the task of imposing political and ideological conformity.

For this the works of Karl Marx are not more directly to blame than the other tendencies of our time. Marx was a typical nineteenth century social theorist, in the same sense as Mill or Comte or Buckle. A policy of deliberate psychological conditioning was as alien to him as to them. He believed that many of the questions of his predecessors were quite genuine, and thought that he had solved them. He supported his solutions with arguments which he honestly supposed to conform to the best scientific and philosophical canons of his time. Whether his outlook was in fact as scientific as he claimed, or his solutions as plausible, is another question. What matters is that he recognized the genuineness of the questions he was attempting to answer and offered a theory with a claim to being scientific in the accepted sense of the term; and thereby poured much light (and darkness) on many vexed problems, and led to much fruitful (and sterile) revaluation and reinterpretation.

But the practice of Communist states and, more logically of Fascist states (since they openly deny and denounce the value of the rational question-and-answer method), is not at all the training of the critical, or solution-finding, powers of their citizens, nor yet the development in them of any capacity for special insights or intuitions regarded as likely to reveal the truth. It consists in something which any nineteenth century thinker with respect for the sciences would have regarded with genuine horror—the training of individuals incapable of being troubled by questions which, when raised and discussed, endanger the stability of the system; the building and elaboration of a strong framework of institutions, "myths," habits of life and thought intended to preserve it from sudden shocks or slow decay. This is the intellectual outlook which attends the rise of totalitarian ideologies—the substance of the hair-raising satires of George Orwell and Aldous Huxley—the state of mind in which troublesome questions appear as a form of mental perturbation, noxious to the mental health of individuals and, when too widely discussed, to the health of societies. This is an attitude which looks on all inner conflict as an evil, or at best as a form of futile self-frustration; which considers the kind of friction, the moral or emotional or intellectual collisions, the particular kind of acute spiritual discomfort which rises to a condition of agony from which great works of the human intellect and imagination, inventions, philosophies, works of art, have sprung, as being no better than purely destructive diseases—neuroses, psychoses, mental derangements, genuinely requiring psychiatric aid; above all as being dangerous deviations from that line to which individuals and societies must adhere if they are to continue in a state of well-ordered, painless, contented, self-perpetuating equilibrium.

This is a truly far-reaching conception, and something far more powerful than the pessimism or cynicism of thinkers like Plato or Machiavelli, Swift or Carlyle, who looked on the majority of mankind as unalterably stupid or incurably vicious, and therefore concerned themselves with how the world might be made safe for the exceptional, enlightened or otherwise superior minority or individual. For their view did at least concede the reality of the painful problems, and merely denied the capacity of the majority to solve them; whereas the more radical attitude looks upon intellectual perplexity as being caused either by a technical problem to be settled in terms of practical policy, or else as a neurosis to be cured, that is made to disappear, if possible without a trace. This leads to a novel conception of the truth and of disinterested ideals in general, which would hardly have been intelligible to previous centuries. To adopt it is to hold that outside the purely technical sphere (where one asks only what are the most efficient means towards this or that practical end) words like "true," or "right," or "free," and the concepts which they denote, are to be defined in terms of the only activity recognized as valuable, namely, the organization of society as a smoothly-working machine providing for the needs of such of its members as are permitted to survive. The words and ideas in such a society will reflect the outlook of the citizens, being adjusted so as to involve as little friction as possible between, and within, individuals, leaving them free to make the "optimum" use of the resources available to them.

This is indeed Dostoevsky's utilitarian nightmare. In the course of their pursuit of social welfare, humanitarian liberals, deeply outraged by cruelty, injustice and inefficiency, discover that the only sound method of preventing these evils is not by providing the widest opportunities for free intellectual or emotional development—for who can tell where this might not lead?—but by eliminating the motives for the pursuit of these perilous ends, by suppressing any tendencies likely to lead to criticism, dissatisfaction, disorderly forms of life. I shall not attempt here to trace historically how this came to pass. No doubt the story must at some stage include the fact that mere disparity in tempo and extent between technical development and social change, together with the fact that the two could not be guaranteed to harmonize— despite the optimistic promises of Adam Smith—and indeed clashed more and more often, led to increasingly destructive and apparently unavertible economic crises. These were accompanied by social, political and moral disasters which the general framework— the patterns of behavior, habits, outlook, language, that is the "ideological superstructure" of the victims—could not sustain. The result was a loss of faith in existing political activities and ideals, and a desperate desire to live in a universe which, however dull and flat, was at any rate secure against the repetition of such catastrophes. An element in this was a growing sense of the greater or lesser meaninglessness of such ancient battle-cries as liberty or equality or civilization or truth, since their application to the surrounding scene was no longer as intelligible as it had been in the nineteenth century.

Together with this development, in the majority of cases, there went a reluctance to face it. But the once hallowed phrases were not abandoned. They were used—robbed of their original value— to cover the different and sometimes diametrically opposed notions of the new morality, which in terms of the old system of values, seemed both unscrupulous and brutal. The Fascists alone did not take the trouble to pretend to retain the old symbols, and while political diehards and the representatives of the more unbridled forms of modern big business clung half cynically, half hopefully, to such terms as freedom or democracy, the Fascists rejected them outright with theatrical gestures of disdain and loathing, and poured scorn upon them as the outworn husks of ideals which had long ago rotted away. But despite the differences of policy concerning the use of specific symbols there is a substantial similarity between all the variants of the new political attitude.

Observers in the twenty-first century will doubtless see these similarities of pattern more easily than we who are involved can possibly do today. They will distinguish them as naturally and clearly from their immediate past—that *hortus inclusus* of the nineteenth century in which so many writers both of history and of journalism and of political addresses today still seem to be living— as we distinguish the growth of romantic nationalism or of naïve positivism from that of enlightened despotism or of patrician re- publics. Still, even we who live in them can discern something novel in our own times. Even we perceive the growth of new character- istics common to widely different spheres. On the one hand, we can see the progressive and conscious subordination of political to social and economic interests. The most vivid symptoms of this sub- ordination are the open self-identification and conscious solidarity of men as capitalists or workers; these cut across, though without destroying, national and religious loyalties. On the other, we meet with the conviction that political liberty is useless without the eco- nomic strength to use it, and consequently implied or open denial of the rival proposition that economic opportunity is of use only to politically free men. This in its turn carries with it a tacit acceptance of the proposition that the responsibilities of the state to its citizens must and will grow and not diminish, a theorem which is today taken for granted by masters and men alike, in Europe perhaps more unquestioningly than in the United States, but accepted even there to a degree which seemed utopian only 30, let alone 50, years ago. This great transformation, with its genuine material gains, and no less genuine growth in social equality in the least liberal societies, is accompanied by something which forms the obverse side of the medal—the elimination, or, at the very best, strong disapproval of those propensities for free inquiry and creation which cannot, without losing their nature, remain as conformist and law-abiding as the twentieth century demands. A century ago Auguste Comte asked why, if there was rightly no demand for freedom to disagree in mathematics, it should be allowed and even encouraged in ethics or the social sciences. And indeed, if the creation of certain "optimum" patterns of behavior and thought and feeling in individuals or entire societies is the main goal of social and individual action, Comte's case is unanswerable. Yet it is the degree of this very right to disregard the forces of order and convention, even the publicly accepted "optimum" goals of action, that forms the glory of that bourgeois culture which reached its zenith in the nineteenth century and of which we have only now begun to witness the beginning of the end.

VI

The new attitude, resting as it does upon the policy of diminishing strife and misery by the atrophy of the faculties capable of causing them, is naturally hostile to, or at least suspicious of, disinterested curiosity (which might end anywhere), and looks upon the practice of all arts not obviously useful to society as being at best forms of social frivolity. Such occupations, when they are not a positive menace, are, in this view, an irritating and wasteful irrelevance, a trivial fiddling, a dissipation or diversion of energy which is difficult enough to accumulate at all and should therefore be directed wholeheartedly and unceasingly to the task of building and maintaining the well-adjusted—sometimes called the "well-integrated"—social whole. In this state of mind it is only natural that such terms as truth or honor or obligation or beauty become transformed into purely offensive or defensive weapons, used by a state or a party in the struggle to create a community impervious to influences beyond its own direct control. The result can be achieved either by rigid censorship and insulation from the rest of the world—a world which remains free at least in the sense that its inhabitants continue to say what they wish, in which words are relatively unorganized, with all the "dangerous" consequences thereby brought about; or else it can be achieved by extending the area of strict control until it stretches over all possible sources of anarchy, *i.e.* the whole of mankind. Only by one of these two expedients can a state of affairs be achieved in which human behavior can be manipulated with relative ease of technically qualified specialists—adjusters of conflicts and promoters of peace both of body and of mind, engineers and other scientific experts, psychologists, sociologists, economic and social planners and so on. Clearly this is not an intellectual climate which favors originality of judgment, moral independence or uncommon powers of insight. The entire trend of such an order is to reduce all issues to technical problems of lesser or greater complexity, in particular the problem of how to survive, get rid of maladjustments, achieve a condition in which the individual's psychological or economic capacities are harnessed to producing the maximum of unclouded social contentment; and this in its turn depends upon the suppression of whatever in him might raise doubt or assert itself against the single all-embracing, all-clarifying, all-satisfying plan.

The tendency has taken acute forms in, for example, the Soviet Union. There subordination to the central plan, and the elimination of disturbing factors, whether by education or repression, has been enacted with that capacity for believing in the literal inspiration of ideologies—in the ability and duty of human beings to translate ideas into practice fully, rigorously and immediately—to which Russian thinkers of all schools seem singularly addicted. The Soviet pattern is clear, simple and correctly deduced from "scientifically demonstrated" premises. The task of realizing it must be entrusted to technically trained believers who look on the human beings at their disposal as material which is infinitely malleable within the confines revealed by the sciences. Stalin's remark that creative artists are "engineers of human souls" is a very precise expression of this spirit. The presence of it in the various Fascist societies destroyed by the recent war, with intuition or instinct substituted for science, and cynicism for hypocrisy, are equally clear for all to see. In Western Europe this tendency has taken the milder form of a shift of emphasis away from disagreement about political principles (and from party struggles which sprang from genuine differences of moral and spiritual outlook) towards disagreements, ultimately technical, about methods—about the best ways of achieving that degree of minimum economic or social stability without which arguments concerned with fundamental principles and the ends of life are felt to be "abstract," "academic" and unrelated to the urgent needs of the hour. Hence that noticeably growing lack of interest in long-term political issues—as opposed to current day-to-day economic or social problems—on the part of the populations of the Western European continent which is occasionally deplored by shocked American and British observers who falsely ascribe it to the growth of cynicism and disenchantment with ideals.

No doubt all abandonment of old values for new must appear to the surviving adherents of the former as conscienceless disregard for morality as such. But this is a great delusion. There is all too little disbelief, whether conscienceless or apathetic, of the new values. On the contrary, they are clung to with unreasoning faith and that blind intolerance towards skepticism which springs, as often as not, from a profound inner bankruptcy, the hope against hope that here is a safe haven at least, narrow, dark, cut off, but secure. Growing numbers of human beings are prepared to purchase this sense of security even at the cost of allowing vast tracts of life to be controlled by persons who, whether consciously or not, act systematically to narrow the horizon of human activity to manageable proportions, to train human beings into more easily combinable parts—interchangeable, almost prefabricated—of a total pattern. In the face of such a strong desire to stabilize, if need be, at the lowest level—upon the floor from which you cannot fall, which cannot betray you, "let you down"—all the ancient political principles begin to vanish, feeble symbols of creeds no longer relevant to the new realities.

This process does not move at a uniform pace everywhere. In the United States perhaps, for obvious economic reasons, the nineteenth century survives far more powerfully than anywhere else. The political issues and conflicts, the topics of discussion, and the idealized personalities of democratic leaders are far more reminiscent of Victorian Europe than anything to be found on that continent now.

Woodrow Wilson was a nineteenth century liberal in a very full and unqualified sense. The New Deal and the personality of President Roosevelt excited political passions far more like those of the battles which raged round Gladstone or Lloyd George, or the anti-clerical governments at the turn of the century in France, than anything actually contemporary with it in Europe; and this great liberal enterprise, certainly the most constructive compromise between individual liberty and economic security which our own time has witnessed, corresponds more closely to the political and economic ideals of John Stuart Mill in his last, humanitarian-Socialist phase than to left-wing thought in Europe in the thirties. The controversy about international organization, about the United Nations and its subsidiaries, as well as the other postwar international institutions, like the controversies which in the years after 1918 surrounded the League of Nations, are fully intelligible in terms of nineteenth century political ideals, and therefore occupied far more attention and meant much more in America than in Europe. The United States may have disavowed President Wilson, but it continued to live in a moral atmosphere not very different from that of Wilson's time—the easily recognizable black-and-white moral world of the Victorian values. The events of 1918 preyed on the American conscience for 25 years, whereas in Europe the *exalté* atmosphere of 1918–1919 disappeared without a trace—a brief moment of illumination which in retrospect seems more American than European, the last manifestation in Europe of a great but dying tradition in a world already living, and fully conscious of living, in a new medium, too well aware of its differences from, and resentful of, its past. The break was not sudden and total, a dramatic *coup de théâtre*. Many of the seeds planted in the eighteenth or nineteenth centuries have flowered only in the twentieth: the political and ethical climate in which trade unions were founded in Germany, or England, or France did of course contain as elements the old, familiar doctrines of human rights and duties which were the common property, avowed or not, of almost all parties and views in the liberal, humanitarian, expansionist hundred years of peaceful progress.

The main current of the nineteenth century does, of course, survive into the present, and especially in America and the British Dominions; but it is not what is most characteristic of our time. For in the past there were conflicts of ideas, whereas what characterizes our time is not the struggle of one set of ideas against another but the mounting wave of hostility to all ideas as such. Since ideas are considered the source of too much disquiet, there is a tendency to suppress the conflict between liberal claims to individual political rights and the economic injustice which results from their satisfaction (which forms the substance of Socialist criticism) by the submersion of both in an authoritarian régime which removes the free area within which such conflicts can occur. What is genuinely typical of our time is a new concept of the society, the values of which derive not from the desires or the moral sense of this or that individual's view of his ultimate ends but from some factual hypothesis or metaphysical dogma about history, or race, or national character in terms of which the answers to the question what is good, right, required, desirable, fitting, can be "scientifically" deduced, or intuited, or expressed in this or that kind of behavior. There is one and only one direction in which a given aggregate of individuals is conceived to be travelling, driven thither by quasi-occult impersonal forces, such as their class structure, or their unconscious selves, or their racial origin, or the "real" social or physical roots of this or that "popular" or "group" "mythology." The direction is alterable only by tampering with the hidden cause of behavior—those who wish to tamper being, according to this view, free to determine their own direction and that of others by having an understanding of the machinery of social behavior and skill in manipulating it.

In this sinister fashion have the words of St. Simon's prophecy finally come true—words which once seemed so brave and optimistic: "The government of man will be replaced by the administration of things." The cosmic forces are conceived as omnipotent and indestructible. Hopes, fears, prayers cannot wish them out of existence; but the élite of experts can canalize them and control them to some extent. The task of these experts is to adjust human beings to these forces and to develop in them an unshakable faith in the new order, and unquestioning loyalty to it, which will anchor it securely and forever. Consequently the technical disciplines which direct natural forces and adjust men to the new order must take primacy over humane pursuits—philosophical, historical, artistic. Such pursuits, at most, will serve only to prop up and embellish the new establishment. Turgenev's naïve materialist, the hero of his novel "Fathers and Sons," the nihilist Bazarov, has finally come into his own, as St. Simon and his more pedestrian follower Comte always felt sure that he would, but for reasons very different from those which seemed plausible a century ago. Bazarov's faith rested on the claim that the dissection of frogs was more important than poetry because it led to the truth, whereas the poetry of Pushkin did not.

The reason given today is more devastating: anatomy is superior to art because it generates no independent ends of life, provides no experiences which act as independent criteria of good or evil, truth or falsehood, and which are therefore liable to clash with the orthodoxy which we have created as the only bulwark strong enough to preserve us from doubts and despairs and all the horrors of maladjustment. To be torn this way and that emotionally or intellectually is a form of *malaise*. Against it nothing will work but the elimination of alternatives so nearly in equal balance that choice between them is—or even appears—possible.

This is, of course, what the Grand Inquisitor in Dostoevsky's "Brothers Karamazov" maintained with deadly eloquence: that what men dreaded most was freedom of choice, to be left alone to grope their way in the dark; and the Church by lifting the responsibility from their shoulders made them willing, grateful and happy slaves. The Grand Inquisitor stood for the dogmatic organization of the life of the spirit: Bazarov for its theoretical opposite—free scientific inquiry, the facing of the "hard" facts, the acceptance of the truth however brutal. But by an irony of history (not unforeseen by Dostoevsky) they have formed a pact, they are allies, and today are almost indistinguishable. Buridan's ass, we are told, unable to choose between two equidistant bundles of hay, starved to death. Against this fate the only remedy is blind obedience and faith. Whether the refuge is a dogmatic religion or a dogmatic natural science matters relatively little: for without such obedience and faith there is no confidence and no hope, no optimistic, "constructive," "positive" form of life.

VII

At this point it might be said that the situation I have described is not altogether new. Has not every authoritarian institution, every irrationalist movement, been engaged upon something of this kind—the artificial stilling of doubts, the attempt either to discredit uncomfortable questions or to educate men not to ask them? Was this not the practice of the great organized churches, indeed of every institution from the national state to small sectarian establishments? Was this not the attitude of the enemies of reason from the earliest mystery cults to the romanticism, anarchistic nihilism or surréalism of the last century and a half? Why should our age be specially accused of addiction to the particular tendency which formed the central theme of the social doctrines of Plato, or of the sect of the mediæval Assassins, or of much Eastern thought and mysticism?

But there are two great differences which separate the political characteristics of our age from their origins in the past. In the first place, the reactionaries or romantics of previous periods, however much they might have advocated the superior wisdom of institutional authority or the revealed word over that of individual reason, did not in their moments of wildest unreason minimize the importance of the questions to be answered. On the contrary they maintained that so crucial was it to obtain the correct answer that only hallowed institutions, or inspired leaders, or mystical revelation, or divine grace could vouchsafe a solution of sufficient depth and universality. No doubt a hierarchy of the relative importance of questions underlies any established social system— a hierarchy the authority of which is itself not intended to be open to question. Moreover, the obscurity of some among the answers offered has in every age concealed their lack of truth or their irrelevance to the questions which they purported to solve. And perhaps much hypocrisy has traditionally been necessary to secure their success. But hypocrisy is very different from cynicism or blindness. Even the censors of opinion and the enemies of the truth felt compelled to pay formal homage to the vital importance of obtaining true answers to the great problems by the best available means. If their practice belied this, at least there was something to be belied: traitors and heretics often keep alive the memory—and the authority—of the beliefs which they are intent on betraying.

The second difference consists in the fact that in the past such attempts to becloud the nature of the issues were associated specifically with the avowed enemies of reason and individual freedom. The alignment of forces has been clear at any rate since the Renaissance; progress and reaction, however much these words have been abused, are not empty concepts. On one side stood the supporters of authority, unreasoning faith, suspicious of, or openly opposed to, the uncontrolled pursuit of truth or the free realization of individual ideals. On the other, whatever their differences, were those supporters of free inquiry and self-expression who looked upon Voltaire and Lessing, Mill and Darwin and Ibsen as their prophets. Their common quality—perhaps their only common quality—was some degree of devotion to the ideals of the Renaissance and a hatred of all that was associated, whether justly or not, with the Middle Ages—darkness, suppression, the stifling of all heterodoxy, the hatred of the flesh and of gaiety and of the love of natural beauty. There were of course many who cannot be classified so simply or so crudely; but until our own day the lines were drawn sharply enough to determine clearly the position of the men who most deeply influenced their age. A combination of devotion to scientific principles with "obscurantist" social theory seemed altogether unthinkable. Today the tendency to circumscribe and confine and limit, to determine the range of what may be asked and what may not, to what may be believed and what may not, is no longer a distinguishing mark of the "reactionaries." On the contrary, it comes as powerfully from the heirs of the radicals, the rationalists, the "progressives," of the nineteenth century as from the descendants of their enemies. There is a persecution not only of science, but by science and in its name; and this is a nightmare scarcely foreseen by the most Cassandra-like prophets of either camp.

We are often told that the present is an age of cynicism and despair, of crumbling values and the dissolution of the fixed standards and landmarks of our civilization. But this is neither true nor even plausible. So far from showing the loose texture of a collapsing order, the world is today stiff with rigid rules and codes and ardent, irrational religions. So far from evincing the toleration which springs from cynical disregard of the ancient sanctions, it treats heterodoxy as the supreme danger.

Whether in the East or West, the danger has not been greater since the ages of faith. Conformities are called for much more eagerly today than yesterday; loyalties are tested far more severely; skeptics and liberals and individuals with a taste for private life and their own inner standards of behavior, if they do not take care to identify themselves with an organized faith, are objects of fear or derision and targets of persecution for either side, execrated or despised by all the embattled parties in the great ideological wars of our time. And although this is less acute in societies traditionally averse to extremes—Great Britain, say, or Switzerland—this makes little difference to the general pattern. In the world today individual stupidity and wickedness are forgiven more easily than failure to be identified with a recognized party or attitude, to achieve an approved political or economic or intellectual status. In earlier periods, when more than one authority ruled human life, a man might escape the pressure of the state by taking refuge in the fortress of the opposition—of an organized church or a dissident feudal establishment. The mere fact of conflict between authorities allowed room for a narrow and shifting, but still never entirely non-existent, no-man's-land, where private lives might still precariously be lived, because neither side dared to go too far for fear of too greatly strengthening the other. Today the very virtues of the paternalistic state, its genuine anxiety to reduce destitution and disease and inequality, to penetrate all the neglected nooks and crannies of life which may stand in need of its justice and its bounty—its very success in those beneficent activities— has narrowed the area within which the individual may commit blunders, has curtailed his liberties in the interest (the very real interest) of his welfare or of his sanity, his health, his security, his freedom from want and fear. His area of choice has grown smaller not in the name of some opposing principle—as in the Dark Ages or during the rise of the nationalities—but in order to create a situation in which the very possibility of opposed principles, with all their unlimited capacity to cause mental stress and danger and destructive collisions, is eliminated in favor of a simpler and better regulated life, a robust faith in an efficiently working order, untroubled by agonizing moral conflict.

Yet this is not a gratuitous development: the social and economic situation in which we are placed, the failure to harmonize the effects of technical progress with the forces of political and economic organization inherited from an earlier phase, do call for a greater measure of social control to prevent chaos and destitution, no less fatal to the development of human faculties than blind conformity. And certainly it is morally unthinkable that we give up our social gains and meditate for an instant the possibility of a return to ancient injustice and inequality and hopeless misery. The progress of technological skill makes it rational and indeed imperative to plan, and anxiety for the success of a particular planned society naturally inclines the planners to seek insulation from dangerous, because incalculable, forces which may jeopardize the plan. And this is a powerful incentive to "autarky" and "Socialism in one country" whether imposed by conservatives, or New Dealers, or isolationists, or Social Democrats, or indeed imperialists. And this in its turn generates artificial barriers and increasingly restricts the planners' own resources. In extreme cases it leads to repression of the discontented and a perpetual tightening of discipline, until it absorbs more and more of the time and ingenuity of those who originally conceived it only as a means to a minimum of efficiency. Presently it grows to be a hideous end in itself, since its realization spells ruin to the system now caught in a vicious circle of repression in order to survive and of survival mainly to repress. So the remedy grows to be worse than the disease, and takes the form of those orthodoxies which rest on the simple puritanical faith of individuals who never knew or have forgotten what *douceur de vivre*, free self-expression, the infinite variety of persons and of the relationships between them, and the right of free choice, difficult to endure but more intolerable to surrender, can ever have been like.

The dilemma is logically insoluble: we cannot sacrifice either freedom or a minimum standard of welfare. The way out must therefore lie in some logically untidy, flexible, and even ambiguous compromise: every situation calls for its own specific policy, since out of the crooked timber of humanity, as Kant once remarked, no straight thing was ever made. What the age calls for is not (as we are so often told) more faith or stronger leadership or more rational organization. Rather is it the opposite—less Messianic ardor, more enlightened skepticism, more toleration of idiosyncrasies, more frequent *ad hoc* and ephemeral arrangements, more room for the attainment of their personal ends by individuals and by minorities whose tastes and beliefs find (whether rightly or wrongly must not matter) little response among the majority. What is required is a less mechanical, less fervent application of general principles, however rational or righteous, a more cautious and less self-confident application of accepted, scientifically tested, general solutions in unexamined individual cases. We must not submit to authority because it is infallible but only for strictly and openly utilitarian reasons, as a necessary evil. Since no solution can be guaranteed against error, no disposition is final. And therefore a loose texture and a measure of inefficiency and even muddle, even a degree of indulgence in idle talk, idle curiosity, aimless pursuit of this or that without authorization—"conspicuous waste" itself—may allow more spontaneous, individual variation (for which the individual must in the end assume full responsibility), and will always be worth far more than the neatest and most delicately fashioned imposed pattern. Above all, it must be realized that the kinds of problems which this or that method of education or system of scientific or religious or social organization of life is guaranteed to solve are *eo facto* not the central questions of human life. They are not, and never have been, the fundamental issues which embody the changing outlook and the most intense preoccupation of their time and generation. It is from absorbed preoccupation with these fundamental issues and these alone, unplanned and at times without technical equipment, more often than not without conscious hope of success, still less of the approbation of the official auditor, that the best moments come in the lives of individuals and peoples.❧

Of Liberty

Benedetto Croce

Foreign Affairs, October 1932

Between the orderly Europe that we used to know and the distracted Europe of today is fixed the great gulf of the World War. We remember the old Europe with its riches, its flourishing trade, its abundance of goods, its ease of life, its bold sense of security; we see today the new Europe—impoverished, discouraged, crisscrossed with high tariff walls, each nation occupied solely with its own affairs, too distraught to pay heed to the things of the spirit and tormented by the fear of worse to come. Gone is the gay international society once the pride of Europe's capitals; extinct, or almost so, is the old community of thought, art, civilization. How many astounding changes there have been in frontiers and in political relationships! In the place of the Germany of the Hohenzollerns we see the German Republic; Austria-Hungary has been dismembered and cut up into new states; French sway has been reëstablished over the provinces lost in 1870, and the Italian frontiers now include the unredeemed territories and extend to the Brenner; Poland has been reconstituted; Russia is ruled, not by the Tsars but by the Soviets; and the United States has become a dominant factor in European policy.

Yet if we pass from externals to essentials and try to identify the controlling forces now at work, we soon discern that these two Europes, so dissimilar in appearance, have continuity and homogeneity. When we leave out superficial impressions and make a

---

BENEDETTO CROCE, Italian Senator, former Minister for Public Instruction, and author of "Filosofia dello Spirito," a philosophic system translated into many languages.

careful analysis we detect the same characteristics in both, though in the Europe of today they have been exaggerated by the war. The same proclivities and the same spiritual conflicts are there, though aggravated by the general intellectual decay which was to be expected after a war which counted its victims by the millions, accustomed its survivors to violence, and destroyed the habit of critical, constructive and concentrated mental labor.

Nationalistic and imperialistic impulses have seized the victorious nations because they are victors, and the vanquished because they are vanquished; while the new states add new nationalisms, new imperialisms to the list. Impatience with free institutions has led to open or masked dictatorships, and, where dictatorships do not exist, to the desire for them. Liberty, which before the war was a faith, or at least a routine acceptance, has now departed from the hearts of men even if it still survives in certain institutions. In its place is an atavistic libertarism which more than ever ponders disorder and destruction, gives rein to extravagant impulses, and produces spectacular and sterile works. Indifferent and contemptuous, its followers scorn meditative and loving labor, labor with a reverent affection for the past and a courageous mastery of the future. They scorn actions which spring from the heart and speak to the heart, speculations which hold the germs of truth, history based on a realization of all that man has achieved by painful struggle, poetry which is beautiful.

Under the name of socialism, communism had already been introduced into the political life and institutions of Europe before the war. Now it has reappeared, crude and disruptive. Liberalism it ridicules as something naively moralistic. Like atavism, into which it often blends, this communism is a sterile thing that kills thought, religion and art: seeking to subjugate them to its own purposes, it can only destroy them. All the distortions and decrepit sophistries of historical materialism have reappeared in the current opinions and theories of the day as if they were new and full of promise, although any man with a slight knowledge of criticism and the history of ideas passed judgment upon them long ago. They have taken on an air of novelty and modernness merely because, although originally introduced by Europe to Russia, they now come out of Russia; if anything they are more immature and shallow than ever; but in this age of unprecedented callowness and crudity they gain unprecedented credence. Catholicism, moreover, which before the war sought to draw new strength from the forces of irrationalism and mysticism, has been gathering into its fold many weak and bewildered souls. Thus once again is heard that chorus of pessimism and decadence which echoed through pre-war literature, this time announcing the decline of western civilization and of the human race itself. According to these prophets it is about to sink back to the level of beasts after having failed to reach the estate of man.

All these are facts, and it is useless to deny them or to say that they are true only of certain people in certain countries. Like the situation from which they spring they are common to all Europe and all the world. And since they are facts, they must have a function to fill in the development of the human spirit and in social and human progress—if not as direct creators of new values, then at least as resources and stimuli for the deepening and broadening of old values. This function, whatever it may be, will be understood and described only by the future historian. He will have before him as a completed story the movement in which we are now involved and its subsequent developments. We cannot understand it or even attempt to describe it as a whole because we are part of it. Being in it, moving with it, we can, it is true, observe and understand many of its aspects, but that is all.

And what practical moral is there for each of us in the fact that we cannot know the future? This: that we must take part in what is going on about us, and not waste our forces in the contemplation of the unknowable, that we must act, to the degree that each of us can, as our conscience and duty command. Those who in disregard of the ancient admonition of Solon strive to understand and judge a life "before it is finished," and who lose themselves in conjecture and surmise, should be on their guard lest these digressions into the unknown prove a snare set by a bad demon to keep them from their goal.

Not "a history of the future" (as the old thinkers used to define prophecy), but a history of the past which is summed up in the present, is what we need for our work, for our action. And what we need most at the moment is to examine, or at least to review, those ideals which are generally accepted today. We must discover whether they contain the power to dissolve or surpass or correct the ideals which we ourselves hold; so that thereafter we may change or modify our ideals, and in any event reëstablish them upon a surer, sounder foundation.

The ideal of a transcendental system of truth, and, corollary to it, of a system of government from on high, exercised on earth by a vicar and represented by a church, has not yet acquired the intellectual proof which past ages found it to lack. Like all obvious statements this one runs the risk of seeming ungenerous. None the less, it is a fact that the spiritual impulse which has prompted many persons to return to Catholicism or to take refuge in it (or in similar if less venerable and authoritative havens) is merely a craving, amid the turmoil of clashing and changing ideals, for a truth that is fixed and a rule of life that is imposed from above. In some cases it may have no nobler basis than fear and renunciation, a childish terror in the presence of the perception that all truth is absolute and at the same time relative. But a moral ideal cannot conform to the needs of the discouraged and the fearful.

Nor can a moral ideal conform to the purposes of those who are drunk with action for action's sake; for action thus conceived leaves only nausea, a profound indifference toward all that has stirred the human race, and an incapacity for objective work. Humanity has drunk deep of nationalism and imperialism and the taste of them is already bitter as gall: *inveni amariorem felle.* Those who love action for its own sake still rage on. But where is their serenity of soul, their joy in life? The best of them are enveloped in gloom; the great mass of them are merely raw and stupid.

Communism, it is the fashion to claim, has passed from theory to practice and is being applied in Russia. But it is being practised not as communism but—in keeping with its inner contradiction— as a form of autocracy, as its critics had always predicted would be the case. Under it the people of Russia are denied even that faint breath of freedom which they managed to obtain under the autocracy of the Tsars. The abolition of the State, that "transition from the régime of necessity to the régime of liberty" about which Marx theorized, has not taken place. Communism has not abolished the State—it could not and never will be able to do so—but, as irony would have it, has forged for itself one of the most oppressive state systems which it is possible to imagine. In saying this we are not trying to deny that perhaps there were circumstances which forced the Russian revolutionists to choose the course they did and no other. Neither do we wish to detract from the immensity of their endeavors to develop, under these circumstances, the productive forces of the country. Neither do we minimize the importance of the lessons to be learned from their endeavors, or fail to admire the mystic enthusiasm, materialistic though it be, which inspires them and keeps them from sinking beneath the load which they have put on their own backs. It is this enthusiasm which gives them courage to trample on religion, thought, poetry, on everything in a word which we in the West revere as sacred or noble.

Nevertheless the Russian Communists have not solved, nor will their violent and repressive methods ever enable them to solve, the fundamental problem of human society, the problem of freedom. For in freedom only can human society flourish and bear fruit. Freedom alone gives meaning to life: without it life is unbearable. Here is an inescapable problem. It cannot be eliminated. It springs from the very vitals of things and stirs in the souls of all those countless human beings whom the Communists are trying to control and reshape in accordance with their arbitrary concepts. And on the day that this problem is faced, the materialistic foundations of the Soviet structure will crumble and new and very different supports will have to be found for it. Then, even as now, pure communism will not be practised in Russia.

Outside of Russia this pseudo-communism has not gained much ground in spite of the fascination that always attaches to things remote in time and space—as the old adage has it, *maior e longinquo reverentia*. Two conditions present in Russia are indeed lacking in Western and Central Europe: the Tsarist tradition and mysticism. Miliukov was not far from the truth when he wrote of

Lenin some twelve or more years ago that "in Russia he was building on the solid foundations of the good old autocratic tradition, but that as far as other countries were concerned he was merely building castles in the air." Even if such experiments should develop in other parts of Europe, the fact that other countries differ so from Russia in religion, civilization, education, customs, traditions—in historical background, in short—would produce something quite new, whatever its name and appearance; or else, after an indeterminate period of blind groping and struggle, there would sooner or later emerge that liberty which is only another name for humanity.

For liberty is the only ideal which unites the stability that Catholicism once possessed with the flexibility which it could never attain, the only ideal which faces the future without proposing to mould it to some particular form, the only ideal that can survive criticism and give human society a fixed point by which from time to time to reëstablish its balance. There are those who question the future of the ideal of freedom. To them we answer that it has more than a future: it has eternity. And today, despite the contempt and ridicule heaped upon it, liberty still endures in many of our institutions and customs and still exercises a beneficent influence upon them. More significant still, it abides in the hearts and minds of many noble men all over the world, men who though scattered and isolated, reduced to a small but aristocratic *res publica literaria*, still keep faith with it, reverently hallow its name, and love it more truly than ever they did in the days when no one denied or questioned its absolute sovereignty, when the mob proclaimed its glory and contaminated it with a vulgarity of which it is now purged.

And not only does freedom abide in such men, and not only does it exist and persist in the constitutions of many important countries and in institutions and customs. Its virtue is operative in things themselves and is gradually opening a way through many difficulties. We see it at work in the present wish for a truce in suspicions, a reduction in armaments and a peaceful settlement among the nations of Europe. That this is true is apparent in the general feeling that somehow these nations must contrive to harmonize their plans and efforts if they are to retain not their political and economic supremacy only, but even their leadership as creators of civilization and the aptitudes for this unending task which they have acquired through centuries of labor and experience.

Disarmament and world peace are the only statesmanlike projects among the many put forward since the war which have not faded out or been dissipated; rather are they gaining ground from year to year and converting many who were once antagonistic or incredulous or faint-hearted. We are entitled to hope that they will not be allowed to fail but will be carried forward to fulfillment in the face of all opposition. It is true that the World War, which future historians may well regard as the *reductio ad absurdum* of nationalism, has embittered the relations of certain states as a result of an unjust and foolish peace treaty; but it also has made the peoples aware in their innermost consciousness that they have common virtues and defects, common strengths and weaknesses, that they share a common destiny, are inspired by the same affections, afflicted by the same sorrows, glory in the same patrimony of ideals. This explains why already in all parts of Europe we are witnessing the birth of a new consciousness, a new nationality—for nations are not, as has been imagined, data of nature but results of conscious acts, historical formations. Just as seventy years ago the Neapolitans and the Piedmontese decided to become Italians, not by abjuring their original nationality but by exalting and merging it in the new one, so Frenchmen and Germans and Italians and all the others will rise to becoming Europeans; they will think as Europeans, their hearts will beat for Europe as they now do for their smaller countries, not forgetting them but loving them the better.

This process of amalgamation is directly opposed to competitive nationalism and will in time destroy it entirely; meanwhile it tends to free Europe from the psychology of nationalism and its attendant habits of thought and action. If and when this happens, the liberal ideal will again prevail in the European mind and resume its sway over European hearts. But we must not see in this rebirth of liberalism merely a way to bring back the "old times" for which the Romantics idly yearn. Present events, those still to take place, will have their due effect; certain institutions of the old liberalism will have to be modified and replaced by ones better adapted to their tasks; new governing classes, made up of different elements, will arise; and experience will bring forth new concepts and give a new direction to the popular will.

In this new mental and moral atmosphere it will be imperative to take up again the so-called "social" problems. They are certainly not of recent making; thinkers and statesmen have struggled with them for centuries, dealing with them as they arose, case by case and in the spirit of the times. During the nineteenth century they were the object of deep attention and most heroic remedies, and were dealt with in such a way as to improve greatly the conditions of the working classes, to raise their standards of living and to better their legal and moral status. "Planned" economy, as it is now being called, although it holds a foremost position in talk today is not essentially new; and the question cannot be seriously raised of finding a collective substitute for individual economy or free individual initiative, both of themselves necessary to human life and economic progress. Discussion can turn only on the proportions, great or small, to be assigned to one form of economic organization rather than to another, differing with different means, places, times and other circumstances. This is primarily a question for technical experts and statesmen, who will have to devise solutions suitable to the times and favorable to an increase of wealth and its more equitable distribution. It is a question for experts and statesmen; but they will be unable to fulfill their function or attain their ends unless liberty be there to prepare and maintain the intellectual and moral atmosphere indispensable to labors so arduous, and to quicken the legal systems within which their duties must be performed.❧

The Position and Prospects of Communism

Harold J. Laski

Foreign Affairs, October 1932

"A spectre is haunting Europe—the spectre of communism."
Eighty-five years have passed since the *Communist Manifesto*
opened with those fateful words. It is little less since Tocqueville
predicted that the democracy, weary of the inadequate results of
their political emancipation, would one day turn to the destruction of the rights of property as the condition precedent to their
economic emancipation. "In matters of social construction," he
wrote,[1] "the field of possibilities is much more extensive than men
living in their various societies are willing to imagine."

After the breakdown of the revolutions of 1848 there was little
disposition among the statesmen of Europe and America to take
the growth of socialism with any profound seriousness until the
epoch of the war. A moment of horror at the events in Paris in 1871,
a sense that the abortive revolution in Russia of 1905 might be the
prelude to a vaster drama, exhausted the sense of doubt about the
foundations of the social system. Neither the experience of France
nor of Germany seemed to point to the likelihood of Socialist governments; and as late as 1908, President Lowell, reflecting upon
the English position at the close of his famous treatise,[2] concluded
that "unless the Labor Party should grow in a way that seems unlikely" there was no prospect of a class-division in English politics

HAROLD J. LASKI, Professor of Political Science in the University
of London; author of "The Dangers of Obedience" and other works.

in the near future. Lord Grey, indeed, on the very eve of the war, was troubled by a sense that its prolongation might result in a repetition of 1848; but the universal welcome which greeted the March Revolution in Russia did not suggest that men had any doubts about the foundations of a capitalist society. At no time in American history prior to the war had the socialist movement made any profound impact upon American life.

The Bolshevik Revolution wrought an immediate and fundamental change in the perspective of public opinion. The very fact that Marxian principles could assume the guise of action made it evident that the foundations of capitalism had nothing like the security that had been assumed. As Lenin consolidated his position against both the attacks of the Allies and the impact of civil war, the Russian Revolution began to reveal itself as the profoundest change in the mental climate of the world since the Reformation. The proletariat in a state of one hundred and thirty millions had not merely challenged the rights of property, it had overthrown them. Before five years had passed it was obvious that the Russian Revolution was not, as its enemies hoped, a temporary portent. It had affected the psychological fabric of all civilization. Ideas like the class-war, the dictatorship of the proletariat, the expropriation of the capitalist, had passed at a single bound from books to action. What seemed in 1914 an underground and unimportant conspiracy had become, ten years later, a state. And it was obvious that the fact of such a state's existence, the knowledge that it could survive and grow, had turned men's thoughts into new directions. For the first time in history, a proletarian state was an actual, and not merely an ideological, inspiration; and for the first time in history, also, capitalist society met a direct and thorough-going challenge.

The impact of Russia upon the old world and the new cannot be expressed in simple terms. Certainly there were few thoughtful minds whom it did not compel to a revaluation, or, at least, a reassessment of the basic principles of politics. The pre-war state-system emerged

---

1 "Recollections," p. 101.

2 "Government of England," II, p. 534.

from the great conflict far more shattered than was apparent in the mood of vindictive triumph embodied in the Peace of Versailles. It had to grapple with a *damnosa hereditas*. The necessities of war had given an enhanced status to the working-classes of the belligerent countries; and it was necessary to satisfy their new claims. National feeling had been profoundly inflamed by the conflict; and since nationalism took the form of an intense revival of neo-mercantilist doctrine, a community of states emerged whose political practices were increasingly at variance with the objective needs of the world-economic market. The problems created by debts and reparations, the control of imports and migration in the interest of the several states, the new levels of taxation rendered necessary by the demands of social legislation, the refusal of the Far East any longer to accept the domination of Western Europe and America, all implied the futility of believing that the old laissez-faire was compatible with the attainment of social good. It had become clear to every careful observer that it was necessary either deliberately to plan the post-war civilization or to perish.

For a brief period, the sudden prosperity of America (though much more confined than was generally realized) concealed from many the realities of the situation. It was argued that the condition of Russia was a special one; that, elsewhere, the problem was rather one of dealing with the excrescences of the capitalist system than with capitalism itself. As late as 1928 President Hoover felt able to announce to an awe-struck world that America had (under God) solved the problem of poverty. Two years later, it was clear that his announcement was premature. The world (including America) was caught in the grips of a depression more intense and more widespread than any recorded in history. The unemployed could be counted in millions in capitalist countries. The mood of pessimism was universal; men spoke gravely of a possible collapse of civilization. At a time when science had made possible a greater productivity than in any previous age, the problem of distribution seemed insoluble. All the nations demanded the removal of barriers against world-trade; despite pious recommendations, like those at Geneva in 1927, they did not seem able to remove them. All the world agreed upon the necessity of disarmament; the conference at Geneva to attain it would have been farcical if it had not been tragic. The dislocation of currency methods deprived commerce of that automatic measure of value upon which the life-blood of trade depended. Thirteen years after the end of the war, the perspective of capitalist civilization revealed an insecurity, both economic and political, which made justifiable the gravest doubts of its future.

Russian development was in striking contrast. The Five Year Plan gave it an integrated and orderly purpose such as no capitalist country could rival. Productivity increased at a remarkable rate; unemployment was non-existent. If the standard of living was low compared with that of Great Britain or the United States, its tendency was to increase and not to decline. The whole population was united in a great corporate effort at material well-being in which there was the promise of equal participation. Where Europe and America were sunk in pessimism, the whole temper of Russia was optimistic. The authority of its government was unchallenged; its power to win amazing response to its demands was unquestionable. Granted all its errors, no honest observer could doubt its capacity both to plan greatly and, in large measure, to realize its plans. No doubt its government was, in a rigorous sense, a dictatorship. No doubt also it imposed upon its subjects a discipline, both spiritual and material, such as a capitalist civilization would hardly dare to attempt. No doubt, again, its subjects paid a heavy price for the ultimate achievement to which they looked forward. Yet, whatever its defects and errors, the mood of the Russian experiment was one of exhilaration. While the rest of the world confronted its future in a temper of skepticism and dismay, Russia moved forward in a belief, religious in the intensity of its emotion, that it had a right to ample confidence in its future.

II

No one can understand the character of the communist challenge to capitalism who does not grasp the significance of this contrast.

A hundred years ago the votaries of capitalism had a religious faith in its prospects. They were, naturally enough, dazzled by the miracles it performed, confident that the aggregation of its individual successes was coincident with the social good, happy in a security about the results of their investment which seemed to entitle them to refashion the whole world in their own image. The successful business man became the representative type of civilization. He subdued all the complex of social institutions to his purposes. Finance, oil, coal, steel, became empires of which the sovereignty was as unchallenged as that of Macedon or of Rome. Men so different as Disraeli and Marx might utter warnings about the stability of the edifice. Broadly speaking, they were unheeded in the triumphs to which the business man could point.

But those triumphs could not conceal the fact that the idol had feet of clay. The price to be paid for their accomplishment was a heavy one. The distribution of the rewards was incapable of justification in terms of moral principle. The state was driven increasingly to intervene to mitigate the inequalities to which capitalism gave rise. Vast and costly schemes of social legislation, militant trade unionism, a nationalism of pathological proportions, imperialist exploitation with its consequential awakening of nationalism among the peoples exploited,[3] were all inherently involved in the technique of a capitalist civilization. Nationalism meant imperialism; imperialism meant war; in the struggle for markets there was involved an inescapable threat to the security of the whole structure. That became finally evident in the Great War and its aftermath. A world of competing economic nationalisms could not avoid inevitable conflict.

Nor is this all. The condition for the survival of an acquisitive society is twofold. There must be no halt in its power to continue its successes; and it must be able so to apportion their results that the proletariat do not doubt their duty to be loyal to its institutions. This condition has not been realized. Economic nationalism has given birth to a body of vested interests which impede in

---

3 See my "Nationalism and the Future of Civilization" (1932).

a fatal way the expansion of world trade. On the one hand, the power of productivity makes the ideal of self-sufficiency incapable of realization; on the other, the capture of foreign markets means commercial warfare which issues into actual warfare. The individual ownership of the means of production is incompatible with the kind of planning necessitated by the interrelations of a world reduced to the unity of interdependence.

The failure to maintain the allegiance of the proletariat, though different in degree in different countries, is, nevertheless, universal. Its danger was foreseen by Tocqueville nearly a century ago. "The manufacturer," he wrote,[4] "asks nothing of the workman but his labor; the workman expects nothing from him but his wages. The one contracts no obligation to protect, nor the other to defend; and they are not permanently connected either by habit or by duty. . . . The manufacturing aristocracy of our age first impoverishes and debases the men who serve it, and then abandons them to be supported by the charity of the public. . . . Between the workman and the master there are frequent relations but no real partnership." Everything that has happened since Tocqueville wrote has combined to give emphasis to his insight. The decay of religion has intensified the appreciation of material well-being. The growth of education has made working-class resentment at the contrast between riches and poverty both keener and more profound. Universal suffrage has made necessary a far wider and more costly response to the demands of the proletariat; and the perfection of party organization has made the struggle for political power one in which the offer of bread and circuses is an essential part.

Men, in short, accept a capitalist society no longer because they believe in it, but because of the material benefits it professes to confer. Once it ceases to confer them, it cannot exercise its old magic over men's minds. It has become, writes Mr. Keynes,[5] "absolutely irreligious, without internal union, without much public spirit, often, though not always, a mere congeries of possessors and pur-

---

4 "Democracy in America," Part II, Book II, Chapter XVIII.
5 "Essays in Persuasion," p. 306.

suers." Once its success is a matter of dubiety, those who do not profit by its results inevitably turn to alternative ways of life. They realize that the essence of a capitalist society is its division into a small number of rich men and a great mass of poor men. They see not only the existence of a wealthy class which lives without the performance of any socially useful function; they realize also that it is inherent in such a society that there should be no proportion between effort and reward. They see this when the decline of capitalist prosperity makes the payment of the price demanded for their allegiance to the system one it is increasingly difficult to pay without destroying the position of advantage which the rich enjoy in society. The social service state can only be maintained at a level which satisfies the worker in a period of increasing returns. Once its benefits have to be diminished, the moral poverty of capitalism becomes apparent to all save those who live by its preservation. There arises an insistent demand for economic and social equality—such a distribution of the social product as can rationally be referred to intelligible principle. Resistance develops to the normal technique by which capitalism adjusts itself to a falling market. The growth of socialism in Great Britain, the dissatisfaction with the historic parties in the United States, the rise of Hitlerism in Germany, the profound and growing interest, all over the world, in the Russian experiment, are all of them, in their various ways, the expression of that resistance. Men have begun to ask, upon a universal scale, whether there is not the possibility of consciously building a classless society in which the ideal of equality is deliberately given meaning.

It is not, I think, excessive to argue that the experience of this generation leads most socially conscious observers to doubt the desirability of relying upon the money motive in individuals automatically to produce a well-ordered community. It is at least a matter of universal recognition that the collective intelligence of society must control all major economic operations. But the translation of that recognition into policy encounters difficulties of which the importance cannot be over-emphasized. For it asks men to part with power on an unexampled scale. It changes a system of established expectations profoundly rooted in the habits of mankind.

It disturbs vested interests which are well organized, both for offense and defense, and accustomed by long tradition to have their way. No governing class in the history of the world has consciously and deliberately sacrificed its authority. It has gone down fighting, as in France and Russia; it has cooperated with the *novi homines* of the industrial revolution, as in England or Germany. But the call to socialism, which the anarchy of capitalist society has produced, is, at bottom, a demand for economic egalitarianism in which the possessors are invited to sacrifice their power, their vested interests, their established expectations, for the attainment of a common good they will no longer be able to manipulate to their own interest.

The socialist parties of Western civilization have conceived a simple formula upon which to place reliance. They will win a majority of the electorate to their side; and they will proceed, by legislative enactment, gradually to introduce the socialist commonwealth. Possessing themselves of the constitution of the state, they assume that they can operate the machinery to their own purposes. They argue that if the pace is not too violently forced, the instinct for law and order will enable them to consummate their revolution with good will because their policy will proceed by reasonable stages. That has been the policy of the two Labor Governments which arrived in office, a little accidentally perhaps, in Great Britain; and in their different ways it has been the policy of such socialist governments as have held office elsewhere. Of them all it is not unfair to say that they nowhere made any essential difference to the foundations of capitalist society. Of them, also, it is true to say that if they showed signs of seriously compromising those foundations, they were driven to surrender power to their rivals. And in that event it was the bankruptcy, rather than the success, of gradualist change which became apparent.

In this context, what is important is the underlying assumption of socialist gradualism: it builds upon the persistence of constitutional democracy. But not only—as Italy, Jugoslavia and the rest make plain—is that persistence a dubious matter in practice; the persistence of constitutional democracy depends upon the further assumption that men are agreed upon the fundamental principles of policy. In a broad way, this was true as between Liberals and Conservatives in the nineteenth century; experience has demonstrated how little ground there is for believing that it is true when the choice is between a capitalist and a socialist way of life. No one who meditates upon the prospect of large-scale socialist experiment can conclude that it is likely to go into operation without grave challenge. No one, either, can argue that such a challenge will permit the principles of constitutional democracy to survive unimpaired.

III

It is at this point that the communist hypothesis becomes of such overwhelming importance. It points to the inherent contradictions of capitalist society. It denies that there is in it any longer the power to resolve those contradictions within its assumptions. It insists that no socialist government can attempt seriously to put its principles into practice without encountering determined resistance which will issue in civil war. To maintain socialist principles, in short, socialists will be driven to become communists or to betray their socialism. If they become communists, they will find themselves involved in the grim logic of Leninism—the dictatorship of the proletariat, the drastic suppression of counter-revolution, the confiscation of the essential instruments of production, the building of the state, in a word, upon the principles of martial law until the security of the new order is firmly established. The transformation of capitalism into socialism means revolution, and that implies an experience akin to that through which Russia has passed.

I do not see how it is reasonable to deny the possibility—to put it no higher—that the communists are right. The threat of war is implicit in our society, and war means revolution all over the world. Even if that revolution assumed a Fascist form, communism would be its inevitable antithesis; and, in that event, sooner or later communism would move to the assault. To avoid the threat of war, the degree of self-reformation which capitalist states must undertake would leave them unrecognizable as capitalist. The observer of

England, of America, of France is entitled to doubt whether there is in the possessing classes of any of them that will to self-reformation which would make it effective. The change of heart required would involve a transvaluation of all values, the supersession by agreement of money as the dominant motive to action. It is only the acceptance of new values with an intensity almost religious in character which could effect that supersession; and that possession of a body of alternative values held with religious intensity is, to put it quite bluntly, practically a monopoly of the communists at the present time.

That, indeed, is the secret of its strength. Its devotees believe in it with a faith so absolute that there is no sacrifice they are not prepared to make in its name. Communism has succeeded in Russia for the same reasons that brought triumph to the Jesuits, the Puritans, the Jacobins in an earlier period. Willing the end, the communists have not shrunk from the application of any means likely to attain that end. They have consistently opposed an unshakable will to the resistance they have encountered. They have disdained both compromise and hesitation. In the service of no other social system in the world today can it be said that these qualities are enlisted. No one defends the acquisitive society save in the most mitigated terms. No capitalist society could attempt experiment on the Russian scale without risking the willingness of the working-classes to observe the demands of law and order. Not even the most intense propaganda in capitalist countries has prevented the working-classes from feeling a proud interest in every success the Russian experiment can show. "Perhaps," wrote Mr. Keynes,[6] "Russian communism does represent the first confused stirrings of a great religion." That is a widespread and growing feeling among all who are disturbed by the contradictions of capitalism; and it is an emotion far more profoundly diffused among the workers than is realized by the rulers of alternative systems.

The unity, in fact, of capitalist society has been broken. No country is prepared to pay the price which its simple rehabilitation demands; and to attempt the enforcement of that price would

---

6 "Essays in Persuasion," p. 309.

involve disorders of which no one could predict the outcome. That is the significance of the point made earlier in this essay that the Russian revolution shapes the perspective of men's thoughts. Lower the standards of life, whether by decreases in wages or by economies in social legislation, diminish the worker's security, sharpen the contrast between poverty and wealth, and it at once comes into the worker's mind that in Russia, if the standard is low, it is rising, and that the hope of still greater rises is profound, that all social legislation is in the proletarian interest, that the contrasts between poverty and wealth are largely without meaning. A state has been built upon the exaltation of the common man; it is inevitable that the common men of other states should have its existence and its possibilities increasingly in their minds.

Capitalist society, in other words, is running a race with communist society for the allegiance of the masses. The terms upon which the former can be successful are fairly clear. It has to solve the contradiction between its power to produce and its inability to distribute income in a rational and morally adequate way. It has to remove the barriers which economic nationalism places in the way of an unimpeded world-market. It has to remove the fear of insecurity by which the worker's life is haunted. It has to end the folly of international competition in wage-rates and hours of labor; it has to find ways of saving Western standards from the slave-labor of the East. It has, not least, to cut away the jungle-growth of vested interests which at present so seriously impair its efficiency. Even a capitalist society will not long endure the spectacle of the cotton and coal industries of Great Britain or the power-trust in the United States. Above all, perhaps, it has to find some way of removing from the clash of competing imperialisms those structures of armed power which, clothed in the garb of national sovereignty, make certain the perpetual threat of insecurity and, born of it, the advent of war.

Let me emphasize again that to meet successfully the challenge of communism a capitalist society has to show itself immensely more successful than the former. This does not, of course, mean that communism, in its Russian expression, does not confront its own grave problems. Broadly, they are of two kinds. It is necessary, by economic success, to maintain the exhilaration, the enthusiastic will to sacrifice, of the first great period of striving; and it is necessary, in the second, to relate Russia more adequately to the conditions of the external world. For, in the context of the first condition, it must not be forgotten that Russia was to some extent fortunate in her situation. Not only was she dealing with a people accustomed to the psychology of an autocratic discipline; she was also able to take advantage of a profound patriotism engendered by external attack. The Soviet State cannot go on perpetually demanding the postponement of consumption for the sake of a future which does not arrive. They must come to a point where the maintenance of enthusiasm for the new régime is the outcome of having conferred tangible benefit. Nor will it be possible over any considerable period to maintain the dominating grip of the Communist Party over the whole political life of Russia. That grip has been acquiesced in because of the social circumstances confronting the new régime; no acquiescence in a dictatorship is ever permanent in character. There must, that is to say, not only be economic success in the new Russia; there must come also a time when restriction is relaxed and room is found for the admission of freedom. The permanence of communist society depends upon its ability to meet these issues creatively. For any new social order that seeks to become universal must be able to correlate its economic advance with spiritual growth.

No doubt, of course, spiritual growth, and especially that temper of tolerance which is the groundwork of all intellectual achievement, is, in its turn, dependent upon economic advance. Periods of revolutionary poverty rarely synchronize with periods of great scientific or literary production; for the atmosphere of dictatorship, the pre-occupation with material well-being, are stifling to that atmosphere of experiment upon which intellectual advance depends. It is not accidental that neither the Puritan nor the French Revolution has left behind it a great cultural impact upon the mind of the world; the spiritual fruits of each were gathered after men could in leisure and in safety seek to probe their implications. It is therefore reasonable to argue that the success of Russian communism depends upon the maintenance, at least for a considerable period, of world peace. For if Russia becomes involved in any serious military conflict the transformation of its energies will dangerously impair the prospect of its economic policy. More than this, the intensification of the dictatorship involved in war might easily, if the struggle were at all prolonged, result in the kind of internal conflicts within the Communist Party which, in the French Revolution, made ultimately possible the emergence of Napoleon.

It would be folly to deny the possibility of Russia becoming involved in war within the next decade.7 The clash of interests with Japan in the Far East is a grave one. The fear of the effect of Russian exports of butter, timber, oil, coal and wheat on a depressed market already gives birth to those economic reprisals out of which war has so often come. The instability of Europe is fed by Russian propaganda; and the very fact that communism expects a world-revolution to come by way of war gives to that propaganda the psychological perspective which so easily makes expectancy fact. The failure of disarmament, the dissatisfaction of minorities, the intensity of social revolutionary movements in the East, all of these point to that kind of collapse in the system of international regulation which is the prelude to conflict. And it is useless to deny that there are, all over the world, important interests which would welcome an attack on Russia before its success is beyond question as the surest way of ending that implicit challenge to capitalist society which it represents. Certainly militant communism and militant capitalism cannot exist side by side, especially in a period of serious economic stress. It is important that Moscow is the Mecca of the discontented and disinherited of the whole world; it is not less important that Moscow is ideologically driven to the encouragement of their hopes. No one who surveys at all objectively the relations of Russia with the external world can possibly be optimistic about their outcome.

---

7 On this see Mr. R. D. Charques' admirable résumé, "The Soviets and the Next War" (1932).

I do not think that a war against Russia would destroy communism there though I believe it would enormously increase the price of its accomplishment; but I do believe it would be fatal to the maintenance of capitalist society at least in Europe and the Far East. Probably its cost would be a period of anarchy comparable to the Dark Ages, with every sort and kind of dictatorship emerging to supply for brief periods an uneasy semblance of order. Ultimately, I think, Russia would be the first state to emerge from that chaos with something like the hope of recovery; and its authority, under those circumstances, would be far more compelling than it is today, its challenge more direct and explicit. In the long run, in a word, the price of challenging communism to military conflict would be not its defeat but its victory.

IV

The future of communism is a function of the capacity of capitalist society to repair its foundations. The success—despite the appalling cost—of the Russian experiment has made it the one effective center of creativeness in a world which, otherwise, does not seem to know how to turn its feet away from the abyss. Capitalist society since the war has adopted every expedient of self-destruction. The Peace of Versailles, the tangled mess of war-debts and reparations, the struggle for power concealed beneath the myth of national sovereignty, the failure to respect the League, all of these were implicit in its ultimate disrespect for moral principle. The social habits of its votaries, its literature with its insistent note of cynical skepticism, its philosophy which sought refuge in mysticism and impulse to shut out the still small voice of reason, a press which (not least notably in its dealing with Russia) could make miraculous propaganda but could not tell the truth, its religions in decay, its political and economic institutions hopelessly remote from the realities they confronted, its leaders like straws caught in the eddies of an ever-quickening stream—it is not in such a society as this that one looks for the spring of a new hope. On the credit side, no doubt, there was a science more renascent than at any time since the seventeenth century; but it was also more dangerous because the formula seemed lost by which it could be bent to social purposes.

Such a society cannot meet the challenge of communism, because its faith in itself is not sufficient to give it a victorious destiny. It may postpone defeat; it cannot finally elude it. For in the conflict of ideologies victory always goes in the end to men who are willing to sacrifice material power for spiritual conquest. Communism interests the new generation because, alone among the welter of competing gospels, it has known how to win sacrifice from its devotees in the name of a great ideal. It offers the prospect—the clue to the success of all the great religions—of losing one's life in order to find it. There is poverty, there is intellectual error, there is grave moral wrong; but there is also unlimited hope. These have been characteristic of all great religious movements. They do not seem to disturb their power eventually to triumph.

The chance for a capitalist society in contest with communism lies in its ability to remake its own creed. Its danger is the ease with which it attacks the symptoms of communism instead of its causes. It is afraid of the propaganda of the Third International instead of the conditions which make that propaganda fall on fertile soil. It is afraid of the bold imagination which underlies the Five Year Plan; but instead of planning more boldly and more imaginatively itself, it spends its time dourly foretelling its inevitable failure. It attacks with passion the outrageous injustices of which communism has been guilty, its stifling of initiative, the reckless cruelty of the Ogpu, the relentless attack on the Kulaks. But it does not stay to remember that its own Sacco-Vanzetti case, the Polish treatment of minorities, the dreary wastage of its own unemployment, bear the same lesson to the masses, and that for them the costs of Russia are expended for the advantage of the many, while the costs of the capitalist society are paid for the profit of a few. There is an uncomfortable sense in the world that what is happening in Russia may be the prelude to a renaissance of the human spirit. There is no such prophetic confidence in capitalist society. Its very leaders look less like great adventurers than men who scan a gray horizon without confidence of a dawn.

The principles which govern capitalist society are, in fact, completely obsolete before the new conditions it confronts; and it seems to lack the energy to bend itself to their revision. It needs a new scheme of motivation, a different sense of values. It needs the power and the will to move from the era of economic chaos to a system which deliberately controls economic forces in the interests of justice and stability. To do so there are required far more pervasive international controls, on the external side, and far greater equality in matters of social constitution, on the internal. To find equilibrium by the blind adjustment of competing interests is simply to court disaster. Yet, generally speaking, the men who govern the old world can think in no other terms.

It is true there are men about us who voice a different philosophy. Rathenau, Keynes, Salter—these have endeavored, as best they could, to insist that the way to survival lies along the road to profound reconstruction. They have seen that a temper is required which gives new significance to the claims of the common man, which recognizes the dangers inherent in a system which identifies self-good and social. They admit the need for sacrifice as the price of reconstruction. They see all the cost involved in a clash of ideologies which seek to test their respective strengths in terms of power. But theirs, if I may say so, is an aristocratic approach, a cool and skeptical impatience of dogma, a passion for the rational solution of questions in their nature essentially rational, of which the appeal is by its nature a limited one. They underestimate the inertia of the existing order, the irrationality with which men will cling to vested interests and established expectations even when their title to response is no longer valid. Given something like a geological time, such rationalism might prevail against the passions which stand in its path. The tragedy of our present position is that the voice of the Mean is unlikely to win attention until humanity has been sacrificed to the call of the Extreme.❧

Nationalism and Economic Life

Leon Trotsky

Foreign Affairs, April 1934

Italian fascism has proclaimed national "sacred egoism" as the sole creative factor. After reducing the history of humanity to national history, German fascism proceeded to reduce nation to race, and race to blood. Moreover, in those countries which politically have not risen—or rather, descended   to fascism, the problems of economy are more and more being forced into national frameworks. Not all of them have the courage to inscribe "autarchy" openly upon their banners. But everywhere policy is being directed toward as hermetic a segregation as possible of national life away from world economy. Only twenty years ago all the school books taught that the mightiest factor in producing wealth and culture is the world-wide division of labor, lodged in the natural and historic conditions of the development of mankind. Now it turns out that world exchange is the source of all misfortunes and all dangers. Homeward ho! Back to the national hearth! Not only must we correct the mistake of Admiral Perry, who blasted the breach in Japan's "autarchy," but a correction must also be made of the much bigger mistake of Christopher Columbus, which resulted in so immoderately extending the arena of human culture.

The enduring value of the nation, discovered by Mussolini and Hitler, is now set off against the false values of the nineteenth

---

LEON TROTSKY, leader in the October Revolution in 1917; Commissar for Foreign Affairs, 1917–1918; Commissar for War, 1919–1923.

century: democracy and socialism. Here too we come into an irreconcilable contradiction with the old primers, and worse yet, with the irrefutable facts of history. Only vicious ignorance can draw a sharp contrast between the nation and liberal democracy. As a matter of fact, all the movements of liberation in modern history, beginning, say, with Holland's struggle for independence, had both a national and a democratic character. The awakening of the oppressed and dismembered nations, their struggle to unite their severed parts and to throw off the foreign yoke, would have been impossible without a struggle for political liberty. The French nation was consolidated in the storms and tempests of democratic revolution at the close of the eighteenth century. The Italian and German nations emerged from a series of wars and revolutions in the nineteenth century. The powerful development of the American nation, which had received its baptism of freedom in its uprising in the eighteenth century, was finally guaranteed by the victory of the North over the South in the Civil War. Neither Mussolini nor Hitler is the discoverer of the nation. Patriotism in its modern sense—or more precisely its bourgeois sense—is the product of the nineteenth century. The national consciousness of the French people is perhaps the most conservative and the most stable of any; and to this very day it feeds from the springs of democratic traditions.

But the economic development of mankind which overthrew mediæval particularism did not stop within national boundaries. The growth of world exchange took place parallel with the formation of national economies. The tendency of this development—for advanced countries, at any rate—found its expression in the shift of the center of gravity from the domestic to the foreign market. The nineteenth century was marked by the fusion of the nation's fate with the fate of its economic life; but the basic tendency of our century is the growing contradiction between the nation and economic life. In Europe this contradiction has become intolerably acute.

The development of German capitalism was of the most dynamic character. In the middle of the nineteenth century the German people felt themselves stifled in the cages of several dozen feudal fatherlands. Less than four decades after the creation of the

German Empire, German industry was suffocating within the framework of the national state. One of the main causes of the World War was the striving of German capital to break through into a wider arena. Hitler fought as a corporal in 1914–1918 not to unite the German nation but in the name of a supra-national imperialistic program that expressed itself in the famous formula "to organize Europe." Unified under the domination of German militarism Europe was to have become the drill-ground for a much bigger job—the organization of the entire planet.

But Germany was no exception. She only expressed in a more intense and aggressive form the tendency of every other national capitalist economy. The clash between these tendencies resulted in the war. The war, it is true, like all the grandiose upheavals of history, stirred up various historical questions and in passing gave the impulse to national revolutions in the more backward sections of Europe—Tsarist Russia and Austria-Hungary. But these were only the belated echoes of an epoch that had already passed away. Essentially the war was imperialist in character. With lethal and barbaric methods it attempted to solve a problem of progressive historic development—the problem of organizing economic life over the entire arena which had been prepared by the world-wide division of labor.

Needless to say, the war did not find the solution to this problem. On the contrary, it atomized Europe even more. It deepened the interdependence of Europe and America at the same time that it deepened the antagonism between them. It gave the impetus to the independent development of colonial countries and simultaneously sharpened the dependence of the metropolitan centers upon colonial markets. As a consequence of the war, all the contradictions of the past were aggravated. One could half-shut one's eyes to this during the first years after the war, when Europe, aided by America, was busy repairing its devastated economy from top to bottom. But to restore productive forces inevitably implied the reinvigorating of all those evils that had led to the war. The present crisis, in which are synthesized all the capitalist crises of the past, signifies above all the crisis of *national* economic life.

The League of Nations attempted to translate from the language of militarism into the language of diplomatic pacts the task which the war left unsolved. After Ludendorff had failed to "organize Europe" by the sword, Briand attempted to create "the United States of Europe" by means of sugary diplomatic eloquence. But the interminable series of political, economic, financial, tariff, and monetary conferences only unfolded the panorama of the bankruptcy of the ruling classes in face of the unpostponable and burning task of our epoch.

Theoretically this task may be formulated as follows: How may the economic unity of Europe be guaranteed, while preserving complete freedom of cultural development to the peoples living there? How may unified Europe be included within a coördinated world economy? The solution to this question can be reached not by deifying the nation, but on the contrary by completely liberating productive forces from the fetters imposed upon them by the national state. But the ruling classes of Europe, demoralized by the bankruptcy of military and diplomatic methods, approach the task today from the opposite end, that is, they attempt by force to subordinate economy to the outdated national state. The legend of the bed of Procrustes is being reproduced on a grand scale. Instead of clearing away a suitably large arena for the operations of modern technology, the rulers chop and slice the living organism of economy to pieces.

In a recent program speech Mussolini hailed the death of "economic liberalism," that is, of the reign of free competition. The idea itself is not new. The epoch of trusts, syndicates and cartels has long since relegated free competition to the back-yard. But trusts are even less reconcilable with restricted national markets than are the enterprises of liberal capitalism. Monopoly devoured competition in proportion as the world economy subordinated the national market. Economic liberalism and economic nationalism became outdated at the same time. Attempts to save economic life by inoculating it with virus from the corpse of nationalism result in blood poisoning which bears the name of fascism.

Mankind is impelled in its historic ascent by the urge to attain the greatest possible quantity of goods with the least expenditure of labor. This material foundation of cultural growth provides also the most profound criterion by which we may appraise social régimes and political programs. The law of the productivity of labor is of the same significance in the sphere of human society as the law of gravitation in the sphere of mechanics. The disappearance of outgrown social formations is but the manifestation of this cruel law that determined the victory of slavery over cannibalism, of serfdom over slavery, of hired labor over serfdom. The law of the productivity of labor finds its way not in a straight line but in a contradictory manner, by spurts and jerks, leaps and zigzags, surmounting on its way geographical, anthropological and social barriers. Whence so many "exceptions" in history, which are in reality only specific refractions of the "rule."

In the nineteenth century the struggle for the greatest productivity of labor took mainly the form of free competition, which maintained the dynamic equilibrium of capitalist economy through cyclical fluctuations. But precisely because of its progressive rôle competition has led to a monstrous concentration of trusts and syndicates, and this in turn has meant a concentration of economic and social contradictions. Free competition is like a chicken that hatched not a duckling but a crocodile. No wonder she cannot manage her offspring!

Economic liberalism has completely outlived its day. With less and less conviction its Mohegans appeal to the automatic interplay of forces. New methods are needed to make skyscraper trusts correspond to human needs. There must be radical changes in the structure of society and economy. But new methods come into clash with old habits and, what is infinitely more important, with old interests. The law of the productivity of labor beats convulsively against barriers which it itself set up. This is what lies at the core of the grandiose crisis of the modern economic system.

Conservative politicians and theorists, taken unawares by the destructive tendencies of national and international economy, incline towards the conclusion that the overdevelopment of technology is the principal cause of present evils. It is difficult to imagine a more tragic paradox! A French politician and financier, Joseph Caillaux, sees salvation in artificial limitations on the process of mechanization. Thus the most enlightened representatives of the liberal doctrine suddenly draw inspiration from the sentiments of those ignorant workers of over a hundred years ago who smashed weaving looms. The progressive task of how to adapt the arena of economic and social relations to the new technology is turned upside down, and is made to seem a problem of how to restrain and cut down productive forces so as to fit them to the old national arena and to the old social relations. On both sides of the Atlantic no little mental energy is wasted on efforts to solve the fantastic problem of how to drive the crocodile back into the chicken egg. The ultra-modern economic nationalism is irrevocably doomed by its own reactionary character; it retards and lowers the productive forces of man.

The policies of a closed economy imply the artificial constriction of those branches of industry which are capable of fertilizing successfully the economy and culture of other countries. They also imply an artificial planting of those industries which lack favorable conditions for growth on national soil. The fiction of economic self-sufficiency thus causes tremendous overhead expenditures in two directions. Added to this is inflation. During the nineteenth century, gold as a universal measure of value became the foundation of all monetary systems worthy of the name. Departures from the gold standard tear world economy apart even more successfully than do tariff walls. Inflation, itself an expression of disordered internal relationships and of disordered economic ties between nations, intensifies the disorder and helps to turn it from a functional into an organic one. Thus the "national" monetary system crowns the sinister work of economic nationalism.

The most intrepid representatives of this school console themselves with the prospect that the nation, while becoming poorer under a closed economy will become more "unified" (Hitler), and that as the importance of the world market declines the causes for external conflicts will also diminish. Such hopes only demonstrate that the doctrine of autarchy is both reactionary and utterly utopian. The fact is that the breeding places of nationalism also are the laboratories of terrific conflicts in the future; like a hungry tiger, imperialism has withdrawn into its own national lair to gather itself for a new leap.

Actually, theories about economic nationalism which seem to base themselves on the "eternal" laws of race show only how desperate the world crisis really is—a classic example of making a virtue of bitter need. Shivering on bare benches in some God-forsaken little station, the passengers of a wrecked train may stoically assure each other that creature comforts are corrupting to body and soul. But all of them are dreaming of a locomotive that would get them to a place where they could stretch their tired bodies between two clean sheets. The immediate concern of the business world in all countries is to hold out, to survive somehow, even if in a coma, on the hard bed of the national market. But all these involuntary stoics are longing for the powerful engine of a new world "conjuncture," a new economic phase.

Will it come? Predictions are rendered difficult, if not altogether impossible, by the present structural disturbance of the whole economic system. Old industrial cycles, like the heartbeats of a healthy body, had a stable rhythm. Since the war we no longer observe the orderly sequence of economic phases; the old heart skips beats. In addition, there is the policy of so-called "state capitalism." Driven on by restless interests and by social dangers, governments burst into the economic realm with emergency measures, the effects of which in most cases it cannot itself foresee. But even leaving aside the possibility of a new war that would upset for a long time the elemental work of economic forces as well as conscious attempts at planned control, we nevertheless can confidently foresee the turning point from the crisis and depression to a revival, whether or not the favorable symptoms present in England and to some degree in the United States prove later on to have been first swallows that did not bring the spring. The destructive work of the crisis must reach the point—if it has not already reached it—where impoverished mankind will need a new mass of goods. Chimneys will smoke, wheels will turn. And when the revival is sufficiently advanced, the business world will shake off its stupor, will promptly forget yesterday's lessons, and will contemptuously cast aside self-denying theories along with their authors.

But it would be the greatest delusion to hope that the scope of the impending revival will correspond to the depth of the present crisis. In childhood, in maturity, and in old age the heart beats at a different tempo. During capitalism's ascent successive crises had a fleeting character and the temporary decline in production was more than compensated at the next stage. Not so now. We have entered an epoch when the periods of economic revival are short-lived, while the periods of depression become deeper and deeper. The lean cows devour the fat cows without a trace and still continue to bellow with hunger.

All the capitalist states will be more aggressively impatient, then, as soon as the economic barometer begins to rise. The struggle for foreign markets will become unprecedentedly sharp. Pious notions about the advantages of autarchy will at once be cast aside, and sage plans for national harmony will be thrown in the waste-paper basket. This applies not only to German capitalism, with its explosive dynamics, or to the belated and greedy capitalism of Japan, but also to the capitalism of America, which still is powerful despite its new contradictions.

The United States represented the most perfect type of capitalist development. The relative equilibrium of its internal and seemingly inexhaustible market assured the United States a decided technical and economic preponderance over Europe. But its intervention in the World War was really an expression of the fact that its internal equilibrium was already disrupted. The changes introduced by the war into the American structure have in turn made entry into the world arena a life and death question for American capitalism. There is ample evidence that this entry must assume extremely dramatic forms.

The law of the productivity of labor is of decisive significance in the interrelations of America and Europe, and in general in determining the future place of the United States in the world. That highest form which the Yankees gave to the law of the productivity of labor is called conveyor, standard, or mass production. It would seem that the spot from which the lever of Archimedes was to turn the world over had been found. But the old planet refuses to be turned over. Everyone defends himself against everybody else, protecting himself by a customs wall and a hedge of bayonets. Europe buys no goods, pays no debts, and in addition arms itself. With five miserable divisions starved Japan seizes a whole country. The most advanced technique in the world suddenly seems impotent before obstacles basing themselves on a much lower technique. The law of the productivity of labor seems to lose its force.

But it only seems so. The basic law of human history must inevitably take revenge on derivative and secondary phenomena. Sooner or later American capitalism must open up ways for itself throughout the length and breadth of our entire planet. By what methods? By *all* methods. A high coefficient of productivity denotes also a high coefficient of destructive force. Am I preaching war? Not in the least. I am not preaching anything. I am only attempting to analyze the world situation and to draw conclusions from the laws of economic mechanics. There is nothing worse than the sort of mental cowardice which turns its back on facts and tendencies when they contradict ideals or prejudices.

Only in the historic framework of world development can we assign fascism its proper place. It contains nothing creative, nothing independent. Its historic mission is to reduce to an absurdity the theory and practice of the economic impasse.

In its day democratic nationalism led mankind forward. Even now, it is still capable of playing a progressive rôle in the colonial countries of the East. But decadent fascist nationalism, preparing volcanic explosions and grandiose clashes in the world arena, bears nothing except ruin. All our experiences on this score during the last twenty-five or thirty years will seem only an idyllic overture compared to the music of hell that is impending. And this time it is not a temporary economic decline which is involved but complete economic devastation and the destruction of our entire culture, in the event that toiling and thinking humanity proves incapable of grasping in time the reins of its own productive forces and of organizing those forces correctly on a European and a world scale.

The Reconstruction of Liberalism

C. H. McIlwain

Foreign Affairs, October 1937

The Good Society. BY WALTER LIPPMANN. Boston: Little, Brown, 1937, 402 pp.

The present generation is rightly concerned, and concerned far more deeply than its immediate forbears ever were, in the ending or mending of the monstrous economic and social inequalities and iniquities which permit and even foster the distress we see about us in the midst of plenty. In sharp contrast with the older notions of an inevitable progressive development that had best be let alone, or even with the recent naïve belief that depressions were a thing of the past, there is a determination among men of the present day, particularly the younger ones, to do something about this; and some would even go so far as to threaten the very existence of plenty itself, in their hatred of the glaring unevenness of its distribution. There is a divine discontent in the air, a discontent which may lead us on to reform if it is wise, or to chaos if it is misdirected. Which shall it be? This is the burning practical question; and it must have an answer very soon, for we are now in the dangerous state of readiness to accept and to act on any suggestion whatever, bad or good, rather than not act at all. Unquestionably one cause of our confusion and bewilderment is the

C. H. McILWAIN, Eaton Professor of the Science of Government in Harvard University; former President of the American Historical Association; author of "The American Revolution," "The Growth of Political Thought in the West" and other works.

suddenness with which events have thrust this question upon us. We have been faced unexpectedly with the necessity of making a quick decision which may in all likelihood involve the fate of our race, and we have had no time to think the question through.

One thing is clear enough: the world in its present mood will never put up with a mere "muddling through" as an answer. The preservation of the *status quo* is a solution that can satisfy none but the contented; and just now most men are not contented. Whether the answer to be made shall be for reform or for annihilation of our institutions, that answer will be given by those who are dissatisfied with existing conditions. These are the ones whose decisions and actions will either mend or end the ingrown abuses of our present social and economic system, will make or mar any system replacing it; and these are the ones therefore to whom all arguments, to be effective, must be directed. The quietists and reactionaries, though they are always with us, have become, for the time at least, practically negligible. Meantime an increasing number of us have grown conscious that these imminent decisions and actions are likely to determine for us and our children no less a question than whether we shall be freemen or slaves in the times to come—and times not far distant. We are becoming more and more concerned that no decision be made that could enslave us all, and, with the present state of Europe in mind, we fear that some present proposals might have that effect.

It is a principle of equity that he who seeks a remedy must come with clean hands. Now we "liberals," advocates of reform, but a constitutional reform, do not come with hands entirely clean. Among our fellows there are doubts of our sincerity, and not altogether without reason; so any cautions or suggestions that may come from us are likely to be received with some suspicion. Why did suspicion of this kind arise? Is it a justifiable suspicion? If not, can we do anything to remove it and thus get a fair hearing for warnings that we believe might, if heeded, save us all from disaster? These are some of the preliminary questions to which the liberal of today must make answer as best he can. I take it, the sum of all the answers, to be effective, will be a plea in confession and avoidance: a frank and full confession of wrongs and blunders past and present—but the wrongs and blunders of liberals, not of liberalism.

If he believes this, it is the liberal's business—or his duty rather—to try to demonstrate it to a discontented, impatient, and hostile world; no easy task, for past mistakes have laid upon him a heavy burden of proof.

Liberals do not differ from others in their conception of the true end of the state, for to all parties at all times the end, actual or professed, has been the good life of the whole; the differences come in determining what is "good" and how this is to be attained. True liberalism can never countenance, even if some "liberals" have, the sacrifice of individual well-being to "reasons of state." There can be no good life for any state whose members live in wretchedness and misery, material or spiritual. National glory or national wealth at the cost of individual welfare is the mark of no true commonwealth, but of a tyranny. The well-being of any state—the common weal—can only be a weal that is common to all. For a state, in the only proper sense of the term, as Cicero said long ago, is not any chance aggregation of men but a multitude united in the common purpose of securing this common good, and that can mean nothing less than the individual good of all, not some, of its members.

But Cicero did not stop there, nor does liberalism stop there. He also said that this multitude must be joined together in consent to law (*juris consensu*), and by law he meant no mere fiat of government. These are his words, among the most memorable in political literature: "True law is right reason consonant with nature, diffused among all men, constant, eternal; which summons to duty by its command and hinders from fraud by its prohibition . . . . To make enactments infringing this law, religion forbids, neither may it be repealed even in part, nor have we power through Senate or people to free ourselves from it."

This, of course, is an idealistic statement to which the sober facts of human life can never fully reach, yet reduced to the level of actual experience its central principle still holds good. It means that "what pleases the prince" may temporarily "have the force of law," but is not law; for the common good for which the state exists requires a stronger guarantee than the nod of any prince or any government. Now this is liberalism pure and simple. For, stripped of all its husks, liberalism is constitutionalism, "a government of laws and not of men," a common weal of individual rights that neither prince nor magistrate nor assembly has any authority to impair. In a word, liberalism means a common welfare with a constitutional guarantee. I maintain that not one part, but both parts of this definition—in essence, Cicero's definition—must be translated into working fact if we mean to live in a true commonwealth and hope to keep it in being. So-called liberals have ignored the first part of the definition and have fouled the nest by invoking the guarantee for privileges of their own, conducive only to the destruction of any true common weal. None have ever prated more of guarantees than these so-called liberals; but they have forgotten, if they ever believed, that these guarantees must secure the rights of all, not the selfish interests of a few. They are the traitors within the gates who have probably done more than all others to betray liberalism to its enemies and put it to its defense. Of all the errors of "liberals" theirs seems the worst; for it is largely the result of greed, and a principal cause of man's recent inhuman exploitation of man.

It is unlikely, however, that this exploitation could ever have reached the proportions it did without more protest, had really liberally minded men not been beguiled by the extreme doctrine of *laissez-faire*, surely one of the strangest fantasies that ever discredited human reason. Thus the self-seekers and the doctrinaires were drawn together into an alliance to maintain the *status quo*, and all its abuses and inequalities were made sacrosanct. This pseudo-liberalism usually exhibited itself in the ineffectiveness of legal guarantees for almost every human right except the right of property, and the acceptance of an unhistorical definition of contract under which the sanction of the law could be obtained for almost any enormity to which men could be induced to agree.

A contract is "an agreement" to do or not to do a particular thing, according to a definition once laid down by Chief Justice Marshall. According to the Roman jurists, a contract is a bond of the law (*vinculum juris*) which the state sees fit to attach to agreements of which it has no reason to disapprove. Between these two definitions the practical difference may not seem great, but in theory and emphasis it is profound.

Under *laissez-faire* and our distorted notions of contract, a lunatic may be protected against the results of his agreement, but of economic inequalities the law can never take notice—*De minimis non curat lex*; there is little or no safeguard for the weak against the strong; protection of the public against an adulterated product would be unthinkable—*Caveat emptor*.

Now this is a return toward Hobbes's "war of every man against every man," without the equality that Hobbes premised. Yet, we are told, the state cannot and should not do anything about it. State interference in such matters would be a violation of a sacred right. What a caricature of liberalism! Few illusions have been more disastrous than the one arising from an uncritical acceptance of Sir Henry Maine's sweeping generalization that human progress has been a development from status to contract.

No doubt conditions such as the ones mentioned above have long been accepted as "natural," or normal, or even desirable by liberals without number. It is equally true that this belief has often led to a callous indifference on their part to many forms of human misery. The indictment that might be drawn against them is a long one, though in fairness it ought to be remembered that this indictment would have been against the great majority of us all, if it had been drawn before the Great War and the awakening caused by that event. The number certainly included more than the justices of the Supreme Court of the United States.

Two wrongs do not make a right; no more do two errors make a truth. The question before us now, the decision we shall have to make before long, is whether we shall renounce these errors and remove these abuses that liberals have allowed to grow up, or whether, once and for all, we shall level with the ground all the bulwarks of our liberty, because some traitors have crept in behind them. This is what the decision we must make really means, for between constitutionalism and despotism there is no tenable middle ground. Of that the recent history of Europe leaves no reasonable doubt for any intelligent man who chooses to look into it.

The men in a hurry are trying to tell us that the only cure for economic inequality is political slavery. They would have us believe that regimentation is the only practical form of liberty. Stripped of all its idealistic phrases, their creed is a creed of pure despotism, and these dreamers could not believe in it if they had not persuaded themselves somehow—honestly enough, no doubt—that despotism will always be altruistic and never selfish. They are willing to entrust to a government without legal limits, and only imperfectly responsible, not only their own present welfare but their children's future fortunes. What a sublime faith in human benevolence! What an opportunity for an adventurer! Much of the bloodshed and misery that history records has been the direct result of this kind of honest, idealistic, but impractical, wishful thinking.

That it should crop up again in this twentieth century is one of the disastrous results of our unfortunate divorce of history and politics. Our public men and even our professed students of government are woefully ignorant—shall I say "blissfully" ignorant?—of the historical "struggle for law," and what it has meant; and they seem equally blind to what it means now. Almost any day they might read in the newspapers of confiscations and banishments and concentration camps and castor oil, of blood-purges and "liquidations" (what a polite term!), of the imprisonment of religious leaders and the beheading of "traitors." But these every-day horrors slip over their minds like water over a duck's back. Terrible as the crimes of liberals have been, are they as bad as these? "You must trust me," this is the whole sum of the "constitution" under a dictatorship. And we are now asked to accept it in place of our bills of rights! With the past and the present before us, dare we then accept as our guides men who thus show that they are unable or unwilling to face the ugly facts, in human nature, in history, and in our world today?

An acceptance might, of course, be not quite irrevocable. History shows cases where such despotic governments have been finally overthrown. But seldom has it been done without distress and bloodshed following a period of intolerable oppression. Would the cost of redressing the wrongs of liberals be likely to be as great as this?

If we look at our present situation, its most ominous aspect is in the cross purposes, the divisions, and even the conflicts we find among those who ought to be presenting a solid front against the forces of reaction. The faults of our liberals and the blindness of our reformers have thus broken up the historic alliance of reformer and constitutionalist through which alone we have gained and kept what little of liberty we still enjoy. And we underrate the present strength of the forces of greed, corruption, and the lust for power, if we think we can hold what we have won from them, to say nothing of winning more, while our own forces are thus divided and weakened. Before we advance to new positions we must secure the ground already won; we must consolidate our gains, and to do it we must restore the old winning combination of reformer and constitutionalist. In the past the reformer may have made these gains, but the constitutionalist enabled him to hold them. The economic and political rights wrested from oppressors have been rendered secure by making them *legal* or constitutional rights, by adding to them the sanction of the law. Only one of two other sanctions is ever possible: physical force, or the acquiescence of the government. The former amounts to a permanent state of civil war, or at best, of armed peace; the latter is a benevolent despotism. Can we then, dare we, exchange our constitutionalism for either of these?

Constitutionalism is more a method than a principle. It is the method of law as contrasted with force or with will. If this law has perpetuated some abuses, it has also preserved all our liberties. The abuses are eradicable and in no way essential to it; without it, the liberties are ours only on sufferance. The moral seems to be that we should guard our legal rights, but see to it that they shall never be economic wrongs. To strip of legal sanction all such wrongs as still exist, to add this sanction to all reforms our times require, this is a program that should enlist the support of every forward-looking man; not half this program, but the whole of it. Before such a program can be realized we must scrap much of the current nonsense about "popular sovereignty." We must discard our traditional notions of sovereignty itself, derived from Hobbes and Austin, and substitute sounder ones. We must strike at the corruption that is eating at the vitals of our body politic. We must modify some of our so-called "checks" that only enfeeble government and that make it responsible to selfish minority groups instead of to all the people. But in it all, and above all, we must retain those legal limits of governmental action which now exist in our bills of rights to protect the personal as well as the proprietary rights of the humblest and even the most hated of our citizens. Not only must we retain them; we must revive and revise, we must clarify and even extend them, for only so can we ever hope to give permanence to our needed reforms themselves. If they are to last, these reforms must have a better guarantee than the passing whim of any dictator; and the only guarantee that men have ever been able to devise, short of actual physical force, is the guarantee of constitutional limitations.

Much of our thinking on these points has been confused, and this has been and is one of the greatest obstacles to sound practical progress. Among the confusions is our conception of what we choose to call "popular sovcreignty."

We live under a government in which the "sovereign" is limited by a superior law, a constituent law, made directly by the whole people themselves, not made and not alterable by the "sovereign" who exists only by virtue of that same constituent law. This is the system which the founders of our state deliberately established and this we think we are trying to preserve. And yet there are many among us today who would emasculate that system by destroying the only means by which it can work or endure, namely, a judicial review which makes sure that no act of the "sovereign" shall exceed the legal authority conferred upon it by the people in the constituent law, or constitution.

In the main, this destructive attitude is not a reasoned one, but in so far as it has any basis at all in thought or theory it seems to come from the common acceptance of the delusion of "popular sovereignty." Popular sovereignty, at bottom, is an identification, contrary to fact, of the government and the people. Now "We the people" do not govern ourselves; we have established a government to do it, and it does it. If the people really governed, it would, of course, be both absurd and impossible to try to limit governmental action by any law. The notion that our government *is* the people, therefore naturally leads to the conclusion that the government has no limits. The logic is sound, the premise is utterly untrue. This unwarranted belief, necessarily destructive of all constitutionalism and of all bills of rights, has been fostered by a strange unhistorical conception of "sovereignty." We are only able to accept "popular" sovereignty, because of our peculiar notions of what sovereignty itself is. Blind followers of the blind have persuaded us—mostly lawyers who have taken Blackstone literally and uncritically—that sovereignty is might, not right, and that this might could not conceivably be the might of any true sovereign if it had any legal limits whatsoever. These men have hopelessly confused authority with power, and apparently have been entirely oblivious of the fact that their conception of political supremacy, fathered by Hobbes and nurtured by John Austin, is completely subversive of the constitutional system under which we all live and to which they themselves have usually paid the most extravagant lip-service.

This is not the place to try to expose the fallacy of Austinianism and its incompatibility with past constitutional development or with the present safeguarding of minority and individual rights, but I do believe that this kind of crooked and dangerous political thinking, though the extent of its influence is hard to estimate, has been one potent cause of our "present discontents."

The generation now at the height of their political activity have been called by Mr. Walter Lippmann "the lost generation." They certainly have no monopoly of the errors and confusions that I have tried to outline above, but it is true that upon them in a peculiar sense has fallen the accumulated burden of these traditional abuses, prejudices, and heresies. They are truly a "lost generation." And not the least interesting aspect of Mr. Lippmann's remarkable book, to a student of contemporary politics, is its autobiographical character. It is nothing less than an *apologia pro vita sua*, the life story of one of the most thoughtful members of this lost generation; an idealist, perplexed and appalled by the present outcome, so sadly different from his earlier confident hopes and expectations, groping for an explanation of this debacle, and finally finding it, not in the defects inherent in liberalism, as some other present-day idealist reformers have, but in the perturbations which have thrown liberalism out of its only true orbit, the fulfillment of the "good life" for all.

The brief summary which I have given above does not follow Mr. Lippmann's discussions very closely, but I hope it contains the gist of his political arguments and conclusions. On the other hand, it conveys no idea whatever of his treatment of the economic aspects of his subject. Much of his book deals with the economic side of the degradation of liberalism and the economic aspect of the changes necessary to restore its integrity. To assess the value of this important part of Mr. Lippmann's work would require the knowledge of a trained economist, to the possession of which I lay no claim. The general inference seems to be that the recrudescence of authoritarianism in our time comes in large part from the belief "that the new machine technology requires the control of an omnipotent state," a belief based on the prior assumption that the concentration of control in modern industry is the result of technical change. The history of industry, however, completely disproves this assumption. "Concentration has its origin in privilege and not in technology." It is "a creation of the state through its laws." As for the rights with which legislatures and courts have gradually invested the modern business corporation, they are conditional only and are subject to alteration by the state. "There is no reason whatever for the assumption, made both by individualists and by collectivists, that corporations must either be allowed to enjoy all their present rights or be taken over and administered by the state." "There is only one purpose to which a whole society can be directed by a deliberate plan. That purpose is war, and there is no other." Hence, "a directed society must be bellicose and poor. If it is not both bellicose and poor, it cannot be directed. . . . A prosperous and peaceable society must be free. If it is not free, it cannot be prosperous and peaceable."

For reactionaries whose liberalism is only protective coloring, there will be scant comfort in this book. It is addressed to sincerely forward-looking men. If these remain deaf to the appeal presented here with such telling force, then the victory of autocracy over liberty seems assured. And let the reformer bear in mind that a victory for autocracy is in the end a victory for reaction. ☯

The Economic Tasks of the Postwar World

Alvin H. Hansen and C. P. Kindleberger

Foreign Affairs, April 1942

The United States is passing through a great psychological crisis. It is having to think out afresh its whole fundamental conception of its place in the world and its relationship with other countries. In the nineteenth century European immigrants by the millions quit the Old World in search of opportunities for a better life in the New. The vast stretches of the American west—its forests and fertile plains, its mineral wealth and latent resources of power—conjured up a restless spirit of enterprise. There was a will to do among Americans of that period, whether old settlers or fresh arrivals, a will to grow, to build a new society in the New World free from the restrictions upon individual opportunity which had been characteristic of the Old. Average Americans in that age felt little direct concern for the affairs of Europe. They wished merely to live their own lives. To be sure, many Americans still have the habit of thinking in those same terms. But even they are beginning to feel uneasy about it. A second World War after only two decades has come as a rude shock to the conception

ALVIN H. HANSEN, Littauer Professor of Political Economy at Harvard University; special economic adviser, Board of Governors of the Federal Reserve System; American chairman of the Joint Economic Committee of Canada and the United States; author of "Economic Stabilization in an Unbalanced World," "Fiscal Policy and Business Cycles" and other works; C. P. KINDLEBERGER, Associate Economist, Board of Governors of the Federal Reserve System; author of "International Short-Term Capital Movement."

that we can handle our own affairs without regard to the reactions of other nations, even ones that are far distant according to former terms of measurement. We begin to see that the problems of Europe, and of Asia as well, have become our problems also.

The task of the nineteenth century was one of engineering— to build up productive capacity, to develop physical resources, to construct capital plant and equipment and to train human skills. The task of the twentieth is to create more secure and mutually profitable relations between the peoples of the world. This task calls for equal inventiveness, equal daring and equally bold leadership. And it requires large outlays of the world's resources.

Prior to this war the United States spent no less than a billion dollars a year to attain physical security. When this war is over we shall need to spend several billion dollars a year as the American contribution towards laying the foundations of international security. Much more will be involved in this than merely maintaining an adequate military force. Alongside the program for international military security must be set a comprehensive program of international economic development, the promotion of full employment and the raising of standards both of production and consumption throughout the world.

During the First World War the planning which was done for the postwar period was mainly political. The feeling was that if a better political world could be constructed the economic problems would adjust themselves as a result of the play of "natural" forces. In actual practice, these operated with a substantial degree of success until 1929. But with the collapse of the world's economic organization in that and succeeding years, the political arrangements planned during World War I and hammered out at Versailles and in Geneva gave way.

The foregoing brief outline admittedly is over-simplified. But it emphasizes how necessary it will be for us to combine economic with political planning after this war. A spate of books, pamphlets and articles on the economic problems that will then confront us testifies that the necessity is widely recognized. It was also given recognition by the inclusion of "freedom from want" among the "Four Freedoms" enunciated by President Roosevelt. The Atlantic

Charter signed by him and by Prime Minister Churchill, and sub-scribed to by the United Nations, recognizes it both in Point IV (access on equal terms to the trade and raw materials of the world) and in Point V (international collaboration for improved labor standards, economic adjustment and social security).

This is the imaginative and dynamic approach. There are still a good many people deeply concerned with problems of international security who think exclusively in terms of political arrangements and economic mechanisms such as tariffs and currencies. We would call that the passive approach. The arrangements and mechanisms which they favor are important, and appropriate means must be found to give them effect. But many economists are coming to think that ac-tion along these traditional lines would by itself be wholly inadequate. It is increasingly understood that the essential foundation upon which the international security of the future must be built is an economic order so managed and controlled that it will be capable of sustaining full employment and developing a rising standard of living as rapidly as technical progress and world productivity will permit. The very sur-vival of our present institutions, including political democracy and private enterprise, depends upon our taking a bolder attitude toward public developmental projects in terms both of human and physical resources, and both in our own country and throughout the world.

Many questions at once arise. What will be the rôle of govern-ment in postwar economic life? Will business enterprise outside of government be organized predominantly along cartel lines, with increasing restraints on competition? Will international trade be based on principles of non-discrimination or will each country make the best bargains it can obtain on a bilateral and separate basis with each of its trading partners? Will the world break up into autarchic countries, pairs of countries, or regions, including empires, continents and hemispheres? Or will each country tend to special-ize in the production of those particular commodities which it can produce most efficiently and trade on the widest possible basis?

These questions are practical ones, and like most practical ques-tions it is impossible to answer them categorically either as a forecast of the future or as a guide to desirable policy under the unforeseeable conditions of the future. It can merely be said that in time of war governments must and do assume more direction of economic life; that after this war they will probably be given increased responsibility for trying to get rid of unemployment in their respective nations and to establish higher minimum standards for the low-income groups; and that while the degree of control exercised in the postwar period will be less than that exercised during the war, it nevertheless will be greater than it used to be before the war. No final answers can be given, however, to questions as to the extent to which a government should intervene or will intervene in the economic life of its citizens. The same is true of attempts to determine now the rôle in the postwar world of such things as cartels, competition, non-discriminatory trade, foreign-exchange control and long-term commodity purchase contracts. We can merely make up our minds what their rôle would be within the framework of a wide range of different conditions. It is important to study such questions during the war in order that we may be cognizant of the new institutional forces at work and plan to adapt them to desirable social and economic ends. In this article, however, we shall consider more fundamental tasks of postwar economic policy, particularly in terms of international collaboration.

Let us start with the aims given expression in the President's "Four Freedoms" speech and the "Atlantic Charter." Those statements are open to criticism on the score that they are at the same time too broad and too narrow. Parts of the latter document, in particular, are Delphic; while the point dealing with equal access to raw materials is a broad pronouncement on the economic organization of the postwar world which calls for applied exegesis if it is to be given definite content. The ideals of freedom from want, improved labor standards, and social security still await a specific program of international collaboration for the elimination of unemployment and the increase of productivity in backward areas.

In view of the foregoing, the larger aims of economic policy in the postwar world seem likely to be the following: 1, a positive expansionist program designed to achieve and to maintain full employment; 2, a program of development designed to raise productivity throughout the world; and 3, the establishment of higher minimum standards of nutrition, health, education and housing everywhere. We venture to assert that international collaboration to achieve each of these three ends will constitute the primary economic task of the postwar period.

II

The elimination of large-scale unemployment must be undertaken through international collaboration rather than by the separate action of individual countries. Primary responsibility evidently rests on each country to find employment for its own labor; but there is an important secondary responsibility which must be added. A country should not, for the sake of creating domestic employment, force exports into areas where that action would displace equally or more efficient labor engaged in making the same products. Similarly, no country should cut off imports from an efficient source of supply for the purpose of shifting the associated employment from foreign to domestic labor.

International responsibility for collaboration in the elimination of unemployment must, however, go much further than this. A country's level of national income is affected—among other influences—by the balance of payments by and to foreigners. When receipts received into the income stream from abroad exceed payments, the national income tends to rise; but in other countries where payments exceed receipts, the income tends to fall.

Because of these cumulative influences of foreign transactions on national income, it is difficult for a single country to restore employment by its own independent action without cutting itself off from world trade. As incomes rise, increasing amounts are spent for imports, i.e. are paid to foreigners who may spend them in their own countries or in third countries. The effects of a purely national anti-depression policy thus spill over into other countries and wither away. But if all countries were to coördinate their anti-depression measures, then no one of them which pursued an expansionist policy would see its efforts dissipated abroad. And no country would find it necessary, as happened so often in the thirties, to cut itself off from world influences in order more effectively to restore employment at home.

The great democratic countries, notably the British Empire and the United States, which command an overwhelming proportion of the world's resources, failed most miserably to achieve the full and efficient use of those resources in the two decades between the two world wars. They made inadequate use of their resources because they permitted vast unemployment to persist over long periods and failed to stop the devastating effect of deflation and depression upon the whole world economy. This failure, and the sense of economic frustration ensuing therefrom, clearly were among the basic causes of the chaos and conflict in which the world is engulfed today. It should not be forgotten that between the two wars we witnessed the destruction of free enterprise and free political institutions in approximately half of the western world. If democratic political institutions are to be preserved from a similar fate again we must learn how to make better use of our economic resources than we have done in the past.

If we do not deliberately adopt a wholly new attitude towards the problem of employment, economic frustration will again lead to chaos and war. International security will not be achieved merely by the defeat of the Axis Powers, and it will not be maintained solely by the establishment and maintenance of an international police force. A well-rounded plan for international security needs also to contain a coördinated program of internal economic expansion in the major industrial countries for the purpose of promoting and maintaining full employment.

Under modern conditions, the most important single factor affecting general world prosperity is the level of income in the great industrial countries. In particular, if the United States continues to be subject to violent industrial fluctuations the world can have little hope of achieving stability. Recent decades have revealed how predominantly American prosperity influences world prosperity. For example, we have seen how responsive American imports are to increases in the American national income. As output in our great mass-production industries rises and our national income approaches the level corresponding to full employment, we increase our imports of raw materials, especially from Canada, the Far East and Latin America, but also from other parts of the world. Moreover, at that income level, in spite of our high tariff, we purchase large quantities of specialty and luxury products from the more advanced industrial countries. There is a further factor. After the last World War our high national income induced us to increase our tourist expenditures abroad to an unprecedented volume. It may be expected that in the future the great development of travel by air will increase this item in our invisible imports even beyond what was known in the twenties. The point is that domestic prosperity in the United States spreads purchasing power throughout the world and tends to increase the volume of world trade in goods and services.

Collaboration among countries for the purpose of eliminating unemployment must also be considered in terms of "economic adjustment." Britain's export problem, and hence her unemployment problem, will not be solved automatically by the mere creation of a prosperous world with large buying power and a high volume of international trade. The hard core of unemployment in England in the period between the wars was in textiles and coal, both of them exporting industries. It was found necessary to shift labor in considerable measure from the north and west of England to the south—into residential building and into consumers' goods industries producing for the home market. In the future, British ingenuity will have to be applied more than ever to finding ways of adapting British productive skills to the requirements of the world market. Intelligent planning of steps for the rehabilitation of blighted areas, with their heritage of unemployment, low productivity and low consumption, is vitally necessary.

We do not claim that the gains from the coördination of anti-depression policies will be revolutionary. In the process of adjustment from war to peace, which will continue long after the armistice and far beyond the period of relief and immediate reconstruction, each of the larger industrial countries must in the main make its way to fairly full employment by itself. But the process of gaining and maintaining full employment will be eased for the larger countries as a group, and for the galaxies of smaller countries which are dependent upon them, if the expansionist policies adopted rule out mercantilistic practices which aim to promote employment by forcing uneconomic exports (through subsidies and otherwise), and which gain for one country at the expense of others; and if expansion in one country is not defeated by contraction in another.

The experience of the thirties showed that deflation tends to spread throughout the world in a cumulative process. Deflation in one country feeds upon deflation in another. The way to halt the cumulative process of deflation at the outset is to adopt coördinated policies which promote employment through measures for internal expansion rather than to rely on unilateral policies which are designed to expand a single nation's exports and which in turn tend to depress employment abroad. In this program the United States has, and must recognize that it has, a vital interest.

III

There is a further task in which the United States must engage in the postwar period in collaboration with other nations. This is the task of increasing world productivity. We have made a start in that direction by such methods as the provision of cheap power, the control of floods, the checking of soil erosion and education in efficient agricultural methods. But much remains to be accomplished. And outside the United States there are even wider differences between actual and potential productivity.

Education as to the need for increasing production has already progressed so far that in practically every nation the government is now fairly well aware of the jobs which have to be done both within its own borders and in conjunction with neighboring nations. Nevertheless a comprehensive world resources survey needs to be made jointly by the industrially advanced nations and those which are relatively undeveloped. A dozen great development projects will have to be undertaken in the postwar period—the reconstruction of Danubian agriculture on the basis of farm machinery instead of peasant labor, the development of the Amazon Valley, the control of the flood of the Yellow River, and others of similar magnitude. Before

World War II, the Soviet Union obtained private technical assistance from abroad to aid in the construction of its hydro-electric plants and steel undertakings. But it borrowed capital in foreign countries only with the greatest difficulty, with the result that the Russian people were obliged to tighten their belts—in some years to the point of starvation—in order to provide the capital outlays required. After the war, other nations which awaken to the opportunities for development and feel the need for capital will be tempted to follow the same unfortunate methods unless foreign capital is forthcoming.

It should be. Capital and technical skill should both be made available under international governmental auspices. The lending governments should of course assure themselves that the projects to be undertaken are reasonably capable of achieving the desired results and that the countries in question are themselves providing as much capital and technical skill as possible and are assuming the maximum responsibility possible for making the undertakings a success. In exchange for these assurances, they should be willing to lend capital. In the first instance it would be money, but actually as time went on this would be transformed into turbines, steel, cement mixers and steam shovels. The rates of interest, if any, should be low and payments should be asked for over extended periods of time. Repayment would become possible in the long run as the productivity of the region in question was increased; and the exchange aspect of repayment would not be unmanageable if world prosperity and full employment were maintained.

Former methods of foreign lending and investment are no longer suitable from the standpoint of either the lending countries or the borrowing countries. New machinery must be devised. The relatively new device of the Government Corporation or the Government Authority might very well be assigned a major rôle. A sort of International R. F. C. might prove a suitable device for stimulating foreign investment. On the one side, there will be need for an international public development corporation to promote large-scale projects in industrially backward countries and areas; on the other side for an international authority under which private corporations seeking foreign investment outlets could obtain minimum guarantees based on the principle of insurance, and under which their operations and conduct could be regularized.

What is the interest of the United States in such a program? It will appeal to some because of the stimulation of exports of capital equipment which would result. To others, the utilization of formerly arid lands or the construction of railroads and highways will offer an occasion for private enterprise to develop new plantations or hitherto inaccessible mines. Still others will hope that the increase in productivity of the improved region will bring increased sales of United States goods—either exported directly or fabricated in branch plants in the countries concerned. Of course, the direct outlays on the sort of development projects which we have in mind will not always bring back 100 cents on the dollar. Nevertheless, it can be said in general that the indirect effects of an international program of expansion will reinforce and sustain our internal program of expansion. Moreover, such a program constitutes an investment on behalf of international security. The cost should be considered in the same category as the cost of educating our youth, maintaining police and firefighting forces and supporting the army and navy. The benefits of these expenditures are real even though they cannot be measured in terms of money or bookkeeping. Increases in the productivity of the Balkan peasant, of the Hindu and Moslem in India, of the Chinese may seem of remote interest to many Americans; but they will contribute in the long run to both the economic and the political security of the United States.

IV

With increasing productivity will go increased consumption and better conditions for millions of people who formerly lived under, or very close to, subsistence standards. Thus it is appropriate that when the time comes for the world to tackle the problem of increased productivity it also shall make a start at increasing the scale and efficiency of consumption. This, like the effort to reduce or eradicate unemployment and the development of unproductive areas, is partly a domestic task, partly an international one.

To the extent that consumption is inefficient and wasteful through lack of knowledge there is a task of education to be performed. This must be undertaken mainly by national governments. Similarly, the improvement of housing standards for lower income groups is a job for domestic authorities. At the same time, an international contribution can be made through the exchange of research information and technological developments. The methods are familiar to us all from the work of the Economic and Intelligence Service of the League of Nations and that of the International Labor Office.

In the special field of nutrition there is a great opportunity for work on an international and collaborative basis. In many countries of the world the masses have entirely inadequate standards of nutrition both as regards quantity and especially as regards quality. They can by degrees be given the proper diet—the right balance of proteins and vitamins, particularly in the so-called "protective foods" such as dairy products, eggs, citrus fruit and leafy vegetables—only through a concerted international effort to improve the methods by which the proper foods are produced and to cheapen them for the ultimate consumer. This involves persuading nations to give up expensive methods of producing staple foods in the interest of national self-sufficiency, turning instead to the production of more dairy products and fresh vegetables, and to undertake the development of diversified production in monoculture areas. An adequate diet for the population of the United States (which is an exporter of agricultural products) would call for us to increase the output of milk in this country by 35 percent over the 1941 figure; of eggs by 25 percent; and of vegetables by 90 percent. Unless agricultural technological progress makes further rapid strides, this procedure would engage a part of our land and farm labor which is now producing food for export. The gradual adoption of a similar standard of diet by other peoples which have been less well fed than Americans have been, and which already are importers of food or else barely are self-sufficient, would require those peoples to increase their food imports on a large scale as well as to undertake an enormous expansion of the acreage now devoted to the production of protective foods.

The need for international collaboration here is plain. Adjustments in the use of land now engaged in agricultural production will have to be planned. The advantages of efficient techniques and machinery will have to be spread from progressive to backward agricultural areas. Means will have to be devised for bringing an adequate diet within the purchasing power of the masses of the population. Public health officials, government agricultural authorities and farm economists have declared that these tasks can be accomplished through international collaboration. Many countries have grown increasingly aware of the problem in the course of the present war as a result of the destruction of crops and the elimination of accustomed channels of international trade. When the war is over, public opinion will doubtless demand that governments undertake broad programs for improving nutrition, health and housing. These domestic programs can be carried out more effectively through international collaboration.

v

These, then, are the basic economic tasks which will confront the world after the war—the elimination, or at any rate the vast reduction, of unemployment; the improvement of wide areas of low economic productivity; and the increase of consumption and its direction into more efficient channels. Together they challenge the courage and creative genius of mankind.

If the United States determines to take the lead in helping attain these goals it must realize that a heavy cost is involved. But that cost would be far less than the costs of new deep depressions and new world wars. *That* is something which we really cannot afford. In the past we have failed to recognize the great responsibility which goes with vast power, political and economic. We must be prepared to make a contribution in both fields. We must recognize our political responsibilities for maintaining world peace; and equally we must recognize our economic responsibilities for achieving and maintaining world prosperity.

Freedom and Control

Geoffrey Crowther

Foreign Affairs, January 1944

At this stage of the last war, friend and foe alike knew the main general principles of the world order that would follow on an Allied victory. The world would be made up of self-determined, independent, sovereign states, linked together by a League of Nations founded on the principles of collective security, arbitration and disarmament. The normal pattern for a state would consist of a two-chamber legislature elected by universal suffrage, a responsible executive, an independent judiciary and guarantees of the civil liberties. Financial relationships between nations would be regulated by the gold standard, buttressed by central banks. Commercial policy would permit only moderate protective tariffs and would frown on such expedients as quotas, discriminations, dumping and official trading. Internally, every state would be dedicated to the principles of free individual enterprise, with a minimum of state interference or control.

It is beside the point that these principles were not completely applied and that some of them which were applied were unsuccessful. In 1918–19 that all lay in the future. The point is that, at the end of the last war, the world knew what an Allied victory would mean. The "triumph of democracy" then had a fairly detailed intellectual substance as well as an emotional content.

But who knows today what an Allied victory would mean? Of the four major Allies, two are democracies, but, apart from the general conviction that people should be allowed to settle their own

GEOFFREY CROWTHER, Editor of *The Economist*, London; author of "The Outline of Money."

affairs, how much of the formulae of democracy do the Americans and British regard as articles of export? To take a specific case, should we recommend the Germans to set up a replica of the Weimar Republic, or the French to restore the Third Republic—supposing that our advice were asked for in either case? And, if not, what do we recommend? Moreover, the other two major Allies do not, in their own affairs, practise anything that we should recognize as democracy. Some allege that the real preference of the western Allies is for legitimist, conservative, monarchist governments in Europe. One may think that it is not so. But can anyone of us say, of full knowledge, that it *is* not so? We want governments to be democratic, yes. But we want them to avoid the mistakes that were made in the name of democracy after the last war. And where does that leave us? Does anyone know?

The confusion is hardly less in the sphere of international organization. The League of Nations is still alive, and the many small nations of the world will not abandon without a very fierce struggle the doctrines of sovereign equality and equal sovereignty on which the League was founded, or the principles of arbitration (*i.e.*, willing submission to arbitration), collective security (*i.e.*, security by the consenting coöperation of all) and disarmament (*i.e.*, equalization of advantages and burdens) by which it hoped to secure peace. But there has been much talk of other conceptions. Much has been heard of the international police force. Some conceive it as a genuinely international body, responsible to a world agency, to which, consequently, the essential attributes of sovereignty would have to be ceded. Others conceive it more in the light of a continuance into the peace of the concept of the present major allies. This latter has become almost a majority concept; and even most of those who criticize the idea of an Anglo-American alliance (should anyone propose it, which no one in authority has done thus far) are usually content if it is enlarged to cover only four of the nations of the world. Does anyone know whether the system to be created will be a "Great Power system" or a generally collective one? If a compromise, will it lean more one way or the other? And do we believe in disarmament, for ourselves, in the practically foreseeable future?

Our economic principles are equally indefinite. Do we still believe in free individual enterprise as the basis of economic activity? Many Americans—probably the majority—say they do, though the vehemence and frequency with which they say it seem to suggest the existence of a doubt. (It was not necessary to make any such profession of faith in 1919.) Most Englishmen have very serious doubts whether private enterprise can any longer be regarded as the sole, or even as the principal, determinant of economic activity. And the Russians have no doubt at all that it cannot. In this supremely important aspect of human society, what would an Allied victory mean? Do we believe in the gold standard? In the old sense, clearly not (for the minority of the faithful is very small). But do we believe in the possibility of universal currency standards in any sense? It is the question that has underlain the recent international discussions, and no answer that is given can be more than experimental. Do we believe in a return to a commercial régime of moderate tariffs only, with the abolition of all the other obnoxious obstructions to world trade that have grown up in the last generation? The American and British Governments share some hopes, but not much confidence. The Russians have not been heard from. And if we do not believe that the international economy of which free trade and the gold standard were the chief symbols can, or should, be re-created, what do we believe in to take its place?

II

This is a formidable list of questions, and if there is any one of my readers who can answer any one of them—answer it, that is to say, not for himself alone, but as expressing the dominant view of the United Nations, or even of the two democratic Great Powers—then he is a far bolder man than I am. It has often been pointed out that there has been nothing in the present war to compare with Woodrow Wilson's magnificent series of definitive and expository speeches in the latter phase of the first World War. The Atlantic Charter was very vague, and subsequent pronouncements have been even less precise. But this is a very small part of the story. It was easy for President Wilson to make his speeches because he knew what to say and he knew that it would command general agreement. He knew this because the western democratic world knew in 1918 what it was after. Last time, we knew what our ideas were. We were putting the finishing touches to a triumphant program. The war of 1914–18 was to be the means of plucking good out of evil, an opportunity to finish off the job on which the western democracies had been engaged for more than a century. The Armistice and the peace were to register the final victory of everything in which the nineteenth century liberal believed. Wilson and everybody else knew what the ideas were because a hundred years had been spent in working them out.

Now nobody knows for sure. We have not yet made up our collective mind (and not many people have made up their individual minds over the whole range) whether there is life in the old dogmas yet, or whether our problems are so different that they cannot be handled by the former body of doctrine, however amended. Is the twentieth century an extension of the nineteenth century, or something different? We do not know, and it is very foolish to cavil at Mr. Roosevelt and Mr. Churchill because they have not taken an afternoon off to tell us. They do not know either. The western democratic world is perilously close to a vacuum of faith.

It is the thesis of E. C. Carr's influential book, "Conditions of Peace," that the dominant ideas of the nineteenth century are dead— or at least that they no longer have sufficient validity to serve as our guiding lights. He defines these dominant ideas as being, in domestic politics, representative democracy; in economics, free individual enterprise; and in international affairs, the sovereignty of self-determined nations. For myself, I would not admit that either representative democracy or free capitalism was dead. But even in our domestic affairs, it seems to me to be very difficult to affirm that they are still the sole or the dominant principles. And as articles for export they are even more doubtful, while between nations it has become clear that national sovereignty, so far from being the only valid principle, is the only certainly disastrous principle. In general, though I would differ from Mr. Carr in matters of degree, I find it impossible to refute the substance of his charge. The twentieth century is *not* simply an extension of the nineteenth. The problems of the postwar world will not be those of the nineteenth century. In many respects they will be directly opposite (*e.g.*, the pressure to create maximum employment rather than maximum income, the need to curb the freedom of nation-states rather than to create them), and in every case they will be different.

Moreover, the people who will face them will be different. Hitherto, the world has been run by men and women who were born in the nineteenth century. Only one man born in the twentieth century has yet sat in an American or British Cabinet. The Russians and Chinese leaders are nineteenth-century-born. So are the chief Nazis. It happens that the children of the nineteenth and twentieth centuries are divided by much more than the accident of a numeral. The eldest child of the twentieth century man who was born on January 1, 1901—was within a few weeks of the draft age when the last war came to an end. He stands just on this side of that great dividing line—a borderline of much greater psychological importance than any that will be created by this war, for all but the very youngest of those who fought in the last war had been brought up to a world of security. They had come to accept a set of absolutes which crumbled in front of their eyes, while the children of the twentieth century have never known what a secure world is. In Britain, though not in America, there is also the great chasm of the "missing generation" dividing the children of the twentieth century from their fathers.

This is not the only accident of history that sets them off. The great technical inventions of the nineteenth century were industrial processes, which the individual rarely saw; they were ways of producing familiar objects in greater numbers and at lower cost, ways of providing for the poor what had formerly been the prerogative of the rich. They extended the spread of comfortable living, but they did not greatly change its content. Round about the turn of the century, however, technical progress began to have a direct impact on social customs and modes of thought. The men and women born in the twentieth century are the first generation to have been familiar, for the whole of their lives, with such revolutionary molders of thought and custom as air travel, individual transport on land by means of the automobile, the moving picture, the radio. They have been influenced by the decline in formal religion. They are the first generation in which it has been more than an impiety to think that the human race could or should control its numbers. In America, they are the first generation in which high-school education has been universal and college education general. In England, the creation of a complete educational ladder from bottom to top dates from 1902.

The historians of the future will have to judge whether these changes were, on balance, for good or evil. My present point is that they make for a greater cleavage of instincts and of instinctive ideas between old and young than has perhaps ever before existed. And just when this strange new generation would in any case be beginning to push its way into the driving seat, there comes the vast catastrophe of the present war to accentuate still further the difference between its environment and that of its fathers. In view of all these facts, I do not believe it is an exaggeration to say that we stand at one of the grand climacterics of world history. If there is any carry-over of dominant principles from the former age to the latter, it will be a matter for marveling.

My quarrel with Mr. Carr is not, then, that I wish to refute his main thesis but that I do not like being left where he leaves me. The dominant doctrines of the nineteenth century, if not dead, are so battered that they will not serve us any longer as our main props. We are, indeed, living in a vacuum of faith. But the trouble about a vacuum is that it gets filled, and if there are no angels available to fill it, fools—or worse—rush in. Let us, then, take Mr. Carr's threefold division of politics, economics and international relations, and consider in each case the alternatives to the old principles which he condemns. What are, not merely the theoretical alternatives, but the actual enemies that have been pushing them off their thrones?

The trend away from liberal democracy has been a trend towards totalitarian dictatorship. The trend away from individualist capitalism has been a trend toward rigid state control exercised in the interest of a war economy—or at least of a war-minded economy. The trend away from the sovereignty of the nation-state has been a trend towards the concentration of aggressive strength in the hands of a few Great Powers. These are not, of course, the only conceivable alternatives; but they are the alternatives that the pressure of the age has been forcing upon us.

That pressure, it will be objected, is about to be lifted by a victory for the United Nations. I am not so certain. I have the suspicion that the Nazi alternatives, diabolical though they are, have far too much of the logic of events in them to be brushed aside by the military defeat of Hitler. If we are realistic, we shall recognize, even though it increases the difficulty of our task, that there is a great deal in the circumstances of our century that leads straight to Fascism. The enormous development in the technique of propaganda and advertising, in the power to sway the minds of people in the mass, plays straight into the hands of the would-be dictator or any other manipulator who, for large ends or small, seeks to muddy the waters of democracy. The growth of large-scale industry, the need for gigantic aggregations of capital, the implications of a maximum employment policy—all these create the danger of a concentration of economic power. The technique of modern war, with its emphasis on the possession of certain complicated weapons which only a handful of highly industrialized states can produce, makes the small nations, or even the league of small nations, quite helpless, and compels the Great Powers to devote quite unprecedented proportions of their resources to the barren purposes of war. We cannot abolish these things, we cannot dodge them. We cannot cancel the invention of the radio and aircraft or unlearn the technique of mass production. But if we accept their existence, we must also accept their consequences. Propaganda *plus* the concentration of economic power *plus* Blitzkrieg technique add up to Fascism; or they may be made to add up to something new that will be compatible with democratic ideals. But whatever else they add up to, they certainly do not add up to the sort of democracy that our fathers thought of. The plain truth is that Hitler has an answer to the problems of the twentieth century and we, as yet, have not. It follows that whatever happens in the present war, Hitler will be hot on our heels for the rest of our lives. We shall have to think very fast, and run very fast, to keep ahead of him. One slip, one stumble, and he will be on our necks.

The central dilemma of the present age is that we can no longer rely on the old principles alone, but that we abominate the alternatives that time and tide, if it is left to them, will produce. This dilemma can be solved in only one way, by the birth of a new faith, adjusted in its instrumentalities to the needs of the new century, but preserving the ultimate objectives of the old. The only way to avoid the murder of nineteenth-century Liberalism by twentieth-century Fascism is through the birth of a twentieth-century democratic faith by the new out of the old. The biological analogy with the conflict of the sexes is exact. If one kills the other, no continuing life is possible. This is what would happen if the crude, raw impact of changed conditions were merely to remove the tried doctrines of an earlier age. Nor is the future to be secured by some hermaphroditic compromise, in which the two elements are so much in conflict that the result is, as Disraeli said of the mule, "without pride of ancestry or hope of posterity." No, the only solution is to take what is strong and good and lasting in the new ideas, to mate it with the old and to conceive something that has elements of both, but has its own life, is new, harmonious, growing, integral. What we need is not a compromise between the old ideas and the new, but a fusion; not a mixture but an amalgam. The nineteenth century, before it dies, must take what is virile in the hostile movements and give birth to something new. Only then can it die in peace.

III

To state the need for such a new democratic faith is one thing. To meet it is another. The task of developing the thesis here presented in every sphere of public policy, political and economic, domestic and international, is probably beyond the power of a single pen; and certainly far beyond the reach of a single article. It may, however, be permissible to proceed a little way further in one particular direction, that of economic organization. What I have to say is chiefly directed to the internal economic problems of nations such as the United States and the United Kingdom—though it is, of course, impossible to treat of these problems in isolation from their international implications.

The air is full at present of wordy warfare on the relative merits of unhampered private enterprise and of government planning of economic developments. Both are being argued in extreme and absolute terms—that is, as principles capable of being applied universally and in unadulterated form. Possibly the protagonists have reservations and modifications in mind, but, if so, they escape but rarely into print or speech. Not often does an advocate of private enterprise make the admission that there are certain economic problems (and among the largest) which must either be tackled by the organizing powers of the government or else left untackled. Still less frequently does an advocate of "planning" pause to concede that over a vast range of industries and occupations either the mainspring of activity will (in any easily foreseeable future) remain that of individual enterprise and ambition or there will be no mainspring at all. No, the argument proceeds in absolutes: the free enterprise party has no use for "bureaucracy" anywhere at any time; and the planners will not admit that a businessman, by serving the interest of his own profit, can ever serve the general interest.

It is, of course, a sham fight. I do not mean that the contestants are not sincere; many of them doubtless (and unhappily) are passionately sincere. It is a sham fight because there is not the slightest chance of either side winning its fight. In the circumstances of the twentieth century, there is no prospect whatever of an industrial democratic state basing its affairs on the principle of unrestricted individual enterprise to the exclusion, or even to the subordination, of other principles. Even less can an industrial democracy contemplate governmental "planning" of the bulk of its activities—at least it cannot do so and remain a democracy.

Perhaps it is worth while pausing for a moment to justify these dogmatic statements. The reasons why unrestricted private enterprise is insufficient by itself are perhaps clearer to a British observer than to an American. The United States, after all, is still in the period of rapid expansion. It is wholly reasonable to suppose that by the end of the present century the American national income may be at least double what it is now—that is to say, at least three times what it was in the late 1930s. And the frontiers of possible achievement are more distant still. The supreme necessity of the American economy remains that of expansion and there is an almost automatic source of demand for great masses of capital. The pioneer is no longer, perhaps, the American archetype— but he is still a socially necessary type, and it is, of course, in a pioneering environment that unregulated private enterprise shows to maximum advantage.

In Great Britain, on the other hand, the end of the rising national income is in sight, owing to the imminence of a stable and even a falling population. It is unlikely that the British national income will ever be more than 50 percent higher than it is now, and even that moderate increase requires optimistic assumptions on the trend both of population and of individual productivity. The peak will be reached in about a generation from now, and thereafter the national income will be preserved from falling only if the rise in individual productivity succeeds in outpacing the fall in total numbers. Clearly, this puts the pioneer and the builder at a discount and the administrator and allocator at a premium. Moreover, there are other problems, hardly more important but possibly more urgent. Britain needs her foreign purchases to live, and the war has knocked a series of holes in the credit side of what was at best a somewhat precarious balance. The task of the postwar years will be not merely to get back the prewar trade, but to find markets for something like a 50 percent increase in the prewar volume of exports. No one but a fanatic would believe uncoördinated private enterprise capable of outfacing these difficulties.

Thus there are reasons why there is less talk in Britain than in America of the sovereign virtues of unregulated individualism. But this does not mean, in my judgment, that there is the slightest possibility of a return to laissez-faire even in America. For one thing, I remain obstinately skeptical about the possibility of making any appreciable headway against the menace of recurrent depressions except by the road of government action. The present attempt, sponsored by the Committee for Economic Development, to demonstrate that a regular and adequate flow of savings into physical investment can be organized by business itself, is a gallant rearguard action. I wish it well, but my money is on the other horse. Secondly, I remain even more obstinately skeptical about the ability of a free-enterprise economy—that is, of an economy where the requirements of free enterprise have priority over other objectives—to bring about any substantial improvement in the unequal distribution of wealth and welfare. Yet if there are two things in the sphere of economic policy that the electorate is going to impose as categorical imperatives on its representatives, regardless of party, they are contained in the current expressions Full Employment and Social Security. Walter Bagehot, the great apostle of the free economy, wrote nearly eighty years ago that "the coöperative, if not the compulsory, agency of the state ought to be used far more than now in applying to our complicated society those results of science which are new to our age." He was thinking, in the main, of physical science. But his remark applies with even greater force to those results of social science (and of social experience) which are new to our age and which must be incorporated into our economy and policy without damaging delay. There are certain objects that society can attain—it has been demonstrated—by means of "the coöperative, if not the compulsory, agency of the state." The Russians have shown that it is possible to secure a very rapid increase in the national income; the Germans have shown that it is possible for a highly industrialized state to remove within a few years one of the largest masses of unemployment known to economic history. We may abominate the methods by which these achievements were secured. But we cannot pretend they do not exist. On the contrary, the electorate is going to insist on emulation of the results, if not on imitation of the methods. Employment of "the coöperative, if not the compulsory, agency of the state" is an inescapable consequence.

But if the wholly free economy is an impossibility, the wholly controlled economy is no less unacceptable. There are two main reasons for this. In the first place, experience seems to show—and common sense would confirm—that it is considerably less efficient in the production of wealth for consumption. The planned economy has had its triumphs. But none of them, I think, has been a triumph in supplying in large quantities at low prices consumption goods of the kinds and in the variety that people want. Yet that must remain one of the fundamental and co-equal objects of any democratic economy. There are examples of planned economics where the strength of the state has been increased, where the capital equipment of the community has been enriched, where mass unemployment has been avoided. I do not know of a wholly planned economy where the consumer has been satisfied. And, in the second place, a wholly planned economy is incompatible with any degree of political freedom. The possibility of a man's earning his own living in his own way, without let or hindrance, is the essential condition of there being any freedom of discussion, any freedom to oppose. If more than a fraction of the electorate come to depend for their livelihood upon the temporary masters of the mechanism of the state—that is, upon the politicians—then democracy is at an end.

It follows from this discussion that the economic system of the next few decades will inevitably have elements both of individual freedom of enterprise and also of purposive direction by the state. This conclusion, by now, is almost a commonplace. What is not so generally realized is that it matters most vitally how the two elements are combined. Neither can, it is true, remove the other; democratic society is not going to be either wholly planned or wholly unplanned. But each opposing principle can very effectively obstruct the other. A society which is based on an active coöperation of the two principles will be a vastly different place from a society based on a deadlock between them.

Deadlock is what the western democracies have been threatened with in the past thirty years. It is easy to see how the desire to plan economic development, the desire to make it follow motives more socially respectable than the incentive of profit, the desire to ensure security in an insecure world—it is easy to see how these desires have clogged and frustrated the free economy. Over far the greater part of the economy, the businessman is still left with the responsibility of initiating activity. He has to make up his mind whether an enterprise is worth the risks involved in it, and unless he gives the word to start the wheels turning, no one else will or can. But the risks of loss have been increased by the great load of prior charges that has been put upon him in the way of rigid wage-rates, wasteful labor practices, social security contributions and the like, while his incentive to take these risks has been dulled by heavy and differential taxation, and his arm has been jogged by all manner of inspectors, controls, regulations, inquisitions, prohibitions and indictments.

The impact on our economy of the idea of planning and of the motive of social welfare has hitherto been almost wholly negative. Few industries have been planned, but a vast number have been bedevilled by planning. In many cases, the approach has been more than negative, it has been punitive, and the entrepreneur has been abused and penalized precisely in proportion to his success in performing his duty of running economic activity at a profit. To date, we are certainly far more planned against than planning.

The other side of the medal is very similar. Wherever the state has tried, by the use of collective methods, to make headway against the problems that beset it, it has been held back by a hundred visible and invisible strings of timidity and orthodoxy. If it wishes to close the deflationary gap by deficit financing, it can do so only within the very narrow field that runs no risk of competing with private enterprise. And every step is taken to the accompaniment of charges ranging from corruption and dictatorship to red ruin.

IV

The result has been deadlock, and if we sometimes wonder why it is that our economy seems to have lost its elasticity, its power to respond to opportunity, if we complain that only in wartime are its potentialities realized, the reason is that we have been busy putting brakes on both the two possible springs of initiative. We make it difficult for the profit motive to work lest it should be anti-social in its effect, and we make it difficult for the social motive to work lest it be too wasteful.

In this struggle, neither side can win. It follows that the most urgent task for all economic statesmen is to work out means by which the two principles of organization can live side by side. If there is to be activity of any sort, there must be some incentive to activity. For a generation or more, we have been hard at work whittling down all incentives, and trying to work out a compromise between freedom and organization on the basis that we shall have as little as possible of either. That is wrong. The right course is to have as much as possible of both, to take the brakes off both the profit incentive and the social incentive.

This is not the place to discuss how this can be done. But the method clearly lies along the way of sorting out the economic activities of the community that are to be powered by each incentive. There are no absolute rules for determining where the line should be drawn, and no doubt it will be drawn in different places in different countries, and at different times in the same country. There are some activities that every country puts on the "organization" side of the line and makes no attempt to run on a profit-earning basis—justice, education and war-making, for example. There are others that every democracy will put on the "freedom" side—the press, entertainments and most luxury trades. Between these extremes, the people will draw the line as they choose and the location of the line is a fit and proper subject for party controversy. What is essential is that, on either side of the line, the dominant incentive should be left as free as possible to stimulate activity. Neither one can be quite exclusive: profit-minded enterprise cannot be allowed to be anti-social, nor can social-minded activity be undertaken without any regard to its economic cost. But in each sphere the interloping considerations should be adjusted to interfere as little as possible with the dominant incentive. The businessman, for example, cannot be relieved of taxation; but his taxes can be designed to interfere as little as possible with the earning of profits.

There will be those among the critics of this doctrine who will shake their heads and say that it cannot be done. They will quote Abraham Lincoln to the effect that a nation cannot live half slave and half free. If so, then the prospect is black indeed for all of us; because, for the reasons given above, it seems to me inconceivable that we shall ever be able to pin our faith on either of the alternatives. If they are so instinctively and inevitably antipathetic to each other that they cannot live in peace, side by side, then we must conclude that democracy is incapable of resolving the contradictions to which it gives rise and must surely perish. I take a more optimistic view. It is true that the opposing principles of economic freedom and of economic organization have, in fact, generated frictions which have perceptibly slowed down the progress of the democratic economy. But this is because they have been stupidly handled and the frictions would not arise if the object of all parties were to avoid them, instead of, as at present, to seek battle on all occasions. Both the British and the American democracies have, each in its own way, over the past 150 years resolved the very similar conflict between freedom and order in the political sphere. I see no overriding reason why the same success should not be achieved in the economic sphere, provided the same essential moderation is shown.

There are those also who hold that there is some inevitability of conflict in the international sphere between nations which draw the line between freedom and organization in different places. This seems to me to be even purer defeatism than the former objection. No state is wholly without compulsory organization in its economy and none is wholly without freedom. The differences are of degree, not of kind, and our affairs are in a sorry posture if differences of ideological degree are going to cause irreconcilable conflicts. The battle, it is said, will come on the management of international trade; a country that exercises conscious management of its trade relations will necessarily have an unfair advantage over one that does not, and thus controlled economics are inevitably aggressive.

But if there is anything at all in this objection, the way to meet it is directly, by securing agreement on the definition of unfair practices and putting a ban on them, whether perpetrated by governments, by cartels or by individuals.

v

This economic argument, as has been said, is intended only as an illustration of the wider thesis that, if western democracy is to confront its twentieth-century problems with any hope of success, there is an urgent necessity for hard thinking on first principles. It is not enough either to demonstrate the inadequacy of the old liberalism or to expatiate on the abomination of the Fascist alternative. Both are destructive exercises, necessary as preliminaries perhaps, but contributing nothing to the positive task of construction. That task involves nothing less than the creation of a new faith, a newly articulated set of principles by which the imperishable objectives of a free humanity can be sought by techniques appropriate to this century. And the first step is to realize that it is not only the theses of the nineteenth century that are dead or dying, but the antitheses also.

I am not one of those who holds that a vacuum of faith will be much handicap to us in winning the war. War is fought mainly by material means, and though it would be an advantage to know what we are fighting for, it is enough to know what we are fighting against. It is after the fighting is over that the trouble will begin. For when material force is removed, it is only the force of ideas that can prevail. At present, in the realm of ideas, we are almost completely disarmed. Rearmament, with modern weapons, cannot begin too soon. ❧

Limits of Economic Planning

Barbara Ward

Foreign Affairs, January 1949

In recent years, the battle between the planners and the anti-planners has become fairly engaged. In the decade before the recent war, the planners tended—in Britain at least—to hold the field of popular theoretical writing and of polemical literature. But since the appearance during the war of Professor Hayek's book, "The Road to Serfdom," a vigorous counterattack has been launched and a number of recent British books on economics have taken the anti-planning side. The debate is being conducted on the whole in terms of forceful dogmatism, and this is not surprising when one remembers how easy it is to be dogmatic about the theoretical basis of a case.

In theory, the planners can claim that they are in the full stream of human progress. What has created the tremendous physical advances of the last century if not man's increasing scientific control over his environment? The masterpieces of modern engineering have all started with the blueprint. Is it not reasonable to argue that the same methods—of plans and blueprints and "social engineering"— will not have equally happy results when society itself is their raw material? To apply planning to human government is simply to rescue one more vital sector—perhaps the most vital sector—of men's lives from the tyranny of the irrational.

The reply of the anti-planner is equally cogent. "Men are not sticks and stones and metals," he protests. "Among men you cannot find—and ought not to induce—the same uniformity of reaction

BARBARA WARD, Assistant Editor of *The Economist*, London; author of "The West At Bay" and other works.

which you find in material things. Nor can you ever be as certain of the purpose to which men ought to be devoted. The best use of a given amount of iron and steel may be to make a bridge, but who can say what is the best use to which a given number of men can be put? Is it not significant that the best examples of planning are to be found either in time of war—when the purpose of every citizen and of society as a whole is singlemindedly to fight for victory—or in totalitarian societies where the uniformity and predictability of all the citizens is the first aim of education? You can, in a word, apply social engineering only by making men resemble the raw materials of ordinary engineering—by depriving them of all liberty of choice, of all variety, and indeed of everything that characterizes a free man."

So long as this debate is unanchored by any reference to fact, there is no reason why it should be brought to any conclusion. And unfortunately the number of facts upon which the observer can call is still strictly limited. The concept of planning the economic life of a community is extremely new. Those who connect it with Communism will look for it in vain in Marx's works. He believed that the maladjustments of capitalist society mainly sprang from the institution of private property and the falsification which private profit introduced into the distribution of wealth. Remove that inhibition and society would function without friction. Nor does the concept of planning figure in the early writings of Socialism. In Britain, for instance, neither the Fabians nor the Guild Socialists ever talked of it at all. And even if they had done so, their talk at that time could only have been theoretical. The statistical data necessary for the drawing up of a national plan was simply not available. The careful statistics of every aspect of the national economy which are kept in certain countries today are essential conditions of any sort of plan and the extent to which the lack of them stultifies government action may be seen any day in 1948 in Paris where 16 governments of vastly varying efficiency seek to draw up four-year forecasts of their production and trade. The figures produced by some governments are so notional as to make impossible any real reliance upon their plans. Thirty years ago, there were not even notional figures. It follows that there could be no plans.

Professor Jewkes in his strong attack upon government direction and control, "Ordeal by Planning," suggests that the first plan worthy of the name was the German attempt at the total planning of their war economy after 1916, the so-called Hindenburg Plan. Its first application to civilian uses was made by Lenin. Professor Jewkes does not hazard a guess whether Lenin was or was not inspired by the German model, but certainly he found nothing in Marxism to tell him how to build a modern economy in a shattered demoralized community which, contrary to all Marx's predictions, had not yet achieved a structure of capitalist industry. Professor Jewkes cites a quotation from Lenin, used by the Webbs to illustrate Lenin's empirical approach: "Couldn't you produce a plan (not a technical but a political scheme) which would be understood by the proletariat? For instance, in 10 years (or 5?) we shall build 20 (or 30 or 50?) power stations covering the country with a network of such stations . . . We need such a plan at once to give the masses a shining unimpeded prospect to work for." Thus planning entered the stage of history, like so many other revolutionary ideas, by a side door, almost unnoticed by the man who first conceived it and aimed at something—propaganda value—which was later to be at best of very secondary importance. When Stalin took up the idea in 1928, he made it the lever of Russia's gigantic plunge into industrialization. And if planning is to have a birthday, 1928 is perhaps the most appropriate year.

It follows that the idea of central planning as a vital instrument of economic and social policy is only 20 years old. That fact alone should encourage caution in making dogmatic estimates of its value or its dangers. Few new techniques have proved themselves in 20 years. This caution is reinforced by a number of other reasons. Most of the concrete examples to which both planners and anti-planners appeal today are drawn from quite exceptional circumstances. The planning with which the world is unfortunately most familiar is planning for war. Planning at such a time is inevitable, for no community left to its own devices will produce enough weapons and armaments to secure victory. War-making coupled with "business as usual" was a fantasy worthy of Mr. Chamberlain and the "phoney war" of 1939 and early 1940. But the planning which diverts a large proportion of the nation's resources—60 percent in Britain—to the making of bombers and tanks has a singleness of purpose which it is hard to repeat in time of peace. This is not to say that some of the administrative techniques may not be usefully studied, but planning for war is not and cannot be an exact analogy of planning for peace.

Some nations—chief among them Britain—have, however, carried their planning over into peacetime. Here surely is the laboratory specimen from which conclusions of scientific accuracy can be drawn. Unfortunately, the conditions of postwar planning are still exceptional since a large part of the planning and control has been not the "purposive direction of the economy" but a desperate rearguard action against acute shortages. So many of the controls which have proved most oppressive to the ordinary queue-standing woman in the street have been dictated not by planning as such but by a desire to make very short supplies go as far as they can and at the same time to avoid the inflationary pressure which free bidding for those scarce supplies would have inevitably produced. The contrast between the British economy, which is controlled but financially exceptionally stable, and the neighboring French economy, where neither the attempt at control nor the attempt at no control has checked galloping inflation, is a warning against too hasty generalizations about the evils of control when controls are being applied at a time of acute scarcity. It may be said in parenthesis that if any vital commodity—such as iron ore or petroleum—were to prove permanently scarce, there can be little doubt that countries most devoted to the ideal of free enterprise would accept governmental supervision of the scarce material.

There is another warning contained in the contrast between Britain and France. It is the difficulty of extending generalizations about planning from one national community to another. However good the theoretical case for planning, it is quite clear that some governments today cannot plan successfully. To give only three preconditions of planning—the civil service must be reasonably efficient and honest, citizens must be reasonably ready to pay their taxes and in general, the conception of respecting the regulations laid down by the government must be reasonably widespread. These conditions are present in Britain, in Holland, in Scandinavia. They are absent in France and Italy. Very few generalizations about the possible scope of planning based on the five former countries would be really applicable to the two latter.

For the same reason, it is difficult to go to Russia for a great deal of guidance on the possibilities of planning. In the first place, accurate and detailed information is exceptionally hard to secure. But even more frustrating is the total difference in political atmosphere. If a society has lost its freedom—or never enjoyed it—the experience of its government can only be applied with difficulty to free communities whose leaders are struggling to combine a measure of direction with the preservation of all essential liberties. To give two instances, planning in a free society has to find ways and means of tempting workers from redundant to expanding areas of employment. It also has to persuade businessmen to adapt themselves to a general policy for the location of industry. Both problems involve delicate questions of incentive and pressure. But what problems do they raise in Russia where the inhabitants of the whole Crimean region were transported *en bloc* to Siberia three years ago and where penal labor camps, starred across the Arctic wastes, forever await the recalcitrant? There are differences in background so vast that the experience of the Russians in planning, interesting though it may be from the point of view of administrative technique, can only be used with the utmost discretion in discussing the problems of free society.

II

These reservations are not introduced to prove that there can be no intelligent discussion of planning. They are simply set down as a guard against excessive dogmatism. The truth is that the world does not yet know very much about the most important issue raised by economic planning—which is the question whether planning is a valuable addition to the techniques of a free society.

To put the question at all admits something which most democrats are ready to admit—that free society is not perfect and that all the various national versions of it in the western world have a long way to go before they make the ideals embodied in them— of freedom and justice and charity and plenty—a living reality. The great claim put forward by the planners is that planning is a technique for curing the observed inadequacies of modern industrial society and possibly the clearest method of examining its claims is to take those shortcomings which are generally admitted to weaken western democracy and to examine the extent to which economic planning offers a cure.

There is, however, one clarification to be made before this examination can be undertaken. The extent to which Socialists have adopted the idea of central planning has led many people to believe that planning, nationalization, workers' share in management and other planks of the Socialist platform are indistinguishable and that to say one is to say them all. This present article, at least, is concerned only with planning; and the questions of state ownership and control will be considered only in so far as they have some direct connection with the practice of planning.

The two concepts—of planning and nationalization—are essentially distinct. Hitler was a great planner, but he left the actual structure and ownership of industry virtually untouched. Or, to give a more topical example of the distinction, the British Government today has on the whole given more attention to nationalization than to planning. The various sessions of parliament have devoted more time to altering the ownership of the coal mines, the Bank of England, land transport and the public utilities than to any other activity. The administration also inherited from the war and has maintained a number of controls, most of them designed to deal with the problems raised by shortage. But any general economic planning, any genuine "purposive direction" of the economy has been almost entirely confined to the efforts of Sir Stafford Cripps. At the Board of Trade, he was first responsible for the dedication of a large part of British industry to the export drive— which this year has achieved a 50 percent increase on the volume of 1938—and when he became Chancellor of the Exchequer, he was able in one year to check inflation and introduce strong elements of deflation into the British economy.

There is only one direct connection between planning and nationalization, and so far it is only a theory. Some Socialists argue that it will be impossible for a government to plan effectively such matters as capital expansion or the control of the trade cycle unless public ownership of an important sector of industry—say, coal mining, transport and iron and steel—gives the planners the last word in determining the investment policy of these industries. This theory assumes that no government could secure the collaboration of industry without taking it over—which is certainly far from being proved in Britain, where, for instance, the steel industry has coöperated fully with the Government even when under the threat of nationalization. In Italy, an even more paradoxical case exists for, although by means of the *Instituto di Ricostruzione Industriale* (IRI), Mussolini's great holding company, a very large sector of heavy industry and transport *is* owned by the Government, the Government has no views on evolving a policy of planned capital development and no intention apparently of using its "public sector" as part of a general policy of planning.

The connection between planning and public ownership can therefore be regarded—for the time being at least—as being to a considerable extent accidental. And it is planning that concerns us here.

III

It is impossible to examine all the shortcomings of modern industrial society which the practice of general economic planning is supposed to counter. There are, however, one or two main difficulties which laissez faire economics apparently do not solve automatically, and it is primarily in relation to these that the case for and against planning can best be examined.

The first is at once an economic and social problem. It is that the unfettered workings of the free enterprise system create wealth but create it very unevenly. The accumulation at the top is far greater than the accumulation at the bottom. This phenomenon creates the economic problem of insufficient demand. The machines pour out the products in greater abundance than the markets can absorb them and the resulting gluts help to produce the alternations of expansion and contraction known as the trade cycle. Nor is it simply a question of lack of demand within the national economy. On a world-wide scale, the failure of demand has produced such imbecilities as textile mills closing in Lancashire and New England while the productivity of Chinese labor suffers for lack of cheap cotton garments. The social problem is even more obvious— the growth of unrest, the resentment of the masses, the spread of Communism.

It is in this field that the most widespread use of "purposive direction" has been made. Almost every government in the western world uses taxation—one of the most flexible instruments of central planning—to redistribute income and to provide out of state funds services and amenities for the mass of the people which were once the preserve of a small minority. The delicacy of all instruments of planning is illustrated by the problem of determining at which point the use of taxation to redistribute wealth in society becomes an obstacle to the accumulation of wealth by society. Taxed beyond a certain point, neither businessman nor worker will create and produce with the necessary zest. Taxation also has unfortunate consequences in relation to the trade cycle which will be discussed later. But in spite of these limitations, taxation as an instrument for regulating the scale of incomes and thus the flow of purchasing power in a community is the most widely accepted method of central planning by the state, and those who extend their dislike of planning even to a frontal attack upon taxation may observe in France today the disastrous economic and social consequences of the existence in a nation of a middle class that refuses to be taxed.

During the war, various experiments were made, particularly in relation to food, to deal with the problem of poverty by other means than those of taxation—although the money provided by taxation has been the basis of the extra services. Free milk, fruit juice and vitamin schemes for mothers and children, school meals for children, subsidies for certain basic foods are all methods used in Britain to plan the diet of the people. Only the last of these—food subsidies—is controversial and it has become the target of all those who believe that taxation is now so high as to check initiative. The figure of some £480,000,000 spent on food subsidies in the last year has become one of the biggest items in the Budget; and since these subsidies assist rich and poor alike and reduce costs in the Ritz equally with the workmen's canteen, their incidence appears somewhat irrational. In Belgium, food subsidies in general were removed while the more poorly paid workers continued to receive special privileges. Experience suggests that, in the long run, the direct intervention of the state as a buyer and provider of foodstuffs is more cumbrous than financial measures, such as children's allowances, rent rebates and tax exemption which leave food prices unaffected but ensure an adequate income to the poorer workers.

The question of food prices brings us to the second field in which government planning and intervention is already a widespread practice. The yields of the world's harvests are so uncertain that unchecked they introduce a dangerous element of instability into economic life. This at least has been recognized for some 30 years and attempts were made after the First World War to regulate supply and in this way to keep some stability of price. Rubber schemes, tea schemes, coffee schemes, organized by the producers, were all tried and in general failed. The great depression of the early 1930s brought the primary producers of the world to their lowest ebb. In Britain it was a time when docks and thistles grew in some of the finest pasture land. In America, the ruin was accentuated by the horrors of drought. The cocoa growers of Nigeria were as hard hit as the rice growers of Siam.

Out of that experience, two policies have grown. The first is support for the farmer at home. One of the biggest American excursions into direct planning is probably its system of price support for agricultural products. This removes a large sector—one of the largest—of the American economy from the free play of supply and demand. It seems certain that, whatever the fall in world demand, wheat at 75 cents the bushel will never appear again in the United States. Similarly in Great Britain, the Government is now pledged to a £100,000,000 development program in agriculture, underpinned at every point by guaranteed prices. In both countries, there are critics who will say that this intervention by the state is false planning, since it has been undertaken without relating the expense of agricultural subsidies to the national income as a whole and without demanding in return any guarantee of increased efficiency and productivity. But if planning be defined as purposive intervention by the state to achieve certain economic ends, the governments of the western world are definitely planners in the agricultural field.

This policy of planning in agriculture has been extended to foreign trade by means of guaranteed import prices and government bulk purchase. Remembering the slump of the thirties, few governments are ready to embark on plans of agricultural expansion unless they receive some guarantee of a continued market. One of the crucial economic discussions at the recent Commonwealth Conference in London concerned the length of time over which the British Government would be prepared to guarantee markets for Australian and New Zealand produce. Both governments were being urged to extend their areas of cultivation. Both in return demanded guarantees which only a government ready to "plan" its agricultural imports could give. The same anxiety for guaranteed markets has appeared at Geneva in the negotiations on trade between Eastern and Western Europe. Poland and Rumania demand guarantees if they are to devote a large part of their agriculture to the grain and fodder and dairy products demanded by the industrialized nations of Western Europe. Finally, with the coming into operation of the Food and Agricultural Organization and its central organ, the World Food Council, the planning of food supplies has now entered the international field.

It is possible to argue that the methods of rigidly guaranteed prices and of bulk purchase are too costly to the importing government to become lasting instruments of economic planning, but it is difficult to contend that planning can be done away with altogether in this field. The very insecurity of production had already led the producers to begin some embryonic planning on their own behalf—and, of all types of planning, planning done by producers for producers tends to be economically the most costly to the consumer. If stability and abundance are to be secured, control must be vested in a governmental agency, at the national or international level, and although the techniques of planning in this vital sector will doubtless improve, there can be little doubt that governmental planning will never be abandoned.

It was the Great Depression that turned so many governments of such very different political complexions to the idea not only of agricultural planning but of planning as such; and it is still true that the greatest single field in which central planning is most generally advocated is in the control of the trade cycle. Such agreement would hardly be possible if there were not now a general agreement on the nature and causes of the trade cycle—an agreement which did not exist 25 years ago, when every kind of explanation still had currency, from Jevons's sun spots to Marx's labor theory of surplus value. Thanks to Lord Keynes's pioneering work, there is now fairly general agreement that trade cycles are caused by fluctuations in the investment of capital and that general prosperity can be secured only by "a high and stable level of capital investment."

There are two ways in which generally unplanned economies can become a prey to instability and stagnation. The case of stagnation may be treated first, since it does not appear to be general. No one, for instance, would criticize American capitalism for being "stagnant." But two older capitalist societies, Britain and France, showed signs of this loss of vitality between the wars. At a time when neither government ventured to plan, when taxation was small, when trade unionism was weak—in a word at a time when the bugbears usually blamed by businessmen were absent, the British and the French economies ceased to expand and, in the case of France, positively diminished.

The reason in both cases appears to have been the same. In any industrial society, it is estimated that economic health can be maintained only if between 10 and 15 percent of the national income is being invested in fresh capital development. In Britain between the wars, the average level was no more than 3 percent. In France between 1929 and 1938 it must have been a minus quantity, since France in 1939 was less highly capitalized than in 1928 and those who remember the "hot money" which was continually escaping from the franc to the safety of the dollar between 1935 and 1939 will not be surprised to learn that the French entrepreneur class indulged in considerable "dis-saving" during that period.

Clearly if those whose function it is to save and invest do not do so, the government must intervene. Significantly, the first aim of the Monnet Plan published in France in 1946 was to bring back the level of France's capital equipment to that of 1929. It may be repeated in passing that the determination of a government to ensure a high level of investment in its economy may or may not be combined with nationalization and state control. Such is not the intention of the Monnet Plan, and in October 1948 Sir Stafford Cripps repeated his government's desire to secure the necessary 10 to 15 percent of annual investment by voluntary means. On the other hand, the stupendous expansion of the Russian planned economy has undoubtedly been due more than anything else to the decision to devote perhaps 30 percent of the annual wealth created by industrialization to fresh capital investment. But, although Russian experience thus confirms the necessity of a high level of capital investment, the economic backwardness and political tyranny of Russian society unfortunately make it difficult to draw detailed conclusions from the Soviet experiment useful to western society. It shows that under a certain set of social and economic conditions, total central economic planning does not break down. Nor—for 300 years—did the elaborate system of slaves and janissaries worked out by the Turks. But not to break down is hardly a proof *per se* of desirability.

The question of the stability and regularity of capitalist society is more important than that of buoyancy, since the phenomenon

of the trade cycle was born almost with the capitalist system itself
and has dogged all communities, progressive or not. It is in this
sphere that there is most general agreement on the possibility and
necessity of central economic planning by the state—the testimony
varying from business colossi such as Lever Brothers and convinced
anti-planners such as Professor Hayek and Professor Jewkes to the
warmest supporters of the Labor Party. The theory is fairly straightforward. It is that capital goods need to be replaced only after a
number of years, and that since confidence is one of the principal
factors in business planning, the new orders for capital goods tend
to be made all together when times are good and to fall off together
when demand begins to slacken. The rise and fall in the capital
goods sector sets the tone for all the rest, and the slump beginning
in the nineteenth century mainly in the textile industry (which
then represented the highest concentration of capital), and in the
twentieth century in iron and steel, spreads to consumers industries
and involves the whole economy in its downward spiral.

Hitherto the practices of the state have served to encourage this
phenomenon. We have seen how taxation is now one of its settled
instruments of planning, but traditional methods of taxation accentuate the trade cycle. When times are good and the call on the government for such services as unemployment pay are small, taxes flood
in from booming industry and the drain on the exchequer is small.
The government therefore tends to remit taxation and may begin
public works on its own account. Thus it sends the rising boom up
another couple of spirals in the process. The boom breaks, business
falls off, receipts from taxation drop, unemployment rises, the drain
on the exchequer mounts. The government therefore increases taxation and cuts its own expenditure—thus deepening the deflation
that is beginning to blight the economy. In other words, government
methods of taxation in the past have been exactly calculated to make
booms more busting and slumps more profound.

From this situation, many statesmen, economists and publicists
have drawn the conclusion that the government can play a vital
part in creating general stability in the community if it will use its
twin instruments of taxation and public expenditure to counteract

the normal workings of the trade cycle. When times are good, taxation should be held steady and perhaps increased, a budget surplus should be secured and reserves laid aside for a carefully drawn out scheme of state expenditure to be undertaken when demand shows sign of slackening. When these deflationary signs appear, the government should remit taxation, particularly all taxation on money devoted to capital expansion—thus guiding industry to phase its development programs and not huddle them all in the upward sweep of the cycle. During this deflationary period, an unbalanced budget might be permissible and budgeting might make the five or ten year period rather than the one year its basis of calculation. Another possibility might lie in the presentation of two budgets, one for the annual income and commitments of the state, the other for its capital expenditure.

These expedients have not yet been tried out, but Sweden during the depression made a limited and successful experiment in the planning of public works and Britain's housing program in the thirties was another instance of state-guided expansion. And it is also true that the industrial upswing of most countries after the Great Depression took the form of that most tragic of all forms of public works—a rearmament program. But these were not part of a coherent policy. No government yet has made a fully consistent and stable attempt to control the trade cycle. Indeed, the postwar trade depression is still only lurking in the wings of history. The stage is still held by wartime dislocation, inflation, full employment and continued shortages. It may be, too, that the Russian menace presages another period of economic activity in part sustained by rearmament. But if the free world secures the chance of peace, sooner or later the problem of the trade cycle will return, and this time the free governments will at least meet its challenge with weapons in their hands.

IV

This very brief survey covers only three of the possible fields of government action—admittedly important ones, but still only three—and no absolute conclusions should be advanced on such relatively scanty evidence. Yet they do at least suggest that not only has some measure of central economic planning come to stay but that this fact offers no inevitable threat to free society. On the contrary, such are the dangers of political shipwreck attendant upon the onslaught of economic depression that control of the trade cycle may well be the condition of preserving free society in this century.

But the admission that some economic planning may be necessary does not throw much light on a secondary but vitally important question—how should this planning be accomplished and by whom? By the government, certainly, for only the central authority can possess the relevant data upon which to base its decisions. But which organ of the government? Ministers? Civil servants? Independent planning boards? And, again, by what means? Should planning be confined to general measures, largely financial in character or should intervention be much more direct and detailed and diffuse?

Some people may feel that in this field at least the experience of different nations in waging war and, in particular, the experience of Great Britain both during and after the war can give valuable examples of what technically is the best (or worst) way to plan. Something certainly can be learnt, but, once again, complete certainty is impossible owing to the very specialized circumstances in which wartime planning was carried out—in particular by the men who have in this first age of planning been called upon to plan. The instances quoted here are drawn from British experience, for it is in Britain that the most determined effort has been made to carry on the experiment of planning into the peace and British experience with the personnel of planning should be particularly relevant.

It is surely not to be thought that if a measure of central planning is adopted as part of the permanent structure of democratic society no change will be made in the type of men called upon to do the planning or in the type of training they receive. The British permanent civil servants upon whom the great burden of planning has fallen were trained on the whole for quite other tasks. Their traditional work was that of administering known regulations with the utmost impartiality and equity, and a large part of their time was spent in seeing that things which went beyond the regulations did not happen. Onto this body of men was thrust the quite opposite task of initiating, directing and guiding the economic life of the country in a positive sense. It is a tremendous tribute to their adaptability that the results have not been more unsatisfactory than has in fact been the case. Yet such training lends itself inevitably to a restrictive attitude. The various officials controlling raw materials, for instance, are far better trained to refuse an application than to stimulate a proper use. They are, moreover, bound by every fiber of their tradition to the principle of equity. To give a concrete instance, they would rather see ten manufacturers receive one windowpane each than that one manufacturer should "secure the advantage" of a single ten-paned window. Yet from the point of view of imparting vigor, energy and encouragement to the men of initiative in the business world, there is no doubt that one window is an incentive, and one windowpane is not.

There is a further problem. The civil service commands financial rewards so totally out of line with those offered by industry that it cannot attract throughout its structure men of the type necessary to make economic planning effective. The "big executive" gravitates naturally to business, not to the civil service. One of the reasons for the relative effectiveness of planning in wartime is the number of able business people who go into the public service. They have all, almost without exception, returned by now to their accustomed work.

It follows that in judging the experience of planning in Britain in the last nine years, and especially in the last three, one must remember that the planners themselves are on the whole not the men a democratic society is likely to put in charge of planning once planning is finally established as a technique of government. Different scales of pay and totally different methods of training will undoubtedly be evolved. What we are judging today is essentially a makeshift.

Having said so much, what should the judgment be? There are certain tentative conclusions which British experience seems to suggest. The first is that the more ruling decisions have to be sent to a single central authority, the more the vigor and speed of the economic machine will be impaired. Ask any businessman what has been the cruellest cross he has had to bear under the present system of control, and he will reply "Delay." Control today can still be excused by the continuance of extreme shortages (of which the most extreme is the dollar shortage). But whatever the excuse, control from the center hampers initiative, and decentralization of decision is essential.

A second point is that physical controls are the hardest and most cumbrous to manage. When a ministry has actual control of the supply of a raw material and it can be obtained only on its allocation, the second greatest time waster becomes inevitable— the filling in of forms and the keeping of records. Moreover, violations of the regulations laid down covering the use of the raw material need to be followed up and prosecuted, and this, in turn, entails supervision at every level of use. Complete supervision is of course impossible, but it nevertheless keeps a great many men controlling and supervising other men, instead of working to produce themselves. The British Civil Service is now larger than at any time in its history. By common agreement, it is much too large.

A point worth mentioning in this context of supervision is that, once acute shortages have been overcome, direct control of prices by the central authority tends to rigidity on the one hand and excessive policing on the other. Control during the period of real shortage is naturally essential, and surely few economic boasts have been so little fulfilled as the claim of American business that to sweep away price controls would bring about a fall in prices. But in normal times the working of the market (within the limits set by supported prices in agriculture, fixed transport charges and the like) is the least cumbrous basis for the calculating of prices. To accept the market rate naturally lays on the government the duty of seeing that no man's income is so small as to exclude him from a share in the market; but the regulation of incomes is a more reliable instrument of planning than the control of prices.

One other conclusion is worth mentioning. No amount of detailed control will be effective if the tide of economic life has set against the controls. In Russia, the government may be able to turn the tide by removing unwilling peasants to Siberia by the million. Such methods are unavailable to free governments, which to a great extent must carry public opinion with them. If, for instance, the financial policy of a government is inflationary and surplus money is constantly tempting manufacturers to the production of high-cost luxuries or amusement parks, no regimentation of controls, however draconic, will prevent precious raw materials from drifting away to nefarious uses. The best method of ending the abuse is, to quote *The Economist*, to control the weather and not to ration the raindrops. Sir Stafford Cripps, by putting an end to Dr. Dalton's senseless inflationary policy, by achieving a genuine budget surplus and by persuading both sides of industry to limit dividends and wage increases, was able between the autumn of 1947 and the summer of 1948 to change the whole economic climate in Britain. And once the climate had changed, the "rationing of the raindrops" began to matter infinitely less.

Now if there is some validity in these conclusions, they suggest that central economic planning will be most effective when it uses financial rather than physical controls. This would seem to be true whatever the structure of society, whatever the system of property, whatever the pattern of classes. Given total public ownership, the various public corporations would still be better managed if they had not to refer everything to centralized ministries. Coöperative undertakings would be in the same case. And the point is obvious in the mixed society of public and private ownership which seems to be the likely democratic pattern for many years to come.

But to say that the state should avoid detailed physical supervision is not to condemn it to ineffectiveness. On the contrary, the budget, taxation, supervision of capital expenditure and the judicious use of allowances and subsidies provide the whole apparatus necessary for ensuring the general well-being of society, provided the politicians who set the course and the public servants who execute policy are fully aware of the aims and methods they ought to pursue. Nor does the confining of general economic planning to the field of finance mean that all kinds of experiments may not be made in the structure and ownership of industry and above all in the ways of associating work people more closely and rationally with the industries in which they work.

And if at the last one step into dogmatism may be permitted, it is to assert that the confining of government to certain essential purposes is more in keeping with the traditions of western political theory than the thoughtless, feckless passion for the state as such which has obscured so much that is generous and sound in the minds of modern reformers. Distrust of government is probably the soundest instinct of western society, doubly sound in a century which has within 40 years produced a Hitler, a Mussolini and a Stalin. No one can doubt the state's duty to secure the welfare of all its citizens. Equally no one can doubt its tendency to eat its citizens up in the process. A theory of economic stability and social progress which nevertheless keeps within reasonable bounds the direct control of government is the only safe theory for free society.

The Split Between Asian and Western Socialism

David J. Saposs

Foreign Affairs, July 1954

The dominating ideology in the international labor movement in the West is still Socialist, but a Socialism with a new look. Marxism has been discarded, although more by force of circumstances than conscious design, and the movement is still influenced by some Marxian reasoning; but, in general, Western Socialism has ceased to be class conscious and become reformist. It seeks the welfare state, but not revolution. The growing Christian (predominantly Catholic) labor movement in Western Europe has also arrived at maturity, and its social philosophy is likewise oriented toward the welfare state.

The old controversy over the interpretation of Marx was not revived in the labor movements in continental Europe after this war, as it was after World War I. This tacit abandonment of Marxism became fully apparent when the Socialist International was revived as a permanent organization in Frankfurt during the summer of 1951. The program and pronouncements of the convention used none of the Marxian terminology so characteristic of prewar Socialist literature, and this momentous omission was not challenged in the discussions there. The 1952 Milan Conference of the Socialist International followed the precedent established at Frankfurt, and

DAVID J. SAPOSS, Special Assistant to the Commissioner of Labor Statistics, Department of Labor; formerly Special Advisor in the European Labor Division, E.C.A., Paris.

at the 1953 Stockholm Conference it was repeated. Such clichés as the materialistic or economic conception of history, exploitation of the workers, expropriating the expropriators, the class struggle, are no longer mentioned. The former sacred tenet that the workers are the class chosen to fulfill the holy mission of bringing about the inevitable capitulation of capitalism has fallen into limbo. The central theme of the new official pronouncements revolves about problems of social justice, economic planning, full employment, democracy and human rights. Emphasis is placed on the need to avoid deflation with its consequent depression and unemployment, and, of course, on the rôle of the trade union movement in promoting social justice.

To be sure, differences exist on policy, with the British Socialists still clinging to nationalization, the Germans featuring "codetermination" in industry and the Scandinavians empirically emphasizing efficiency and production, with better distribution of the proceeds. But the Communists are the only group within the Western democracies still consistently quoting Marx—albeit hyphenated to Lenin and Stalin—and talking revolution, often obfuscated by their need to adapt their pronouncements and activities to the changing tactics of Soviet foreign policy.

In Asia and other underdeveloped areas, however, the situation is different. A deep schism seems to be developing in the world Socialist movement, led by the Asian Socialist parties. The separatist group revealed itself at the 1951 congress of the Socialist International in Frankfurt; and at the succeeding Milan Congress this group announced the intention of organizing an independent Asian Socialist movement. Its Congress convened in Rangoon in January 1953. European Socialist notables, including Clement R. Attlee, attended as fraternal delegates and urged the conference to remain an organic part of the Socialist International, arguing strongly against the formation of a separate Asian Socialist Conference. Notwithstanding the prominence of these fraternal delegates from the Socialist Parties of the Western democracies and the eloquence of their appeal, their advice was not heeded. A separate and independent Asian Socialist Conference was formed.

The only concession made to the Socialist International was the proviso that the affiliates with the Asian Socialist Conference could retain affiliation with the Socialist International if they desired. It was further announced that the Asian organization would undertake to maintain close contact with the Socialist International, but it was emphatically stipulated that the Asian Conference would have no organic connection with the International.

The new Asian organization differs basically from the Western-oriented Socialists, although its thinking has not yet been clarified. Many of its adherents, like the left-wing Socialist Party of Japan, feature revolutionary radicalism and hail Marx as their true prophet. With mild reservations they regard Russia as the Socialist fatherland, uncritically accepting its claims of accomplishments and looking to it for inspiration. Such left-wing elements point to the United States and the capitalist world as the enemy; Soviet interpretations of events and accusations against the Western democracies are unquestioningly supported. Similarly, this faction supports all proposals made by the Communists for ostensibly improving relations between the East and the West.

However, such left-wing Socialists have resisted the Communist efforts to take over their parties, and, so far, have maintained their independence. They have no open relations with the Cominform and its affiliates, differing in this respect from the Nenni Socialists in Italy, for example. On the other hand, they are devout champions of revolutionary radicalism, seeking the overthrow of the present social order and its replacement by a Socialist society. In Japan, the right-wing Socialist Party reflects the prevailing national sentiment which believes in a strong domestic police force, but it opposed Japanese rearmament and does not want the government to lean toward the United States and the other Western democracies.

In some Asian countries—Burma and India, for example—Socialists tend to blend their doctrine with the prevailing religious or social philosophies, most of them steering clear of Marxism and revolutionary radicalism and advocating an advanced program of social reform, stimulated by the existing feudalism. Thus they emphasize land reform, anti-imperialism and national independence, to be attained through moderate means. Like the more extreme faction, however, they too are friendly toward Russia. Even the more moderate elements, influenced by Communist anti-imperialist and anti-capitalist propaganda, which is reinforced by their own suspicion of the motives of the West (particularly the United States) and by their fear of offending their Communist neighbor, China, are inclined to equate Russia with the United States. Neutralism in international affairs is their watchword. The Asian Conference disapproved of Communist totalitarian policies, such as the use of force, denial of freedom and negation of human rights, but the tendency is to regard these features as transitory and incidental. Even the moderates tend to accept the professions of accomplishment by the Communist countries at face value, hoping that they themselves can achieve their objectives without resort to brutality.

Thus both wings of the Socialist movement in Asia are neutralist. Some, as in Burma, are primarily influenced by their juxtaposition to Communist countries; others in India are still operating under the spell of Gandhi. Their conceptions of neutrality sometimes transcend normal understanding. Recently the Socialist Government of Burma refused economic aid from the United States so that its neutrality would not be compromised. However, it proposes to negotiate an economic treaty with Soviet Russia. This same Government has deported deserting Chinese Communist army personnel that claimed political asylum in Burma, justifying this inhuman action by the contention that its neutral policy forced it to deny political asylum to offenders against "a friendly nation," notwithstanding that these soldiers were returned to certain death. But such neutralists were horrified at the execution of the Rosenberg atom spies in the United States.

Such states of mind can be only temporary, although it is clear that the Asian Socialist Parties of both right and left are determined to separate themselves from the movement dominated by the Western democratic Socialists. The left wing, which clings to the doctrine of the overthrow of capitalism, by revolutionary means if need be, predicates its doctrine on Marxist reasoning and tempers its neutralism by being "neutral against" the United States in favor of Russia. The right wing sponsors moderate procedures and immediate social reform with emphasis on particular Asian problems. It is not critical of Russia and is more readily attracted by Soviet claims than is its Western Socialist counterpart. However, it favors accepting Western economic and technological assistance, with no military or diplomatic alliances. It considers itself a firm adherent of democracy.

The Communists are using the Asian neutralist Socialists to their advantage, but whether they will capture them is questionable. They seem to be making headway in Japan, both with the left-wing Socialists and the principal trade union organizations; the Sohyo trade-union group shifted from "neutralism" to "worldwide collaboration of peace forces," the line now advocated by the Communists, and some of its leaders even declared that Soviet Russia and China were the forces making for peace. However, when leaders of the left-wing Socialist Party criticized this attitude as contrary to neutralism, the Sohyo spokesman retreated. On the whole, it does not seem likely that the Communists will capture the Asian Socialist Conference.

The determination to maintain a separate organization is rationalized by the Asian Socialists on the ground that Asia is confronted with problems which differ from those of the rest of the world. They point out that Asia is primarily agricultural and underdeveloped, that it still suffers from imperialism and colonialism, and that these are problems which the Western World does not understand: only by separate organization, the Asians say, can they cope with the particular problems of the Far East.

This rationale, as well as many of the current demands of the Asian Socialist Conference, highlight the contrast with the conditions that generated the Western Socialist movement in its earlier stages. Socialism in the Western countries was founded on an emerging industrialism, and it adapted its principles, policies and tactics to the expansion and growing stability of capitalism. On the other hand, most of Asia and the other underdeveloped countries of the world still operate under feudalistic customs and régimes. Insofar as there is an emerging industrialism, it is based primarily on plantation and extractive industries closely allied to agriculture. Nevertheless, the thinking of Socialists in these countries is complicated by their desire to seek salvation through industrialism. Some of these countries have enacted most advanced social legislation, as recommended in I.L.O. conventions, but little effort is made to enforce these laws.

Politically, the Asian Socialists, in common with the rest of the population in Asia, are still thinking in colonial and semi-colonial terms; their reactions are chiefly based on past experience, influenced by resentment at the fact that they are either still linked to Western countries, or obligated to them. They know that they are economically dependent on Western capital, equipment, technological know-how and supervisory skill, but psychologically they are disturbed at having to accept such assistance. Hence, in emphasizing immediate demands for social improvements, the Asian Socialist Parties have nationalistic, racial, economic and political issues uppermost in their minds. Their pragmatic demands are limited primarily to the solution of agrarian problems and those related to agriculture, such as stimulation and regulation of cottage industries, use of small machines in manufacturing as well as in agriculture, cheap power development. Even the few that look to industrialism for ultimate salvation find it necessary to fall in line with those who stress these immediate demands in order to alleviate pressing social evils.

In contrast, the Socialist parties of the Western democracies, with a rationale stimulated by an emerging industrialism, called for social and labor legislation that would promote the interests of the new wage-earning class—demands for sanitary working conditions, proper light in the factories, accident prevention, workmen's compensation, maximum hours of labor and minimum wages, abolition of child labor, special protection for women workers and social insurance. They also sought to promote better living conditions through housing programs, price controls and food subsidies, and consumer coöperative movements. In time the Asian Socialists will probably adjust their program accordingly.

There is little or no prospect for the old-fashioned revolutionary radicalism in countries and areas with a highly stabilized social structure and a mature industrialization, where workers enjoy "status" and a feeling of belonging. In the viable Western democracies, the small residue of Socialists still attracted by the siren-call of revolution will gravitate, if they have not already done so, toward the Communist movement. It should be noted that the Communist movement has been rapidly losing ground in the countries enjoying a relatively stable social structure—Western Europe (except France and Italy), Australasia, North America. In Italy and France, the Communists seem to be gaining in the political field, and, judging from elections of representatives to works councils, are either retaining their strength or gaining in the industrial field. Outside of these exceptions there are few regions where the Communists have succeeded in maintaining their position. In general their strength has so receded that they are a minor element in the labor movement.

Even in Japan in the recent election the Communists polled only 700,000 votes and elected only one member to the Lower House of Parliament; but there they are growing stronger in the unions. They made a more formidable showing in the first election in India and are a considerable threat to the Congress Party in many areas—a development that has alerted the dominant political organization to the necessity of seeking alliances with other non-Communist elements. On the whole, open Communist strength is receding in effectiveness in the democratic world. It is naturally more difficult to gauge its conspiratorial and surreptitious activities. Since the Catholic trade-union movement, in common with the Canadian and American labor movements, is clearly committed to an advanced program of social reform and some form of the welfare state, the labor movements of the Western democracies are drawing closer together ideologically.

Thus three political internationals operating in the labor movement are likely to emerge as a result of the new developments— the Western group, the Communists and the Asian neutralists. The last-named, in a sense a "third-force" group, will probably have a strong appeal to the people in other underdeveloped countries, such as in Africa and Latin America. It should prove to be a rival of the Communists, in that it will appeal to the outspoken anti-capitalist, anti-imperialist, race-conscious elements, who shy away from aligning themselves with either the Western-oriented movements or the totalitarian forces behind the Iron Curtain. Though there seems little danger that it will be captured by the Communists, it might be tempted to collaborate with them, and it may experience defections. It will, however, be playing the Communist game indirectly, and will thereby render a serious disservice to the democratic world. It will no doubt prosper in underdeveloped areas, particularly among peoples who are still laboring under the shell-shock of colonialism and imperialism, and who have suffered from discrimination because of color. The ultra-radical element which used to be temperamentally attracted to syndicalism in the West, and which thrived in the countries with the most unstable social structures, might also gravitate toward this group.

Eventually, the relations of the Communists to this neutralist group are certain to become strained. At present, Asian Socialism is an obstacle to the strengthening of democratic forces; but it is also a barrier between the Communists and the masses. If the Communists come to believe that the neutralism of the Asian Socialists is hindering them more than it is helping them, they are bound to turn on it, as they have on other movements which they have failed to direct or control. ❧

The Myth of
Post–Cold War Chaos

G. John Ikenberry

Foreign Affairs, May/June 1996

THE 1945 ORDER LIVES ON

A great deal of ink has been shed in recent years describing various versions of the post–Cold War order. These attempts have all failed, because there is no such creature. The world order created in the 1940s is still with us, and in many ways stronger than ever. The challenge for American foreign policy is not to imagine and build a new world order but to reclaim and renew an old one—an innovative and durable order that has been hugely successful and largely unheralded.

The end of the Cold War, the common wisdom holds, was a historical watershed. The collapse of communism brought the collapse of the order that took shape after World War II. While foreign policy theorists and officials scramble to design new grand strategies, the United States is rudderless on uncharted seas.

The common wisdom is wrong. What ended with the Cold War was bipolarity, the nuclear stalemate, and decades of containment of the Soviet Union—seemingly the most dramatic and consequential features of the postwar era. But the world order created in the middle to late 1940s endures, more extensive and in some respects more robust than during its Cold War years. Its basic

G. JOHN IKENBERRY, Co-Director of the Lauder Institute of Management and International Studies and Associate Professor of Political Science at the University of Pennsylvania.

principles, which deal with organization and relations among the Western liberal democracies, are alive and well.

These less celebrated, less heroic, but more fundamental principles and policies—the real international order—include the commitment to an open world economy and its multilateral management, and the stabilization of socioeconomic welfare. And the political vision behind the order was as important as the anticipated economic gains. The major industrial democracies took it upon themselves to "domesticate" their dealings through a dense web of multilateral institutions, intergovernmental relations, and joint management of the Western and world political economies. Security and stability in the West were seen as intrinsically tied to an array of institutions—the United Nations and its agencies and the General Agreement on Tariffs and Trade (GATT) only some among many—that bound the democracies together, constrained conflict, and facilitated political community. Embracing common liberal democratic norms and operating within interlocking multilateral institutions, the United States, Western Europe, and, later, Japan built an enduring postwar order.

The end of the Cold War has been so disorienting because it ended the containment order—40 years of policies and bureaucratic missions and an entire intellectual orientation. But the watershed of postwar order predated hostilities with the Soviet Union. The turning point was not a Cold War milestone such as the announcement of the Truman Doctrine in 1947 or the creation of the Atlantic alliance in 1948–49. It might have come as early as 1941, when Roosevelt and Churchill issued the Atlantic Charter declaring the liberal principles that were to guide the postwar settlement. The process became irreversible in 1944, when representatives at the Bretton Woods conference laid down the core principles and mechanisms of the postwar Western economic order and those at Dumbarton Oaks gave the political aspect of the vision concrete form in their proposals for a United Nations. The Cold War may have reinforced the liberal democratic order, by hastening the reintegration of Germany and Japan and bringing the United States much more directly into the management of the system. But it did not call it forth.

In world historical terms, the end of the Cold War is an over-rated event. Former Secretary of State James A. Baker III observes in his 1995 memoir, *The Politics of Diplomacy*, "In three and a half years [from the late 1980s to the early 1990s] . . . the very nature of the international system as we know it was transformed." To be sure, large parts of the non-Western world are undergoing a tremendous and difficult transformation. A great human drama is playing itself out in the former communist states, and the future there hangs in the balance. But the system the United States led the way in creating after World War II has not collapsed; on the contrary, it remains the core of world order. The task today is not to discover or define some mythic new order but to reclaim the policies, commitments, and strategies of the old.

A TALE OF TWO DOCTRINES

World War II produced two postwar settlements. One, a reaction to deteriorating relations with the Soviet Union, led to the containment order, which was based on the balance of power, nuclear deterrence, and political and ideological competition. The other, a reaction to the economic rivalry and political turmoil of the 1930s and the resulting world war, can be called the liberal democratic order. It culminated in a wide range of new institutions and relations among the Western industrial democracies, built around economic openness, political reciprocity, and multilateral management of an American-led liberal political system.

Distinct political visions and intellectual rationales animated the two settlements, and at key moments the American president gave voice to each. On March 12, 1947, President Truman delivered his celebrated speech before Congress announcing aid to Greece and Turkey, wrapping it in an American commitment to support the cause of freedom worldwide. The declaration of the Truman Doctrine was a founding moment of the containment order, rallying Americans to a new great struggle, this one against what was thought to be Soviet communism's quest for world domination. A "fateful hour" had struck, Truman said, and the people of the world "must choose between two alternate ways of life." If the United States failed to exercise leadership, he warned, "we may endanger the peace of the world."

It is often forgotten that six days before, Truman had delivered an equally sweeping speech at Baylor University. On this occasion he spoke of the lessons the world must learn from the disasters of the 1930s. "As each battle of the economic war of the Thirties was fought, the inevitable tragic result became more and more apparent," said Truman. "From the tariff policy of Hawley and Smoot, the world went on to Ottawa and the system of imperial preferences, from Ottawa to the kind of elaborate and detailed restrictions adopted by Nazi Germany." Truman reaffirmed America's commitment to "economic peace," which would involve tariff reductions and rules and institutions of trade and investment. When economic differences arose, he said, "the interests of all will be considered, and a fair and just solution will be found." Conflicts would be captured and tamed in a cage of multilateral rules, standards, safeguards, and procedures for dispute resolution. According to Truman, "This is the way of a civilized community."

But it was the containment order that impressed itself on the popular imagination. In celebrated American accounts of the early years after World War II, intrepid officials struggled to make sense of Soviet military power and geopolitical intentions. A few "wise men" fashioned a reasoned and coherent response to the global challenge of Soviet communism, and their containment strategy gave clarity and purpose to several decades of American foreign policy. Over those decades, sprawling bureaucratic and military organizations were built around containment. The bipolar division of the world, nuclear weapons of growing size and sophistication, the ongoing clash of two expansive ideologies—all these gave life to and reinforced the centrality of the containment order.

By comparison, the thinking behind the liberal democratic order was more diffuse. The liberal democratic agenda was less obviously a grand strategy designed to advance American security interests, and it was inevitably viewed during the Cold War as secondary, a preoccupation of economists and businessmen. The policies and institutions that supported free trade among the advanced industrial societies seemed the stuff of low politics. But the liberal democratic agenda was actually built on a robust yet sophisticated set of ideas about American security interests, the causes of war and depression, and a desirable postwar political order. Although containment overshadowed it, the postwar liberal democratic order was more deeply rooted in the American experience and an understanding of history, economics, and the sources of political stability.

The proper foundations of political order have preoccupied American thinkers from the nation's founding onward, and innovative institutions and practices were developed in response to independence, continental expansion, civil war, economic depression, and world war. The liberal ideal was held high: open and decentralized political institutions could limit and diffuse conflict while integrating diverse peoples and interests. Moreover, a stable and legitimate political order was assured by its grounding in the Constitution, which specified rights, guarantees, and an institutionalized political process. When American officials began to contemplate postwar order, they were drawing on a wellspring of ideas, experiments, and historical lessons and sifting these with an abiding liberal belief in the possibility of peaceful and mutually beneficial international relations.

The most basic conviction underlying the postwar liberal agenda was that the closed autarkic regions that had contributed to the world-wide depression and split the globe into competing blocs before the war must be broken up and replaced by an open, nondiscriminatory economic system. Peace and security, proponents had decided, were impossible in the face of exclusive economic regions. The challengers of liberal multilateralism, however, occupied almost every corner of the advanced industrial world. Germany and Japan were the most overtly hostile; both had pursued a dangerous path that combined authoritarian capitalism with military dictatorship and coercive regional autarky. But the British Commonwealth and its imperial preference system also challenged liberal multilateral order.

The hastily drafted Atlantic Charter was an American effort to ensure that Britain signed on to its liberal democratic war aims.[1] The joint statement of principles affirmed free trade, equal access to natural resources for all interested buyers, and international economic collaboration to advance labor standards, employment security, and social welfare. Roosevelt and Churchill declared before the world that they had learned the lessons of the interwar years—and those lessons were fundamentally about the proper organization of the Western political economy. America's enemies, its friends, and even America itself had to be reformed and integrated into the postwar economic system.

THE LIBERAL MANIFESTO

The postwar liberal democratic order was designed to solve the internal problems of Western industrial capitalism. It was not intended to fight Soviet communism, nor was it simply a plan to get American business back on its feet after the war by opening up the world to trade and investment. It was a strategy to build Western solidarity through economic openness and joint political governance. Four principles pursued in the 1940s gave shape to this order.

The most obvious principle was economic openness, which would ideally take the form of a system of nondiscriminatory trade and investment. As American strategic thinkers of the 1930s watched the world economy collapse and the German and Japanese blocs emerge, they pondered whether the United States could remain a great industrial power within the confines of the western hemisphere. What were the minimum geographical requirements for the country's economic and military viability? For all practical purposes they had their answer by the time the United States entered the war. An American hemispheric bloc would not be sufficient; the United States needed secure markets

1 Churchill insisted that the charter not mandate the dismantling of the British Empire and its system of trade preferences, and only last-minute sidestepping of this controversial issue made agreement possible.

and supplies of raw materials in Asia and Europe. Experts in a Council on Foreign Relations study group reached a similar conclusion when considering the necessary size of the area on which the United States depended for economic vitality.

American thinking was that economic openness was an essential element of a stable and peaceful world political order. "Prosperous neighbors are the best neighbors," remarked Roosevelt administration Treasury official Harry Dexter White. But officials were convinced that American economic and security interests demanded it as well. Great liberal visionaries and hard-nosed geopolitical strategists could agree on the notion of open markets; it united American postwar planners and was the seminal idea informing the work of the Bretton Woods conference on postwar economic cooperation. In his farewell remarks to the conference, Secretary of the Treasury Henry Morgenthau asserted that the agreements creating the International Monetary Fund and the World Bank marked the end of economic nationalism, by which he meant not that countries would give up pursuit of their national interest but that trade blocs and economic spheres of influence would no longer be their vehicles.

The second principle was joint management of the Western political-economic order. The leading industrial democratic states must not only lower barriers to trade and the movement of capital but must govern the system. This also was a lesson from the 1930s: institutions, rules, and active mutual management by governments were necessary to avoid unproductively competitive and conflictual economic practices. Americans believed such cooperation necessary in a world where national economies were increasingly at the mercy of developments abroad. The unwise or untoward policies of one country threatened contagion, undermining the stability of all. As Roosevelt said at the opening of Bretton Woods, "The economic health of every country is a proper matter of concern to all its neighbors, near and far."

The belief in cooperative economic management also drew inspiration from the government activism of Roosevelt's New Deal. The postwar Western system was organized at a high tide of optimism about the capability of experts, economic and technical knowledge, and government intervention. The rise of Keynesian economics in Europe in the 1930s had begun to encourage an activist role for the state in the economy and society. International economic governance was a natural and inevitable extension of the policies being tried in individual Western industrial societies.

A third principle of liberal democratic order held that the rules and institutions of the Western world economy must be organized to support domestic economic stability and social security. This new commitment was foreshadowed in the Atlantic Charter's call for postwar international collaboration to ensure employment stability and social welfare. It was a sign of the times that Churchill, a conservative Tory, could promise a historic expansion of the government's responsibility for the people's well-being. In their schemes for postwar economic order, both Britain and the United States sought a system that would aid and protect their nascent social and economic commitments. They wanted an open world economy, but one congenial to the emerging welfare state as well as business.

The discovery of a middle way between old political alternatives was a major innovation of the postwar Western economic order. British and American planners began their discussion in 1942 deadlocked, Britain's desire for full employment and economic stabilization after the war running up against the American desire for free trade. The breakthrough came in 1944 with the Bretton Woods agreements on monetary order, which secured a more or less open system of trade and payments while providing safeguards for domestic economic stability through the International Monetary Fund. The settlement was a synthesis that could attract a new coalition of conservative free traders and the liberal prophets of economic planning.

A final element of the liberal democratic system might be termed "constitutionalism"—meaning simply that the Western nations would make systematic efforts to anchor their joint commitments in principled and binding institutional mechanisms. In fact, this may be the order's most basic aspect, encompassing the other principles and policies and giving the whole its distinctive domestic character. Governments might ordinarily seek to keep their options open, cooperating with other states but retaining the possibility of disengagement. The United States and the other Western nations after the war did exactly the opposite. They built long-term economic, political, and security commitments that were difficult to retract, and locked in the relationships, to the extent that sovereign states can. Insofar as the participating governments attempted to construct a political order based on commonly embraced norms and principles along with institutional mechanisms for resolving conflicts and reaching specific agreements, they practiced constitutionalism.

Democracies are particularly capable of making constitutional commitments to each other. For self-regarding states to agree to pursue their interests within binding institutions, they must perceive in their partners a credible sense of commitment—an assurance that they will not exit at the least sign of disagreement. Because policymaking in democracies tends to be decentralized and open, the character of commitments can be more clearly determined and there are opportunities to lobby policymakers in the other democracies. Democracies do not just sign agreements; they create political processes that reduce uncertainty and build confidence in mutual commitments.

A CONSTITUTION FOR THE WEST

The constitutional political order was constructed in the West around economic, political, and security institutions. In the economic realm, the Bretton Woods accords were the first permanent international arrangements for cooperation between states. Rules and institutions were proposed to ensure a stable and expansionary world economy and an orderly exchange rate system. Many of the original agreements for a rule-based monetary order gave way to ad hoc arrangements based more on the American dollar, but the vision of jointly managed, multilateral order remained. The organization of postwar trade relations also had an uncertain start, but ultimately an elaborate system of rules and obligations was developed, with quasi-judicial procedures for adjudicating disputes. In effect, the Western governments created an array of transnational political arenas organized by function. The postwar years were filled with economic disputes, but they were largely contained within these arenas.

The constitutional vision informed the creation of the United Nations, which combined political, economic, and security aspirations. To be sure, the U.N. system preserved the sovereign rights of member states. Intent on avoiding the failures of the League of Nations, the architects of the new international body drafted a charter under which the great powers would retain their freedom of action. But despite its weak rules and obligations, the United Nations reflected American and European desires to insure against a relapse of American isolation, to establish principles and mechanisms of conflict resolution, and to mute conflicts between states within a semi-institutionalized political process.

Cold War security structures provided additional constitutional architecture. Lord Ismay's observation that NATO was created to keep the Russians out, the Germans down, and the Americans in encapsulates the alliance's importance in locking in long-term commitments and expectations. The American-Japanese security pact had a similar dual-containment character. These institutions not only served as alliances in the ordinary sense of organized efforts to balance external threats, but offered mechanisms and venues for building relations, conducting business, and regulating conflict. The recent French decision to rejoin NATO can be understood only in this light. If NATO were simply a balancing alliance, the organization would be in an advanced stage of decay. It is NATO's broader political function—binding the democracies together and reinforcing political community—that explains its remarkable durability.

The democratic character of the United States and its partners facilitated construction of these dense interstate connections. The decentralized and open character of domestic institutions encouraged political give-and-take across the advanced industrial world.

Thus the Western liberal democratic order was not only defined by a set of institutions and agreements but made for a particular kind of politics—transnational, pluralistic, reciprocal, legitimate.

The constitutional features of the Western order have been especially important for Germany and Japan. Both countries were reintegrated into the advanced industrial world as semisovereign powers that had accepted unprecedented constitutional limits on their military capacity and independence. As such, they became unusually reliant on Western regional and multilateral economic and security institutions. The Western order in which they were embedded was integral to their stability and their very functioning. The Christian Democratic politician Walther Leisler Kiep argued in 1972 that "the German-American alliance is not merely one aspect of modern German history, but a decisive element as a result of its preeminent place in our politics. In effect, it provides a second constitution for our country." Western economic and security institutions were and are for Germany and Japan a political bulwark that provides stability and transcends those institutions' more immediate purposes.

WHAT ENDURES

For those who thought cooperation among the advanced industrial democracies was driven primarily by Cold War threats, the last few years must appear puzzling. Relations between the major Western countries have not broken down. Germany has not rearmed, nor has Japan. What the Cold War focus misses is an appreciation of the other, less heralded, postwar American project—the building of a liberal order in the West. Archaeologists remove one stratum only to discover an older one beneath; the end of the Cold War allows us to see a deeper and more enduring layer of the postwar political order that was largely obscured by the more dramatic struggles between East and West.

Fifty years after its founding, the Western liberal democratic world is robust, and its principles and policies remain the core of world order. The challenges to liberal multilateralism both from within and from outside the West have mainly disappeared. Although regional experiments abound, they are fundamentally different from the autarkic blocs of the 1930s. The forces of business and financial integration are moving the globe inexorably toward a more tightly interconnected system that ignores regional as well as national borders. Recent proposals for an Atlantic free trade agreement and a Transatlantic Treaty, whatever their economic merits, reflect the trend toward increased integration across regions. The successful conclusion of the Uruguay Round of international trade talks in 1994 and the launching of the World Trade Organization on January 1, 1995, testify to the vigor of liberal multilateral principles.

Some aspects of the vision of the 1940s have faded. The optimism about government activism and economic management that animated the New Deal and Keynesianism has been considerably tempered. Likewise, the rule-based, quasi-judicial functions of liberal multilateralism have eroded, particularly in monetary relations. Paradoxically, although the rules of cooperation have become less coherent, cooperation itself has increased. Formal rules governing the Western world economy have gradually been replaced by a convergence of thinking on economic policy. The consensus on the broad outlines of desirable domestic and international economic policies has both reflected and promoted increased economic growth and the incorporation of emerging economies into the system.

The problems the liberal democratic order confronts are mostly problems of success, foremost among them the need to integrate the newly developing and post-communist countries. Here one sees most clearly that the post–Cold War order is really a continuation and extension of the Western order forged during and after World War II. The difference is its increasingly global reach. The world has seen an explosion in the desire of countries and peoples to move toward democracy and capitalism. When the history of the late twentieth century is written, it will be the struggle for more open and democratic polities throughout the world that will mark the era, rather than the failure of communism.

Other challenges to the system are boiling up in its leading states. In its early years, rapid and widely shared economic growth buoyed the system, as working- and middle-class citizens across the advanced industrial world rode the crest of the boom. Today economic globalization is producing much greater inequality between the winners and the losers, the wealthy and the poor. How the subsequent dislocations, dashed expectations, and political grievances are dealt with—whether the benefits are shared and the system as a whole is seen as socially just—will affect the stability of the liberal world order more than regional conflict, however tragic, in places like the Balkans.

To be sure, the Cold War reinforced solidarity and a sense of common identity among the liberal democracies, so it would be a mistake to take these binding forces for granted now. Trade disputes, controversies over burden-sharing, and regional conflict will test the durability of the liberal order. Without a Cold War threat to unite their countries, leaders in the advanced democracies will have to work harder to manage the inevitable conflicts and fissures. An agenda of reform and renewal would be an intelligent move to protect 50 years of investment in stable and thriving relations. Policies, institutions, and political symbols can all be directed at reinforcing liberal order, just as they are in individual liberal polities. At the very least, Western leaders could spend much more time acknowledging and celebrating the political space they share.

It is fashionable to say that the United States after the Cold War faces its third try at forging a durable world order, at reinventing the basic rules of world politics, just as after both world wars. But this view is more rhetorically compelling than historically valid. The end of the Cold War was less the end of a world order than the collapse of the communist world into an expanding Western order. If that order is to be defended and strengthened, its historical roots and accomplishments must be reclaimed. The United States built and then managed the containment order for 40 years, but it also built and continues to enjoy the rewards of an older liberal democratic order. America is not adrift in uncharted seas. It is at the center of a world of its own making.☯

The Return of Authoritarian Great Powers

Azar Gat

Foreign Affairs, July / August 2007

THE END OF THE END OF HISTORY

Today's global liberal democratic order faces two challenges. The first is radical Islam—and it is the lesser of the two challenges. Although the proponents of radical Islam find liberal democracy repugnant, and the movement is often described as the new fascist threat, the societies from which it arises are generally poor and stagnant. They represent no viable alternative to modernity and pose no significant military threat to the developed world. It is mainly the potential use of weapons of mass destruction—particularly by nonstate actors—that makes militant Islam a menace.

The second, and more significant, challenge emanates from the rise of nondemocratic great powers: the West's old Cold War rivals China and Russia, now operating under authoritarian capitalist, rather than communist, regimes. Authoritarian capitalist great powers played a leading role in the international system up until 1945. They have been absent since then. But today, they seem poised for a comeback.

Capitalism's ascendancy appears to be deeply entrenched, but the current predominance of democracy could be far less secure. Capitalism has expanded relentlessly since early modernity, its lower-priced goods and superior economic power eroding and

AZAR GAT, Ezer Weizman Professor of National Security at Tel Aviv University and the author of *War in Human Civilization*.

transforming all other socioeconomic regimes, a process most memorably described by Karl Marx in *The Communist Manifesto*. Contrary to Marx's expectations, capitalism had the same effect on communism, eventually "burying" it without the proverbial shot being fired. The triumph of the market, precipitating and reinforced by the industrial-technological revolution, led to the rise of the middle class, intensive urbanization, the spread of education, the emergence of mass society, and ever greater affluence. In the post–Cold War era (just as in the nineteenth century and the 1950s and 1960s), it is widely believed that liberal democracy naturally emerged from these developments, a view famously espoused by Francis Fukuyama. Today, more than half of the world's states have elected governments, and close to half have sufficiently entrenched liberal rights to be considered fully free.

But the reasons for the triumph of democracy, especially over its nondemocratic capitalist rivals of the two world wars, Germany and Japan, were more contingent than is usually assumed. Authoritarian capitalist states, today exemplified by China and Russia, may represent a viable alternative path to modernity, which in turn suggests that there is nothing inevitable about liberal democracy's ultimate victory—or future dominance.

CHRONICLE OF A DEFEAT NOT FORETOLD

The liberal democratic camp defeated its authoritarian, fascist, and communist rivals alike in all of the three major great-power struggles of the twentieth century—the two world wars and the Cold War. In trying to determine exactly what accounted for this decisive outcome, it is tempting to trace it to the special traits and intrinsic advantages of liberal democracy.

One possible advantage is democracies' international conduct. Perhaps they more than compensate for carrying a lighter stick abroad with a greater ability to elicit international cooperation through the bonds and discipline of the global market system. This explanation is probably correct for the Cold War, when a greatly expanded global economy was dominated by the democratic powers, but it does not apply to the two world wars. Nor is it true that liberal democracies succeed because they always cling together. Again, this was true, at least as a contributing factor, during the Cold War, when the democratic capitalist camp kept its unity, whereas growing antagonism between the Soviet Union and China pulled the communist bloc apart. During World War I, however, the ideological divide between the two sides was much less clear. The Anglo-French alliance was far from preordained; it was above all a function of balance-of-power calculations rather than liberal cooperation. At the close of the nineteenth century, power politics had brought the United Kingdom and France, bitterly antagonistic countries, to the brink of war and prompted the United Kingdom to actively seek an alliance with Germany. Liberal Italy's break from the Triple Alliance and joining of the Entente, despite its rivalry with France, was a function of the Anglo-French alliance, as Italy's peninsular location made it hazardous for the country to be on a side opposed to the leading maritime power of the time, the United Kingdom. Similarly, during World War II, France was quickly defeated and taken out of the Allies' side (which was to include nondemocratic Soviet Russia), whereas the right-wing totalitarian powers fought on the same side. Studies of democracies' alliance behavior suggest that democratic regimes show no greater tendency to stick together than other types of regimes.

Nor did the totalitarian capitalist regimes lose World War II because their democratic opponents held a moral high ground that inspired greater exertion from their people, as the historian Richard Overy and others have claimed. During the 1930s and early 1940s, fascism and Nazism were exciting new ideologies that generated massive popular enthusiasm, whereas democracy stood on the ideological defensive, appearing old and dispirited. If anything, the fascist regimes proved more inspiring in wartime than their democratic adversaries, and the battlefield performance of their militaries is widely judged to have been superior.

Liberal democracy's supposedly inherent economic advantage is also far less clear than is often assumed. All of the belligerents in the twentieth century's great struggles proved highly effective in producing for war. During World War I, semiautocratic Germany committed its resources as effectively as its democratic rivals did. After early victories in World War II, Nazi Germany's economic mobilization and military production proved lax during the critical years 1940–42. Well positioned at the time to fundamentally alter the global balance of power by destroying the Soviet Union and straddling all of continental Europe, Germany failed because its armed forces were meagerly supplied for the task. The reasons for this deficiency remain a matter of historical debate, but one of the problems was the existence of competing centers of authority in the Nazi system, in which Hitler's "divide and rule" tactics and party functionaries' jealous guarding of their assigned domains had a chaotic effect. Furthermore, from the fall of France in June 1940 to the German setback before Moscow in December 1941, there was a widespread feeling in Germany that the war had practically been won. All the same, from 1942 onward (by which time is was too late), Germany greatly intensified its economic mobilization and caught up with and even surpassed the liberal democracies in terms of the share of GDP devoted to the war (although its production volume remained much lower than that of the massive U.S. economy). Likewise, levels of economic mobilization in imperial Japan and the Soviet Union exceeded those of the United States and the United Kingdom thanks to ruthless efforts.

Only during the Cold War did the Soviet command economy exhibit deepening structural weaknesses—weaknesses that were directly responsible for the Soviet Union's downfall. The Soviet system had successfully generated the early and intermediate stages of industrialization (albeit at a frightful human cost) and excelled at the regimentalized techniques of mass production during World War II. It also kept abreast militarily during the Cold War. But because of the system's rigidity and lack of incentives, it proved ill equipped to cope with the advanced stages of development and the demands of the information age and globalization.

There is no reason, however, to suppose that the totalitarian capitalist regimes of Nazi Germany and imperial Japan would have proved inferior economically to the democracies had they survived. The inefficiencies that favoritism and unaccountability typically create in such regimes might have been offset by higher levels of social discipline. Because of their more efficient capitalist economies, the right-wing totalitarian powers could have constituted a more viable challenge to the liberal democracies than the Soviet Union did; Nazi Germany was judged to be such a challenge by the Allied powers before and during World War II. The liberal democracies did not possess an inherent advantage over Germany in terms of economic and technological development, as they did in relation to their other great-power rivals.

So why did the democracies win the great struggles of the twentieth century? The reasons are different for each type of adversary. They defeated their nondemocratic capitalist adversaries, Germany and Japan, in war because Germany and Japan were medium-sized countries with limited resource bases and they came up against the far superior—but hardly preordained—economic and military coalition of the democratic powers and Russia or the Soviet Union. The defeat of communism, however, had much more to do with structural factors. The capitalist camp—which after 1945 expanded to include most of the developed world—possessed much greater economic power than the communist bloc, and the inherent inefficiency of the communist economies prevented them from fully exploiting their vast resources and catching up to the West. Together, the Soviet Union and China were larger and thus had the potential to be more powerful than the democratic capitalist camp. Ultimately, they failed because their economic systems limited them, whereas the nondemocratic capitalist powers, Germany and Japan, were defeated because they were too small. Contingency played a decisive role in tipping the balance against the nondemocratic capitalist powers and in favor of the democracies.

AMERICAN EXCEPTION

The most decisive element of contingency was the United States. After all, it was little more than a chance of history that the scion of Anglo-Saxon liberalism would sprout on the other side of the Atlantic, institutionalize its heritage with independence, expand across one of the most habitable and thinly populated territories in the world, feed off of massive immigration from Europe, and so create on a continental scale what was—and still is—by far the world's largest concentration of economic and military might. A liberal regime and other structural traits had a lot to do with the United States' economic success, and even with its size, because of its attractiveness to immigrants. But the United States would scarcely have achieved such greatness had it not been located in a particularly advantageous and vast ecological-geographic niche, as the counterexamples of Canada, Australia, and New Zealand demonstrate. And location, of course, although crucial, was but one necessary condition among many for bringing about the giant and, indeed, *United* States as the paramount political fact of the twentieth century. Contingency was at least as responsible as liberalism for the United States' emergence in the New World and, hence, for its later ability to rescue the Old World.

Throughout the twentieth century, the United States' power consistently surpassed that of the next two strongest states combined, and this decisively tilted the global balance of power in favor of whichever side Washington was on. If any factor gave the liberal democracies their edge, it was above all the existence of the United States rather than any inherent advantage. In fact, had it not been for the United States, liberal democracy may well have lost the great struggles of the twentieth century. This is a sobering thought that is often overlooked in studies of the spread of democracy in the twentieth century, and it makes the world today appear much more contingent and tenuous than linear theories of development suggest. If it were not for the U.S. factor, the judgment of later generations on liberal democracy would probably have echoed the negative verdict on democracy's performance, issued by the fourth-century-BC Greeks, in the wake of Athens' defeat in the Peloponnesian War.

THE NEW SECOND WORLD

But the audit of war is, of course, not the only one that societies—democratic and nondemocratic—undergo. One must ask how the totalitarian capitalist powers would have developed had they not been defeated by war. Would they, with time and further development, have shed their former identity and embraced liberal democracy, as the former communist regimes of eastern Europe eventually did? Was the capitalist industrial state of imperial Germany before World War I ultimately moving toward increasing parliamentary control and democratization? Or would it have developed into an authoritarian oligarchic regime, dominated by an alliance between the officialdom, the armed forces, and industry, as imperial Japan did (in spite of the latter's liberal interlude in the 1920s)? Liberalization seems even more doubtful in the case of Nazi Germany had it survived, let alone triumphed. Because all these major historical experiments were cut short by war, the answers to these questions remain a matter of speculation. But perhaps the peacetime record of other authoritarian capitalist regimes since 1945 can offer a clue.

Studies that cover this period show that democracies generally outdo other systems economically. Authoritarian capitalist regimes are at least as successful—if not more so—in the early stages of development, but they tend to democratize after crossing a certain threshold of economic and social development. This seems to have been a recurring pattern in East Asia, southern Europe, and Latin America. The attempt to draw conclusions about development patterns from these findings, however, may be misleading, because the sample set itself may be polluted. Since 1945, the enormous gravitational pull exerted by the United States and the liberal hegemony has bent patterns of development worldwide.

Because the totalitarian capitalist great powers, Germany and Japan, were crushed in war, and these countries were subsequently threatened by Soviet power, they lent themselves to a sweeping restructuring and democratization. Consequently, smaller countries that chose capitalism over communism had no rival political and economic model to emulate and no powerful international players to turn to other than the liberal democratic camp. These small and medium-sized countries' eventual democratization probably had as much to do with the overwhelming influence of the Western liberal hegemony as with internal processes. Presently, Singapore is the only example of a country with a truly developed economy that still maintains a semiauthoritarian regime, and even it is likely to change under the influence of the liberal order within which it operates. But are Singapore-like great powers that prove resistant to the influence of this order possible?

The question is made relevant by the recent emergence of nondemocratic giants, above all formerly communist and booming authoritarian capitalist China. Russia, too, is retreating from its postcommunist liberalism and assuming an increasingly authoritarian character as its economic clout grows. Some believe that these countries could ultimately become liberal democracies through a combination of internal development, increasing affluence, and outside influence. Alternatively, they may have enough weight to create a new nondemocratic but economically advanced Second World. They could establish a powerful authoritarian capitalist order that allies political elites, industrialists, and the military; that is nationalist in orientation; and that participates in the global economy on its own terms, as imperial Germany and imperial Japan did.

It is widely contended that economic and social development creates pressures for democratization that an authoritarian state structure cannot contain. There is also the view that "closed societies" may be able to excel in mass manufacturing but not in the advanced stages of the information economy. The jury on these issues is still out, because the data set is incomplete. Imperial and Nazi Germany stood at the forefront of the advanced scientific and manufacturing economies of their times, but some would argue that their success no longer applies because the information economy is much more diversified. Nondemocratic Singapore has a highly successful information economy, but Singapore is a city-state, not a big country. It will take a long time before China reaches the stage when the possibility of an authoritarian state with an advanced capitalist economy can be tested. All that can be said at the moment is that there is nothing in the historical record to suggest that a transition to democracy by today's authoritarian capitalist powers is inevitable, whereas there is a great deal to suggest that such powers have far greater economic and military potential than their communist predecessors did.

China and Russia represent a return of economically successful authoritarian capitalist powers, which have been absent since the defeat of Germany and Japan in 1945, but they are much larger than the latter two countries ever were. Although Germany was only a medium-sized country uncomfortably squeezed at the center of Europe, it twice nearly broke out of its confines to become a true world power on account of its economic and military might. In 1941, Japan was still behind the leading great powers in terms of economic development, but its growth rate since 1913 had been the highest in the world. Ultimately, however, both Germany and Japan were too small—in terms of population, resources, and potential—to take on the United States. Present-day China, on the other hand, is the largest player in the international system in terms of population and is experiencing spectacular economic growth. By shifting from communism to capitalism, China has switched to a far more efficient brand of authoritarianism. As China rapidly narrows the economic gap with the developed world, the possibility looms that it will become a true authoritarian superpower.

Even in its current bastions in the West, the liberal political and economic consensus is vulnerable to unforeseen developments, such as a crushing economic crisis that could disrupt the global trading system or a resurgence of ethnic strife in a Europe increasingly troubled by immigration and ethnic minorities. Were the West to be hit by such upheavals, support for liberal democracy in Asia, Latin America, and Africa—where adherence to that model is more recent, incomplete, and insecure— could be shaken. A successful nondemocratic Second World could then be regarded by many as an attractive alternative to liberal democracy.

MAKING THE WORLD
SAFE FOR DEMOCRACY

Although the rise of authoritarian capitalist great powers would not necessarily lead to a nondemocratic hegemony or a war, it might imply that the near-total dominance of liberal democracy since the Soviet Union's collapse will be short-lived and that a universal "democratic peace" is still far off. The new authoritarian capitalist powers could become as deeply integrated into the world economy as imperial Germany and imperial Japan were and not choose to pursue autarky, as Nazi Germany and the communist bloc did. A great-power China may also be less revisionist than the territorially confined Germany and Japan were (although Russia, which is still reeling from having lost an empire, is more likely to tend toward revisionism). Still, Beijing, Moscow, and their future followers might well be on antagonistic terms with the democratic countries, with all the potential for suspicion, insecurity, and conflict that this entails—while holding considerably more power than any of the democracies' past rivals ever did.

So does the greater power potential of authoritarian capitalism mean that the transformation of the former communist great powers may ultimately prove to have been a negative development for global democracy? It is too early to tell. Economically, the liberalization of the former communist countries has given the global economy a tremendous boost, and there may be more in store. But the possibility of a move toward protectionism by them in the future also needs to be taken into account—and assiduously avoided. It was, after all, the prospect of growing protectionism in the world economy at the turn of the twentieth century and the protectionist bent of the 1930s that helped radicalize the nondemocratic capitalist powers of the time and precipitate both world wars.

On the positive side for the democracies, the collapse of the Soviet Union and its empire stripped Moscow of about half the resources it commanded during the Cold War, with eastern Europe absorbed by a greatly expanded democratic Europe. This is perhaps the most significant change in the global balance of power since the forced postwar democratic reorientation of Germany and Japan under U.S. tutelage. Moreover, China may still eventually democratize, and Russia could reverse its drift away from democracy. If China and Russia do not become democratic, it will be critical that India remain so, both because of its vital role in balancing China and because of the model that it represents for other developing countries.

But the most important factor remains the United States. For all the criticism leveled against it, the United States—and its alliance with Europe—stands as the single most important hope for the future of liberal democracy. Despite its problems and weaknesses, the United States still commands a global position of strength and is likely to retain it even as the authoritarian capitalist powers grow. Not only are its GDP and productivity growth rate the highest in the developed world, but as an immigrant country with about one-fourth the population density of both the European Union and China and one-tenth of that of Japan and India, the United States still has considerable potential to grow—both economically and in terms of population—whereas those others are all experiencing aging and, ultimately, shrinking populations. China's economic growth rate is among the highest in the world, and given the country's huge population and still low levels of development, such growth harbors the most radical potential for change in global power relations. But even if China's superior growth rate persists and its GDP surpasses that of the United States by the 2020s, as is often forecast, China will still have just over one-third of the United States' wealth per capita and, hence, considerably less economic and military power. Closing that far more challenging gap with the developed world would take several more decades. Furthermore, GDP alone is known to be a poor measure of a country's power, and evoking it to celebrate China's ascendency is highly misleading. As it was during the twentieth century, the U.S. factor remains the greatest guarantee that liberal democracy will not be thrown on the defensive and relegated to a vulnerable position on the periphery of the international system.☯

How Development Leads to Democracy

What We Know About Modernization

Ronald Inglehart and Christian Welzel

Foreign Affairs, March/April 2009

In the last several years, a democratic boom has given way to a democratic recession. Between 1985 and 1995, scores of countries made the transition to democracy, bringing widespread euphoria about democracy's future. But more recently, democracy has retreated in Bangladesh, Nigeria, the Philippines, Russia, Thailand, and Venezuela, and the Bush administration's attempts to establish democracy in Afghanistan and Iraq seem to have left both countries in chaos. These developments, along with the growing power of China and Russia, have led many observers to argue that democracy has reached its high-water mark and is no longer on the rise

That conclusion is mistaken. The underlying conditions of societies around the world point to a more complicated reality. The bad news is that it is unrealistic to assume that democratic institutions can be set up easily, almost anywhere, at any time. Although the outlook is never hopeless, democracy is most likely to emerge and survive when certain social and cultural conditions are in place. The Bush administration ignored this reality

RONALD INGLEHART, Professor of Political Science at the University of Michigan and Director of the World Values Survey. CHRISTIAN WELZEL, Professor of Political Science at Jacobs University Bremen, in Germany. They are the co-authors of *Modernization, Cultural Change, and Democracy.*

when it attempted to implant democracy in Iraq without first establishing internal security and overlooked cultural conditions that endangered the effort.

The good news, however, is that the conditions conducive to democracy can and do emerge—and the process of "modernization," according to abundant empirical evidence, advances them. Modernization is a syndrome of social changes linked to industrialization. Once set in motion, it tends to penetrate all aspects of life, bringing occupational specialization, urbanization, rising educational levels, rising life expectancy, and rapid economic growth. These create a self-reinforcing process that transforms social life and political institutions, bringing rising mass participation in politics and—in the long run—making the establishment of democratic political institutions increasingly likely. Today, we have a clearer idea than ever before of why and how this process of democratization happens.

The long-term trend toward democracy has always come in surges and declines. At the start of the twentieth century, only a handful of democracies existed, and even they fell short of being full democracies by today's standards. There was a major increase in the number of democracies following World War I, another surge following World War II, and a third surge at the end of the Cold War. Each of these surges was followed by a decline, although the number of democracies never fell back to the original base line. By the start of the twenty-first century, about 90 states could be considered democratic.

Although many of these democracies are flawed, the overall trend is striking: in the long run, modernization brings democracy. This means that the economic resurgence of China and Russia has a positive aspect: underlying changes are occurring that make the emergence of increasingly liberal and democratic political systems likely in the coming years. It also means that there is no reason to panic about the fact that democracy currently appears to be on the defensive. The dynamics of modernization and democratization are becoming increasingly clear, and it is likely that they will continue to function.

THE GREAT DEBATE

The concept of modernization has a long history. During the nineteenth and twentieth centuries, a Marxist theory of modernization proclaimed that the abolition of private property would put an end to exploitation, inequality, and conflict. A competing capitalist version held that economic development would lead to rising living standards and democracy. These two visions of modernization competed fiercely throughout much of the Cold War. By the 1970s, however, communism began to stagnate, and neither economic development nor democratization was apparent in many poor countries. Neither version of utopia seemed to be unfolding, and critics pronounced modernization theory dead.

Since the end of the Cold War, however, the concept of modernization has taken on new life, and a new version of modernization theory has emerged, with clear implications for our understanding of where global economic development is likely to lead. Stripped of the oversimplifications of its early versions, the new concept of modernization sheds light on ongoing cultural changes, such as the rise of gender equality; the recent wave of democratization; and the democratic peace theory.

For most of human history, technological progress was extremely slow and new developments in food production were offset by population increases—trapping agrarian economies in a steady-state equilibrium with no growth in living standards. History was seen as either cyclic or in long-term decline from a past golden age. The situation began to change with the Industrial Revolution and the advent of sustained economic growth—which led to both the capitalist and the communist visions of modernization. Although the ideologies competed fiercely, they were both committed to economic growth and social progress and brought mass participation in politics. And each side believed that the developing nations of the Third World would follow its path to modernization.

At the height of the Cold War, a version of modernization theory emerged in the United States that portrayed underdevelopment as a direct consequence of a country's psychological and cultural traits. Underdevelopment was said to reflect irrational traditional religious and communal values that discouraged achievement. The rich Western democracies, the theory went, could instill modern values and bring progress to "backward" nations through economic, cultural, and military assistance. By the 1970s, however, it had become clear that assistance had not brought much progress toward prosperity or democracy—eroding confidence in this version of modernization theory, which was increasingly criticized as ethnocentric and patronizing. It came under heavy criticism from "dependency theorists," who argued that trade with rich countries exploits poor ones, locking them into positions of structural dependence. The elites in developing countries welcomed such thinking, since it implied that poverty had nothing to do with internal problems or the corruption of local leaders; it was the fault of global capitalism. By the 1980s, dependency theory was in vogue. Third World nations, the thinking went, could escape from global exploitation only by withdrawing from global markets and adopting import-substitution policies.

More recently, it has become apparent that import-substitution strategies have failed: the countries least involved in global trade, such as Cuba, Myanmar (also called Burma), and North Korea, have not been the most successful—they have actually grown the least. Export-oriented strategies have been far more effective in promoting sustained economic growth and, eventually, democratization. The pendulum, accordingly, has swung back, and a new version of modernization theory has gained credibility. The rapid economic development of East Asia, and the subsequent democratization of South Korea and Taiwan, seem to confirm its basic claims: producing for the world market enables economic growth; investing the returns in human capital and upgrading the work force to produce high-tech goods brings higher returns and enlarges the educated middle class; once the middle class becomes large and articulate enough, it presses for liberal democracy—the most effective political system for advanced industrial societies. Nevertheless, even today, if one mentions modernization at a conference on economic development, one is likely to hear a reiteration of dependency theory's critique of the "backward nations" version of modernization theory, as if that were all there is to modernization theory—and as if no new evidence had emerged since the 1970s.

THE NEW MODERNIZATION

In retrospect, it is obvious that the early versions of modernization theory were wrong on several points. Today, virtually nobody expects a revolution of the proletariat that will abolish private property, ushering in a new era free from exploitation and conflict. Nor does anyone expect that industrialization will automatically lead to democratic institutions; communism and fascism also emerged from industrialization. Nonetheless, a massive body of evidence suggests that modernization theory's central premise was correct: economic development does tend to bring about important, roughly predictable changes in society, culture, and politics. But the earlier versions of modernization theory need to be corrected in several respects.

First, modernization is not linear. It does not move indefinitely in the same direction; instead, the process reaches inflection points. Empirical evidence indicates that each phase of modernization is associated with distinctive changes in people's worldviews. Industrialization leads to one major process of change, resulting in bureaucratization, hierarchy, centralization of authority, secularization, and a shift from traditional to secular-rational values. The rise of postindustrial society brings another set of cultural changes that move in a different direction: instead of bureaucratization and centralization, the new trend is toward an increasing emphasis on individual autonomy and self-expression values, which lead to a growing emancipation from authority.

Thus, other things being equal, high levels of economic development tend to make people more tolerant and trusting, bringing more emphasis on self-expression and more participation in decision-making. This process is not deterministic, and any forecasts can only be probabilistic, since economic factors are not the only influence; a given country's leaders and nation-specific events also shape what happens. Moreover, modernization is not irreversible. Severe economic collapse can reverse it, as happened during the Great Depression in Germany, Italy, Japan, and Spain and during the 1990s in most of the Soviet successor states. Similarly, if the current economic crisis becomes a twenty-first-century Great Depression, the world could face a new struggle against renewed xenophobia and authoritarianism.

Second, social and cultural change is path dependent: history matters. Although economic development tends to bring predictable changes in people's worldviews, a society's heritage—whether shaped by Protestantism, Catholicism, Islam, Confucianism, or communism—leaves a lasting imprint on its worldview. A society's value system reflects an interaction between the driving forces of modernization and the persisting influence of tradition. Although the classic modernization theorists in both the East and the West thought that religion and ethnic traditions would die out, they have proved to be highly resilient. Although the publics of industrializing societies are becoming richer and more educated, that is hardly creating a uniform global culture. Cultural heritages are remarkably enduring.

Third, modernization is not westernization, contrary to the earlier, ethnocentric version of the theory. The process of industrialization began in the West, but during the past few decades, East Asia has had the world's highest economic growth rates, and Japan leads the world in life expectancy and some other aspects of modernization. The United States is not the model for global cultural change, and industrializing societies in general are not becoming like the United States, as a popular version of modernization theory assumes. In fact, American society retains more traditional values than do most other high-income societies.

Fourth, modernization does not automatically lead to democracy. Rather, it, in the long run, brings social and cultural changes that make democratization increasingly probable. Simply attaining a high level of per capita GDP does not produce democracy: if it did, Kuwait and the United Arab Emirates would have become model democracies. (These countries have not gone through the modernization process described above.) But the emergence of postindustrial society brings certain social and cultural changes that are specifically conducive to democratization. Knowledge societies cannot function effectively without highly educated publics that have become increasingly accustomed to thinking for themselves. Furthermore, rising levels of economic security bring a growing emphasis on a syndrome of self-expression values—one that gives high priority to free choice and motivates political action. Beyond a certain point, accordingly, it becomes difficult to avoid democratization, because repressing mass demands for more open societies becomes increasingly costly and detrimental to economic effectiveness. Thus, in its advanced stages, modernization brings social and cultural changes that make the emergence and flourishing of democratic institutions increasingly likely.

The core idea of modernization theory is that economic and technological development bring a coherent set of social, cultural, and political changes. A large body of empirical evidence supports this idea. Economic development is, indeed, strongly linked to pervasive shifts in people's beliefs and motivations, and these shifts in turn change the role of religion, job motivations, human fertility rates, gender roles, and sexual norms. And they also bring growing mass demands for democratic institutions and for more responsive behavior on the part of elites. These changes together make democracy increasingly likely to emerge, while also making war less acceptable to publics.

EVALUATING VALUES

New sources of empirical evidence provide valuable insights into how modernization changes worldviews and motivations. One important source is global surveys of mass values and attitudes. Between 1981 and 2007, the World Values Survey and the European Values Study carried out five waves of representative national surveys in scores of countries, covering almost 90 percent of the world's population. (For the data from the surveys, visit www.worldvaluessurvey.org.) The results show large cross-national differences in what people believe and value. In some countries, 95 percent of the people surveyed said that God was very important in their lives; in others, only 3 percent did. In some societies, 90 percent of the people surveyed said they believed that men have more of a right to a job than women do; in others, only 8 percent said they thought so. These cross-national differences are robust and enduring, and they are closely correlated with a society's level of economic development: people in low-income societies are much likelier to emphasize religion and traditional gender roles than are people in rich countries.

These values surveys demonstrate that the worldviews of people living in rich societies differ systematically from those of people living in low-income societies across a wide range of political, social, and religious norms. The differences run along two basic dimensions: traditional versus secular-rational values and survival versus self-expression values. (Each dimension reflects responses to scores of questions asked as part of the values surveys.) The shift from traditional to secular-rational values is linked to the shift from agrarian to industrial societies. Traditional societies emphasize religion, respect for and obedience to authority, and national pride. These characteristics change as societies become more secular and rational.

The shift from survival to self-expression values is linked to the rise of postindustrial societies. It reflects a cultural shift that occurs when younger generations emerge that have grown up taking survival for granted. Survival values give top priority to economic and physical security and conformist social norms. Self-expression values give high priority to freedom of expression, participation in decision-making, political activism, environmental protection, gender equality, and tolerance of ethnic minorities, foreigners, and gays and lesbians. A growing emphasis on these latter values engenders a culture of trust and tolerance in which people cherish individual freedom and self-expression and have activist political orientations. These attributes are crucial to democracy—and thus explain how economic growth, which takes societies from agrarian to industrial and then from industrial to postindustrial, leads to democratization.

The unprecedented economic growth of the past 50 years has meant that an increasing share of the world's population has grown up taking survival for granted. Time-series data from the values surveys indicate that mass priorities have shifted from an overwhelming emphasis on economic and physical security to an emphasis on subjective well-being, self-expression, participation in decision-making, and a relatively trusting and tolerant outlook.

Both dimensions are closely linked to economic development: the value systems of high-income countries differ dramatically from those of low-income countries. Every nation that the World Bank defines as having a high income ranks relatively high on both dimensions—with a strong emphasis on both secular-rational and self-expression values. All the low-income and lower-middle-income countries rank relatively low on both dimensions. The upper-middle-income countries fall somewhere in between. To a remarkable degree, the values and beliefs of a given society reflect its level of economic development—just as modernization theory predicts.

This strong connection between a society's value system and its per capita GDP suggests that economic development tends to produce roughly predictable changes in a society's beliefs and values, and time-series evidence supports this hypothesis. When one compares the positions of given countries in successive waves of the values surveys, one finds that almost all the countries that experienced rising per capita GDPs also experienced predictable shifts in their values.

The values survey evidence also shows, however, that cultural change is path dependent; a society's cultural heritage also shapes where it falls on the global cultural map. This map shows distinctive clusters of countries: Protestant Europe, Catholic Europe, ex-communist Europe, the English-speaking countries, Latin America, South Asia, the Islamic world, and Africa. The values emphasized by different societies fall into a remarkably coherent pattern that reflects both those societies' economic development and their religious and colonial heritage. Still, even if a society's cultural heritage continues to shape its prevailing values, economic development brings changes that have important consequences. Over time, it reshapes beliefs and values of all kinds—and it brings a growing mass demand for democratic institutions and for more responsive elite behavior. And over the quarter century covered by the values surveys, the people of most countries placed increasing emphasis on self-expression values. This cultural shift makes democracy increasingly likely to emerge where it does not yet exist and increasingly likely to become more effective and more direct where it does.

DEVELOPMENT AND DEMOCRACY

Fifty years ago, the sociologist Seymour Martin Lipset pointed out that rich countries are much more likely than poor countries to be democracies. Although this claim was contested for many years, it has held up against repeated tests. The causal direction of the relationship has also been questioned: Are rich countries more likely to be democratic because democracy makes countries rich, or is development conducive to democracy? Today, it seems clear that the causality runs mainly from economic development to democratization. During early industrialization, authoritarian states are just as likely to attain high rates of growth as are democracies. But beyond a certain level of economic development, democracy becomes increasingly likely to emerge and survive. Thus, among the scores of countries that democratized around 1990, most were middle-income countries: almost all the high-income countries already were democracies, and few low-income countries made the transition. Moreover, among the countries that democratized between 1970 and 1990, democracy has survived in every country that made the transition when it was at the economic level of Argentina today or higher; among the countries that made the transition when they were below this level, democracy had an average life expectancy of only eight years.

The strong correlation between development and democracy reflects the fact that economic development is conducive to democracy. The question of why, exactly, development leads to democracy has been debated intensely, but the answer is beginning to emerge. It does not result from some disembodied force that causes democratic institutions to emerge automatically when a country attains a certain level of GDP. Rather, economic development brings social and political changes only when it changes people's behavior. Consequently, economic development is conducive to democracy to the extent that it, first, creates a large, educated, and articulate middle class of people who are accustomed to thinking for themselves and, second, transforms people's values and motivations.

Today, it is more possible than ever before to measure what the key changes are and how far they have progressed in given countries. Multivariate analysis of the data from the values surveys makes it possible to sort out the relative impact of economic, social, and cultural changes, and the results point to the conclusion that economic development is conducive to democracy insofar as it brings specific structural changes (particularly the rise of a knowledge sector) and certain cultural changes (particularly the rise of self-expression values). Wars, depressions, institutional changes, elite decisions, and specific leaders also influence what happens, but structural and cultural change are major factors in the emergence and survival of democracy.

Modernization brings rising educational levels, moving the work force into occupations that require independent thinking and making people more articulate and better equipped to intervene in politics. As knowledge societies emerge, people become accustomed to using their own initiative and judgment on the job and are also increasingly likely to question rigid and hierarchical authority.

Modernization also makes people economically more secure, and self-expression values become increasingly widespread when a large share of the population grows up taking survival for granted. The desire for freedom and autonomy are universal aspirations. They may be subordinated to the need for subsistence and order when survival is precarious, but they take increasingly high priority as survival becomes more secure. The basic motivation for democracy—the human desire for free choice—starts to play an increasingly important role. People begin to place a growing emphasis on free choice in politics and begin to demand civil and political liberties and democratic institutions.

EFFECTIVE DEMOCRACY

During the explosion of democracy that took place between 1985 and 1995, electoral democracy spread rapidly throughout the world. Strategic elite agreements played an important role in this process, facilitated by an international environment in which the end of the Cold War opened the way for democratization. Initially, there was a tendency to view any regime that held free and fair elections as a democracy. But many of the new democracies suffered from massive corruption and failed to apply the rule of law, which is what makes democracy effective. A growing number of observers today thus emphasize the inadequacy of "electoral democracy," "hybrid democracy," "authoritarian democracy," and other forms of sham democracy in which mass preferences are something that political elites can largely ignore and in which they do not decisively influence government decisions. It is important, accordingly, to distinguish between effective and ineffective democracies.

The essence of democracy is that it empowers ordinary citizens. Whether a democracy is effective or not is based on not only the extent to which civil and political rights exist on paper but also the degree to which officials actually respect these rights. The first of these two components—the existence of rights on paper—is measured by Freedom House's annual rankings: if a country holds free elections, Freedom House tends to rate it as "free," giving it a score at or near the top of its scale. Thus, the new democracies of eastern Europe receive scores as high as those of the established democracies of western Europe, although in-depth analyses show that widespread corruption makes these new democracies far less effective in responding to their citizens' choices. Fortunately, the World Bank's governance scores measure the extent to which a country's democratic institutions are actually effective. Consequently, a rough index of effective democracy can be obtained by multiplying these two scores: formal democracy, as measured by Freedom House, and elite and institutional integrity, as measured by the World Bank.

Effective democracy is a considerably more demanding standard than electoral democracy. One can establish electoral democracy almost anywhere, but it will probably not last long if it does not transfer power from the elites to the people. Effective democracy is most likely to exist alongside a relatively developed infrastructure that includes not only economic resources but also widespread participatory habits and an emphasis on autonomy. Accordingly, it is closely linked to the degree to which a given public emphasizes self-expression values. Indeed, the correlation between a society's values and the nature of the country's political institutions is remarkably strong.

Virtually all the stable democracies show strong self-expression values. Most Latin American countries are underachievers, showing lower levels of effective democracy than their publics' values would predict. This suggests that these societies could support higher levels of democracy if the rule of law were strengthened there. Iran is also an underachiever—a theocratic regime that allows a much lower level of democracy than that to which its people aspire. Surprising as it may seem to those who focus only on elite-level politics, the Iranian public shows relatively strong support for democracy. Conversely, Cyprus, Estonia, Hungary, Poland, Latvia, and Lithuania are overachievers, showing higher levels of democracy than their publics' values would predict—perhaps reflecting the incentives to democratize provided by membership in the European Union.

But do self-expression values lead to democracy, or does democracy cause self-expression values to emerge? The evidence indicates that these values lead to democracy. (For the full evidence for this claim, see our book *Modernization, Cultural Change, and Democracy*.) Democratic institutions do not need to be in place for self-expression values to emerge. Time-series evidence from the values surveys indicates that in the years preceding the wave of democratization in the late 1980s and early 1990s, self-expression values had already emerged through a process of an intergenerational change in values—not only in the Western democracies but also within many authoritarian societies. By 1990, the publics of East Germany and Czechoslovakia—which had been living under two of the most authoritarian regimes in the world—had developed high levels of self-expression values. The crucial factor was not the political system but the fact that these countries were among the most economically advanced countries in the communist world, with high levels of education and advanced social welfare systems. Thus, when the Soviet leader Mikhail Gorbachev renounced the Brezhnev Doctrine, removing the threat of Soviet military intervention, they moved swiftly toward democracy.

In recent decades, self-expression values have been spreading and getting stronger, making people more likely to directly intervene in politics. (Indeed, unprecedented numbers of people took part in the demonstrations that helped bring about the most recent wave of democratization.) Does this mean that authoritarian systems will inevitably crumble? No. A rising emphasis on self-expression values tends to erode the legitimacy of authoritarian systems, but as long as determined authoritarian elites control the army and the secret police, they can repress pro-democratic forces. Still, even repressive regimes find it costly to check these tendencies, for doing so tends to block the emergence of effective knowledge sectors.

MODERN STRATEGY

This new understanding of modernization has broad implications for international relations. For one thing, it helps explain why advanced democracies do not fight one another. Recent research provides strong empirical support for the claim that they do not, which goes back to Adam Smith and Immanuel Kant. Since they emerged in the early nineteenth century, liberal democracies have fought a number of wars, but almost never against one another. This new version of modernization theory indicates that the democratic peace phenomenon is due more to cultural changes linked to modernization than to democracy per se.

In earlier periods of history, democracies fought one another frequently. But the prevailing norms among them have evolved over time, as is illustrated by the abolition of slavery, the gradual expansion of the franchise, and the movement toward gender equality in virtually all modern societies. Another cultural change that has occurred in modern societies—which tend to be democracies—is that war has become progressively less acceptable and people have become more likely to express this preference and try to affect policy accordingly. Evidence from the World Values Survey indicates that the publics of high-income countries have much lower levels of xenophobia than do the publics of low-income countries, and they are much less willing to fight for their country than are the publics of low-income countries. Moreover, economically developed democracies behave far more peacefully toward one another than do poor democracies, and economically developed democracies are far less prone to civil war than are poor democracies.

Modernization theory has both cautionary and encouraging implications for U.S. foreign policy. Iraq, of course, provides a cautionary lesson. Contrary to the appealing view that democracy can be readily established almost anywhere, modernization theory holds that democracy is much more likely to flourish under certain conditions than others. A number of factors made it unrealistic to expect that democracy would be easy to establish in Iraq, including deep ethnic cleavages that had been exacerbated by Saddam Hussein's regime. And after Saddam's defeat, allowing physical security to deteriorate was a particularly serious mistake. Interpersonal trust and tolerance flourish when people feel secure. Democracy is unlikely to survive in a society torn by distrust and intolerance, and Iraq currently manifests the highest level of xenophobia of any society for which data are available. A good indicator of xenophobia is the extent to which people say they would not want to have foreigners as neighbors. Across 80 countries, the median percentage of those surveyed who said this was 15 percent. Among Iraqi Kurds, 51 percent of those polled said they would prefer not to have foreigners as neighbors. Among Iraqi Arabs, 90 percent of those polled said they would not want foreigners as neighbors. In keeping with these conditions, Iraq (along with Pakistan and Zimbabwe) shows very low levels of both self-expression values and effective democracy.

Modernization theory also has positive implications for U.S. foreign policy. Supported by a large body of evidence, it points to the conclusion that economic development is a basic driver of democratic change—meaning that Washington should do what it can to encourage development. If it wants to bring democratic change to Cuba, for example, isolating it is counterproductive. The United States should lift the embargo, promote economic development, and foster social engagement with, and other connections to, the world. Nothing is certain, but empirical evidence suggests that a growing sense of security and a growing emphasis on self-expression values there would undermine the authoritarian regime.

Similarly, although many observers have been alarmed by the economic resurgence of China, this growth has positive implications for the long term. Beneath China's seemingly monolithic political structure, the social infrastructure of democratization is emerging, and it has progressed further than most observers realize. China is now approaching the level of mass emphasis on self-expression values at which Chile, Poland, South Korea, and Taiwan made their transitions to democracy. And, surprising as it may seem to observers who focus only on elite-level politics, Iran is also near this threshold. As long as the Chinese Communist Party and Iran's theocratic leaders control their countries' military and security forces, democratic institutions will not emerge at the national level. But growing mass pressures for liberalization are beginning to appear, and repressing them will bring growing costs in terms of economic inefficiency and low public morale. On the whole, increasing prosperity for China and Iran is in the United States' national interest.

More broadly, modernization theory implies that the United States should welcome and encourage economic development around the world. Although economic development requires difficult adjustments, its long-term effects encourage the emergence of more tolerant, less xenophobic, and ultimately more democratic societies. 🌐

The Post-Washington Consensus

Development After the Crisis

Nancy Birdsall and Francis Fukuyama

Foreign Affairs, March / April 2011

The last time a global depression originated in the United States, the impact was devastating not only for the world economy but for world politics as well. The Great Depression set the stage for a shift away from strict monetarism and laissez-faire policies toward Keynesian demand management. More important, for many it delegitimized the capitalist system itself, paving the way for the rise of radical and antiliberal movements around the world.

This time around, there has been no violent rejection of capitalism, even in the developing world. In early 2009, at the height of the global financial panic, China and Russia, two formerly noncapitalist states, made it clear to their domestic and foreign investors that they had no intention of abandoning the capitalist model. No leader of a major developing country has backed away from his or her commitment to free trade or the global capitalist system. Instead, the established Western democracies are the ones that have highlighted the risks of relying too much on market-led globalization and called for greater regulation of global finance.

NANCY BIRDSALL, President of the Center for Global Development. FRANCIS FUKUYAMA, Olivier Nomellini Senior Fellow at the Freeman Spogli Institute for International Studies at Stanford University. They are the editors of *New Ideas in Development After the Financial Crisis* (Johns Hopkins University Press, 2011), from which this essay is adapted.

Why has the reaction in developing countries been so much less extreme after this crisis than it was after the Great Depression? For one, they blame the United States for it. Many in the developing world agreed with Brazilian President Luiz Inácio Lula da Silva when he said, "This is a crisis caused by people, white with blue eyes." If the global financial crisis put any development model on trial, it was the free-market or neoliberal model, which emphasizes a small state, deregulation, private ownership, and low taxes. Few developing countries consider themselves to have fully adopted that model.

Indeed, for years before the crisis, they had been distancing themselves from it. The financial crises of the late 1990s in East Asia and Latin America discredited many of the ideas associated with the so-called Washington consensus, particularly that of unalloyed reliance on foreign capital. By 2008, most emerging-market countries had reduced their exposure to the foreign financial markets by accumulating large foreign currency reserves and maintaining regulatory control of their banking systems. These policies provided insulation from global economic volatility and were vindicated by the impressive rebounds in the wake of the recent crisis: the emerging markets have posted much better economic growth numbers than their counterparts in the developed world.

Thus, the American version of capitalism is, if not in full disrepute, then at least no longer dominant. In the next decade, emerging-market and low-income countries are likely to modify their approach to economic policy further, trading the flexibility and efficiency associated with the free-market model for domestic policies meant to ensure greater resilience in the face of competitive pressures and global economic trauma. They will become less focused on the free flow of capital, more concerned with minimizing social disruption through social safety net programs, and more active in supporting domestic industries. And they will be even less inclined than before to defer to the supposed expertise of the more developed countries, believing—correctly—that not only economic but also intellectual power are becoming increasingly evenly distributed.

THE FOREIGN FINANCE FETISH

One of the central features of the old, pre-crisis economic consensus was the assumption that developing countries could benefit substantially from greater inflows of foreign capital—what the economist Arvind Subramanian has labeled "the foreign finance fetish." The idea that the unimpeded flow of capital around the globe, like the free flow of goods and services, makes markets more efficient was more or less taken for granted in policy circles. In the 1990s, the United States and international financial institutions such as the International Monetary Fund (IMF) pushed developing-country borrowers to open up their capital markets to foreign banks and dismantle exchange-rate controls.

Although the benefits of free trade have been well documented, the advantages of full capital mobility are much less clear. The reasons for this have to do with the fundamental differences between the financial sector and the "real" economy. Free capital markets can indeed allocate capital efficiently. But large interconnected financial institutions can also take risks that impose huge negative externalities on the rest of the economy in a way that large manufacturing firms cannot.

One of the paradoxical consequences of the 2008–9 financial crisis may thus be that Americans and Britons will finally learn what the East Asians figured out over a decade ago, namely, that open capital markets combined with unregulated financial sectors is a disaster in the waiting. At the conclusion of the Asian financial crisis, many U.S. policymakers and economists walked back their previous stress on quick liberalization and started promoting "sequencing," that is, liberalization only after a strong regulatory system with adequate supervision of banks has been put in place. But they devoted little thought to whether certain developing countries were capable of enacting such regulation quickly or what an appropriate regulatory regime would look like. And they overlooked the relevance of their new message to their own case, failing to warn against the danger of the huge, unregulated, and overleveraged shadow financial sector that had emerged in the United States.

The first clear consequence of the crisis has thus been the end of the foreign finance fetish. The countries that pursued it the most enthusiastically, such as Iceland, Ireland, and those in eastern Europe, were the hardest hit and face the toughest recoveries. Just as for Wall Street, the strong growth records these countries amassed from 2002 to 2007 proved to be partly a mirage, reflecting the easy availability of credit and high leverage ratios rather than strong fundamentals.

CARING ABOUT CARING

The second consequence is a new respect among developing countries for the political and social benefits of a sensible social policy. Before the crisis, policymakers tended to downplay social insurance and safety net programs in favor of strategies that emphasized economic efficiency. U.S. President Ronald Reagan and British Prime Minister Margaret Thatcher had come to power in the late 1970s and 1980s attacking the modern welfare state, and many of their critiques were well taken: state bureaucracies had become bloated and inefficient in many countries, and an entitlement mentality had taken hold. The Washington consensus did not necessarily reject the use of social policy, but its focus on efficiency and fiscal discipline often led to cuts in social spending.

What the crisis did, however, was to underscore the instability inherent in capitalist systems—even ones as developed and sophisticated as the United States. Capitalism is a dynamic process that regularly produces faultless victims who lose their jobs or see their livelihoods threatened. Throughout the crisis and its aftermath, citizens have expected their governments to provide some level of stability in the face of economic uncertainty. This is a lesson that politicians in developing-country democracies are not likely to forget; the consolidation and legitimacy of their fragile democratic systems will depend on their ability to deliver a greater measure of social protection.

Consider how continental Europe has reacted in comparison to the United States. Until now, with the eurozone crisis, western Europe experienced a far less painful recovery, thanks to its more developed system of automatic countercyclical social spending, including for unemployment insurance. In contrast, the jobless recovery in the United States makes the U.S. model even less attractive to policymakers in the developing world, particularly those who are increasingly subject to political pressure to attend to the needs of the middle class.

A good example of the new stress on social policy can be found in China. Reacting to the country's rapidly aging population, its leadership is struggling behind the scenes to build a modern pension system, something that represents a shift from the traditional tactic of concentrating solely on generating new jobs to maintain social and political stability. In Latin America, the same pressures are playing out differently. After experiencing fatigue in the wake of liberalizing reforms in the 1990s that did not seem to produce the growth that was expected, the region has moved to the left in this century, and the new governments have increased social spending to reduce poverty and inequality. Many countries have followed the successful example of Brazil and Mexico and instituted cash transfer schemes targeted to poor households (which require beneficiaries to keep their children in school or meet other conditions). In Brazil and Mexico, the approach has contributed to the first visible declines in income inequality in many years and helped shelter the poorest households from the recent crisis.

The question, of course, is whether programs like these that target the poor (and thus keep fiscal outlays surprisingly low) will have difficulty attracting long-term support from the region's growing middle class, and how these and other emerging economies, including China, will manage the fiscal costs of more universal health, pension, and other social insurance programs. Will they be better at handling the problems associated with these unfunded universal entitlement programs, the kinds of problems now facing Europe and the United States as their populations age?

THE VISIBLE HAND

The third consequence of the crisis has been the rise of a new round of discussions about industrial policy—a country's strategy to develop specific industrial sectors, traditionally through such support as cheap credit or outright subsidies or through state management of development banks. Such policies were written off as dangerous failures in the 1980s and 1990s for sustaining inefficient insider industries at high fiscal cost. But the crisis and the effective response to it by some countries are likely to bolster the notion that competent technocrats in developing countries are capable of efficiently managing state involvement in the productive sectors. Brazil, for example, used its government-sponsored development bank to direct credit to certain sectors quickly as part of its initial crisis-driven stimulus program, and China did the same thing with its state-run banks.

However, this new industrial policy is not about picking winners or bringing about large sectoral shifts in production. It is about addressing coordination problems and other barriers that discourage private investment in new industries and technologies, difficulties that market forces alone are unlikely to overcome. To promote an innovative clothing industry in West Africa, for example, governments might ensure a constant supply of textiles or subsidize the construction of ports to avoid export bottlenecks. The idea is that by bearing some of the initial financial or other risks and more systematically targeting public infrastructure, governments can help private investors overcome the high costs of being the first movers and innovators in incipient sectors.

For the last three decades, Washington-based development institutions have taken the view that growth is threatened more by government incompetence and corruption than by market failures. Now that American-style capitalism has fallen from its pedestal, might this view begin to shift? Might the idea that the state can take a more active role get far more traction? The answer depends, for any single developing country, on an assessment of its state capacity and overall governance. This is because the most significant critique of industrial policy was never economic but political, contending that economic decision-making in developing countries could not be shielded from political pressure. Critics argued that policymakers would retain protectionist measures long after they had fulfilled their original purpose of jump-starting domestic industries. Industrial policies such as reducing dependency on imports and promoting infant industries, although later derided in Washington, did in fact produce impressive rates of economic growth in the 1950s and 1960s in East Asia and Latin America. The problem, however, was that governments in the latter region were politically unable to unwind that protection, and so their domestic industries failed to become globally competitive.

Therefore, technocrats in developing countries contemplating the use of industrial policies must consider the politics of doing so. Does a bureaucracy exist that is sufficiently capable and autonomous from political pressure? Is there enough money to sustain such an agenda? Will it be possible to make hard political decisions, such as eliminating the policies when they are no longer needed? Most of the successful uses of industrial policy have been in East Asia, which has a long tradition of strong technocratic bureaucracies. Countries without such a legacy need to be more careful.

MAKING BUREAUCRACY WORK

If countries are to promote industrial development and provide a social safety net, they will need to reform their public sectors; indeed, the fourth consequence of the crisis has been a painful reminder of the costs of not doing so. In the United States, regulatory agencies were underfunded, had difficulty attracting high-quality personnel, and faced political opposition. This was not surprising: implicit in the Reagan-Thatcher doctrine was the belief that markets were an acceptable substitute for efficient government. The crisis demonstrated that unregulated or poorly regulated markets can produce extraordinary costs.

Leaders in both the developing world and the developed world have marveled at China's remarkable ability to bounce back after the crisis, a result of a tightly managed, top-down policymaking machine that could avoid the delays of a messy democratic process. In response, political leaders in the developing world now associate efficiency and capability with autocratic political systems. But there are plenty of incompetent autocratic regimes. What sets China apart is a bureaucracy that, at its upper levels at least, is capable of managing and coordinating sophisticated policies. Among low-income countries, that makes China an exception.

Promoting effective public sectors is one of the most daunting development challenges that the world faces. Development institutions such as the World Bank and the United Kingdom's Department for International Development have supported programs that strengthen public sectors, promote good governance, and combat corruption for the last 15 years with little to show for it. The fact that even financial regulators in the United States and the United Kingdom failed to use their existing powers or to keep pace with rapidly evolving markets is a humbling reminder that effective public sectors are a challenge to maintain in even the most developed countries.

Why has so little progress been made in improving developing countries' public sectors? The first problem is that their bureaucracies often serve governments that are rent-seeking coalitions acting according to self-interest, instead of an ideal of impersonal public service. Outside donors typically do not have the leverage to force them to change, with the partial exception of mechanisms such as the European Union's accession process. Second, effective institutions have to evolve indigenously, reflecting a country's own political, social, and cultural realities. The development of impersonal bureaucracies in the West was the product of a long and painful process, with factors exogenous to the economy (such as the need to mobilize for war) playing a large part in creating strong state institutions (such as Prussia's famously efficient bureaucracy). Institutions such as the rule of law will rarely work if they are simply copied from abroad; societies must buy into their content. Finally, public-sector reform requires a parallel process of nation building. Unless a society has a clear sense of national identity and a shared public interest, individuals will show less loyalty to it than to their ethnic group, tribe, or patronage network.

MOVING TO MULTIPOLARITY

Years from now, historians may well point to the financial crisis as the end of American economic dominance in global affairs. But the trend toward a multipolar world began much earlier, and the implosion of Western financial markets and their weak recoveries have merely accelerated the process. Even before the crisis, the international institutions created after World War II to manage economic and security challenges were under strain and in need of reform. The IMF and the World Bank suffered from governance structures that reflected outdated economic realities. Starting in the 1990s and continuing into the new century, the Bretton Woods institutions have come under increasing pressure to grant more voting power to emerging-market countries such as Brazil and China. Meanwhile, the G-7, the elite group of the six most economically important Western democracies plus Japan, remained the world's informal steering committee when it came to issues of global economic coordination, even as other power centers emerged.

The financial crisis finally led to the demise of the G-7 as the primary locus of global economic policy coordination and its replacement by the G-20. In November 2008, heads of state from the G-20 gathered in Washington, D.C., to coordinate a global stimulus program—a meeting that has since grown into an established international institution. Since the G-20, unlike the G-7, includes emerging countries such as Brazil, China, and India, the expansion of economic coordination represents an overdue recognition of a new group of global economic players.

The crisis also breathed new life and legitimacy into the IMF and the World Bank. Beforehand, the IMF had looked like it was rapidly becoming obsolete. Private capital markets provided countries with financing on favorable terms without the conditions often attached to IMF loans. The organization was having trouble funding its own activities and was in the process of reducing its staff.

But the outlook changed in 2009, when the G-20 leaders agreed to ensure that the Bretton Woods institutions would have as much as $1 trillion in additional resources to help countries better weather future financing shortfalls. Countries such as Brazil and China were among the contributors to the special funds, which have ended up supporting Greece, Hungary, Iceland, Ireland, Latvia, Pakistan, and Ukraine.

By requesting that emerging markets take on a bigger leadership role in global affairs, the Western democracies are implicitly admitting that they are no longer able to manage global economic affairs on their own. But what has been called "the rise of the rest" is not just about economic and political power; it also has to do with the global competition of ideas and models. The West, and in particular the United States, is no longer seen as the only center for innovative thinking about social policy. Conditional cash transfer schemes, for example, were first developed and implemented in Latin America. As for industrial policy, the West has contributed little innovative thinking in that realm in the last 30 years. One has to turn to emerging-market countries, rather than the developed world, to see successful models in practice. And when it comes to international organizations, the voices and ideas of the United States and Europe are becoming less dominant. Those of emerging-market countries—states that have become significant funders of the international financial institutions—are being given greater weight.

All this signals a clear shift in the development agenda. Traditionally, this was an agenda generated in the developed world that was implemented in—and, indeed, often imposed on—the developing world. The United States, Europe, and Japan will continue to be significant sources of economic resources and ideas, but the emerging markets are now entering this arena and will become significant players. Countries such as Brazil, China, India, and South Africa will be both donors and recipients of resources for development and of best practices for how to use them. A large portion of the world's poor live within their borders, yet they have achieved new respect on the global scene in economic, political, and intellectual terms. In fact, development has never been something that the rich bestowed on the poor but rather something the poor achieved for themselves. It appears that the Western powers are finally waking up to this truth in light of a financial crisis that, for them, is by no means over.

The Future of History

Can Liberal Democracy Survive the Decline of the Middle Class?

Francis Fukuyama

Foreign Affairs, January/February 2012

Something strange is going on in the world today. The global financial crisis that began in 2008 and the ongoing crisis of the euro are both products of the model of lightly regulated financial capitalism that emerged over the past three decades. Yet despite widespread anger at Wall Street bailouts, there has been no great upsurge of left-wing American populism in response. It is conceivable that the Occupy Wall Street movement will gain traction, but the most dynamic recent populist movement to date has been the right-wing Tea Party, whose main target is the regulatory state that seeks to protect ordinary people from financial speculators. Something similar is true in Europe as well, where the left is anemic and right-wing populist parties are on the move.

There are several reasons for this lack of left-wing mobilization, but chief among them is a failure in the realm of ideas. For the past generation, the ideological high ground on economic issues has been held by a libertarian right. The left has not been able to make a plausible case for an agenda other than a return to an unaffordable form of old-fashioned social democracy. This absence of a plausible

FRANCIS FUKUYAMA, Senior Fellow at the Center on Democracy, Development, and the Rule of Law at Stanford University and the author, most recently, of *The Origins of Political Order: From Prehuman Times to the French Revolution.*

progressive counternarrative is unhealthy, because competition is good for intellectual debate just as it is for economic activity. And serious intellectual debate is urgently needed, since the current form of globalized capitalism is eroding the middle-class social base on which liberal democracy rests.

THE DEMOCRATIC WAVE

Social forces and conditions do not simply "determine" ideologies, as Karl Marx once maintained, but ideas do not become powerful unless they speak to the concerns of large numbers of ordinary people. Liberal democracy is the default ideology around much of the world today in part because it responds to and is facilitated by certain socioeconomic structures. Changes in those structures may have ideological consequences, just as ideological changes may have socioeconomic consequences.

Almost all the powerful ideas that shaped human societies up until the past 300 years were religious in nature, with the important exception of Confucianism in China. The first major secular ideology to have a lasting worldwide effect was liberalism, a doctrine associated with the rise of first a commercial and then an industrial middle class in certain parts of Europe in the seventeenth century. (By "middle class," I mean people who are neither at the top nor at the bottom of their societies in terms of income, who have received at least a secondary education, and who own either real property, durable goods, or their own businesses.)

As enunciated by classic thinkers such as Locke, Montesquieu, and Mill, liberalism holds that the legitimacy of state authority derives from the state's ability to protect the individual rights of its citizens and that state power needs to be limited by the adherence to law. One of the fundamental rights to be protected is that of private property; England's Glorious Revolution of 1688–89 was critical to the development of modern liberalism because it first established the constitutional principle that the state could not legitimately tax its citizens without their consent.

At first, liberalism did not necessarily imply democracy. The Whigs who supported the constitutional settlement of 1689 tended to be the wealthiest property owners in England; the parliament of that period represented less than ten percent of the whole population. Many classic liberals, including Mill, were highly skeptical of the virtues of democracy: they believed that responsible political participation required education and a stake in society—that is, property ownership. Up through the end of the nineteenth century, the franchise was limited by property and educational requirements in virtually all parts of Europe. Andrew Jackson's election as U.S. president in 1828 and his subsequent abolition of property requirements for voting, at least for white males, thus marked an important early victory for a more robust democratic principle.

In Europe, the exclusion of the vast majority of the population from political power and the rise of an industrial working class paved the way for Marxism. *The Communist Manifesto* was published in 1848, the same year that revolutions spread to all the major European countries save the United Kingdom. And so began a century of competition for the leadership of the democratic movement between communists, who were willing to jettison procedural democracy (multiparty elections) in favor of what they believed was substantive democracy (economic redistribution), and liberal democrats, who believed in expanding political participation while maintaining a rule of law protecting individual rights, including property rights.

At stake was the allegiance of the new industrial working class. Early Marxists believed they would win by sheer force of numbers: as the franchise was expanded in the late nineteenth century, parties such as the United Kingdom's Labour and Germany's Social Democrats grew by leaps and bounds and threatened the hegemony of both conservatives and traditional liberals. The rise of the working class was fiercely resisted, often by nondemocratic means; the communists and many socialists, in turn, abandoned formal democracy in favor of a direct seizure of power.

Throughout the first half of the twentieth century, there was a strong consensus on the progressive left that some form of socialism—government control of the commanding heights of the economy in order to ensure an egalitarian distribution of wealth—was unavoidable for all advanced countries. Even a conservative economist such as Joseph Schumpeter could write in his 1942 book, *Capitalism, Socialism, and Democracy*, that socialism would emerge victorious because capitalist society was culturally self-undermining. Socialism was believed to represent the will and interests of the vast majority of people in modern societies.

Yet even as the great ideological conflicts of the twentieth century played themselves out on a political and military level, critical changes were happening on a social level that undermined the Marxist scenario. First, the real living standards of the industrial working class kept rising, to the point where many workers or their children were able to join the middle class. Second, the relative size of the working class stopped growing and actually began to decline, particularly in the second half of the twentieth century, when services began to displace manufacturing in what were labeled "postindustrial" economies. Finally, a new group of poor or disadvantaged people emerged below the industrial working class—a heterogeneous mixture of racial and ethnic minorities, recent immigrants, and socially excluded groups, such as women, gays, and the disabled. As a result of these changes, in most industrialized societies, the old working class has become just another domestic interest group, one using the political power of trade unions to protect the hard-won gains of an earlier era.

Economic class, moreover, turned out not to be a great banner under which to mobilize populations in advanced industrial countries for political action. The Second International got a rude wake-up call in 1914, when the working classes of Europe abandoned calls for class warfare and lined up behind conservative leaders preaching nationalist slogans, a pattern that persists to the present day. Many Marxists tried to explain this, according to the scholar Ernest Gellner, by what he dubbed the "wrong address theory": "Just as extreme Shi'ite Muslims hold that Archangel Gabriel made a mistake, delivering the Message to Mohamed when it was intended for Ali, so Marxists basically like to think that the spirit of history or human consciousness made a terrible boob. The awakening message was intended for classes, but by some terrible postal error was delivered to nations." Gellner went on to argue that religion serves a function similar to nationalism in the contemporary Middle East: it mobilizes people effectively because it has a spiritual and emotional content that class consciousness does not. Just as European nationalism was driven by the shift of Europeans from the countryside to cities in the late nineteenth century, so, too, Islamism is a reaction to the urbanization and displacement taking place in contemporary Middle Eastern societies. Marx's letter will never be delivered to the address marked "class."

Marx believed that the middle class, or at least the capital-owning slice of it that he called the bourgeoisie, would always remain a small and privileged minority in modern societies. What happened instead was that the bourgeoisie and the middle class more generally ended up constituting the vast majority of the populations of most advanced countries, posing problems for socialism. From the days of Aristotle, thinkers have believed that stable democracy rests on a broad middle class and that societies with extremes of wealth and poverty are susceptible either to oligarchic domination or populist revolution. When much of the developed world succeeded in creating middle-class societies, the appeal of Marxism vanished. The only places where leftist radicalism persists as a powerful force are in highly unequal areas of the world, such as parts of Latin America, Nepal, and the impoverished regions of eastern India.

What the political scientist Samuel Huntington labeled the "third wave" of global democratization, which began in southern Europe in the 1970s and culminated in the fall of communism in Eastern Europe in 1989, increased the number of electoral democracies around the world from around 45 in 1970 to more than 120 by the late 1990s. Economic growth has led to the emergence of new middle classes in countries such as Brazil, India, Indonesia, South Africa, and Turkey. As the economist Moisés Naím has pointed out, these middle classes are relatively well educated, own property, and are technologically connected to the outside world.

They are demanding of their governments and mobilize easily as a result of their access to technology. It should not be surprising that the chief instigators of the Arab Spring uprisings were well-educated Tunisians and Egyptians whose expectations for jobs and political participation were stymied by the dictatorships under which they lived.

Middle-class people do not necessarily support democracy in principle: like everyone else, they are self-interested actors who want to protect their property and position. In countries such as China and Thailand, many middle-class people feel threatened by the redistributive demands of the poor and hence have lined up in support of authoritarian governments that protect their class interests. Nor is it the case that democracies necessarily meet the expectations of their own middle classes, and when they do not, the middle classes can become restive.

THE LEAST BAD ALTERNATIVE?

There is today a broad global consensus about the legitimacy, at least in principle, of liberal democracy. In the words of the economist Amartya Sen, "While democracy is not yet universally practiced, nor indeed uniformly accepted, in the general climate of world opinion, democratic governance has now achieved the status of being taken to be generally right." It is most broadly accepted in countries that have reached a level of material prosperity sufficient to allow a majority of their citizens to think of themselves as middle class, which is why there tends to be a correlation between high levels of development and stable democracy.

Some societies, such as Iran and Saudi Arabia, reject liberal democracy in favor of a form of Islamic theocracy. Yet these regimes are developmental dead ends, kept alive only because they sit atop vast pools of oil. There was at one time a large Arab exception to the third wave, but the Arab Spring has shown that Arab publics can be mobilized against dictatorship just as readily as those in Eastern Europe and Latin America were. This does not of course mean that the path to a well-functioning democracy will be easy or straightforward in Tunisia, Egypt, or Libya, but it does suggest that the desire for political freedom and participation is not a cultural peculiarity of Europeans and Americans.

The single most serious challenge to liberal democracy in the world today comes from China, which has combined authoritarian government with a partially marketized economy. China is heir to a long and proud tradition of high-quality bureaucratic government, one that stretches back over two millennia. Its leaders have managed a hugely complex transition from a centralized, Soviet-style planned economy to a dynamic open one and have done so with remarkable competence—more competence, frankly, than U.S. leaders have shown in the management of their own macroeconomic policy recently. Many people currently admire the Chinese system not just for its economic record but also because it can make large, complex decisions quickly, compared with the agonizing policy paralysis that has struck both the United States and Europe in the past few years. Especially since the recent financial crisis, the Chinese themselves have begun touting the "China model" as an alternative to liberal democracy.

This model is unlikely to ever become a serious alternative to liberal democracy in regions outside East Asia, however. In the first place, the model is culturally specific: the Chinese government is built around a long tradition of meritocratic recruitment, civil service examinations, a high emphasis on education, and deference to technocratic authority. Few developing countries can hope to emulate this model; those that have, such as Singapore and South Korea (at least in an earlier period), were already within the Chinese cultural zone. The Chinese themselves are skeptical about whether their model can be exported; the so-called Beijing consensus is a Western invention, not a Chinese one.

It is also unclear whether the model can be sustained. Neither export-driven growth nor the top-down approach to decision-making will continue to yield good results forever. The fact that the Chinese government would not permit open discussion of the disastrous high-speed rail accident last summer and could not bring the Railway Ministry responsible for it to heel suggests that there are other time bombs hidden behind the façade of efficient decision-making.

Finally, China faces a great moral vulnerability down the road. The Chinese government does not force its officials to respect the basic dignity of its citizens. Every week, there are new protests about land seizures or environmental violations or revelations of gross corruption on the part of some official. While the country is growing rapidly, these abuses can be swept under the carpet. But rapid growth will not continue forever, and the government will have to pay a price in pent-up anger. The regime no longer has any guiding ideal around which it is organized; it is run by a Communist Party supposedly committed to equality that presides over a society marked by dramatic and growing inequality.

So the stability of the Chinese system can in no way be taken for granted. The Chinese government argues that its citizens are culturally different and will always prefer benevolent, growth-promoting dictatorship to a messy democracy that threatens social stability. But it is unlikely that a spreading middle class will behave all that differently in China from the way it has behaved in other parts of the world. Other authoritarian regimes may be trying to emulate China's success, but there is little chance that much of the world will look like today's China 50 years down the road.

DEMOCRACY'S FUTURE

There is a broad correlation among economic growth, social change, and the hegemony of liberal democratic ideology in the world today. And at the moment, no plausible rival ideology looms. But some very troubling economic and social trends, if they continue, will both threaten the stability of contemporary liberal democracies and dethrone democratic ideology as it is now understood.

The sociologist Barrington Moore once flatly asserted, "No bourgeois, no democracy." The Marxists didn't get their communist utopia because mature capitalism generated middle-class societies, not working-class ones. But what if the further development of technology and globalization undermines the middle class and makes it impossible for more than a minority of citizens in an advanced society to achieve middle-class status?

There are already abundant signs that such a phase of development has begun. Median incomes in the United States have been stagnating in real terms since the 1970s. The economic impact of this stagnation has been softened to some extent by the fact that most U.S. households have shifted to two income earners in the past generation. Moreover, as the economist Raghuram Rajan has persuasively argued, since Americans are reluctant to engage in straightforward redistribution, the United States has instead attempted a highly dangerous and inefficient form of redistribution over the past generation by subsidizing mortgages for low-income households. This trend, facilitated by a flood of liquidity pouring in from China and other countries, gave many ordinary Americans the illusion that their standards of living were rising steadily during the past decade. In this respect, the bursting of the housing bubble in 2008–9 was nothing more than a cruel reversion to the mean. Americans may today benefit from cheap cell phones, inexpensive clothing, and Facebook, but they increasingly cannot afford their own homes, or health insurance, or comfortable pensions when they retire.

A more troubling phenomenon, identified by the venture capitalist Peter Thiel and the economist Tyler Cowen, is that the benefits of the most recent waves of technological innovation have accrued disproportionately to the most talented and well-educated members of society. This phenomenon helped cause the massive growth of inequality in the United States over the past generation. In 1974, the top one percent of families took home nine percent of GDP; by 2007, that share had increased to 23.5 percent.

Trade and tax policies may have accelerated this trend, but the real villain here is technology. In earlier phases of industrialization—the ages of textiles, coal, steel, and the internal combustion engine—the benefits of technological changes almost always flowed down in significant ways to the rest of society in terms of employment. But this is not a law of nature. We are today living in what the scholar Shoshana Zuboff has labeled "the age of the smart machine," in which technology is increasingly able to substitute for more and higher human functions. Every great advance for Silicon Valley likely means a loss of low-skill jobs elsewhere in the economy, a trend that is unlikely to end anytime soon.

Inequality has always existed, as a result of natural differences in talent and character. But today's technological world vastly magnifies those differences. In a nineteenth-century agrarian society, people with strong math skills did not have that many opportunities to capitalize on their talent. Today, they can become financial wizards or software engineers and take home ever-larger proportions of the national wealth.

The other factor undermining middle-class incomes in developed countries is globalization. With the lowering of transportation and communications costs and the entry into the global work force of hundreds of millions of new workers in developing countries, the kind of work done by the old middle class in the developed world can now be performed much more cheaply elsewhere. Under an economic model that prioritizes the maximization of aggregate income, it is inevitable that jobs will be outsourced.

Smarter ideas and policies could have contained the damage. Germany has succeeded in protecting a significant part of its manufacturing base and industrial labor force even as its companies have remained globally competitive. The United States and the United Kingdom, on the other hand, happily embraced the transition to the postindustrial service economy. Free trade became less a theory than an ideology: when members of the U.S. Congress tried to retaliate with trade sanctions against China for keeping its currency undervalued, they were indignantly charged with protectionism, as if the playing field were already level. There was a lot of happy talk about the wonders of the knowledge economy, and how dirty, dangerous manufacturing jobs would inevitably be replaced by highly educated workers doing creative and interesting things. This was a gauzy veil placed over the hard facts of deindustrialization. It overlooked the fact that the benefits of the new order accrued disproportionately to a very small number of people in finance and high technology, interests that dominated the media and the general political conversation.

THE ABSENT LEFT

One of the most puzzling features of the world in the aftermath of the financial crisis is that so far, populism has taken primarily a right-wing form, not a left-wing one.

In the United States, for example, although the Tea Party is anti-elitist in its rhetoric, its members vote for conservative politicians who serve the interests of precisely those financiers and corporate elites they claim to despise. There are many explanations for this phenomenon. They include a deeply embedded belief in equality of opportunity rather than equality of outcome and the fact that cultural issues, such as abortion and gun rights, crosscut economic ones.

But the deeper reason a broad-based populist left has failed to materialize is an intellectual one. It has been several decades since anyone on the left has been able to articulate, first, a coherent analysis of what happens to the structure of advanced societies as they undergo economic change and, second, a realistic agenda that has any hope of protecting a middle-class society.

The main trends in left-wing thought in the last two generations have been, frankly, disastrous as either conceptual frameworks or tools for mobilization. Marxism died many years ago, and the few old believers still around are ready for nursing homes. The academic left replaced it with postmodernism, multiculturalism, feminism, critical theory, and a host of other fragmented intellectual trends that are more cultural than economic in focus. Postmodernism begins with a denial of the possibility of any master narrative of history or society, undercutting its own authority as a voice for the majority of citizens who feel betrayed by their elites. Multiculturalism validates the victimhood of virtually every out-group. It is impossible to generate a mass progressive movement on the basis of such a motley coalition: most of the working- and lower-middle-class citizens victimized by the system are culturally conservative and would be embarrassed to be seen in the presence of allies like this.

Whatever the theoretical justifications underlying the left's agenda, its biggest problem is a lack of credibility. Over the past two generations, the mainstream left has followed a social democratic program that centers on the state provision of a variety of services, such as pensions, health care, and education. That model is now exhausted: welfare states have become big, bureaucratic, and inflexible; they are often captured by the very organizations that administer them, through public-sector unions; and, most important, they are fiscally unsustainable given the aging of populations virtually everywhere in the developed world. Thus, when existing social democratic parties come to power, they no longer aspire to be more than custodians of a welfare state that was created decades ago; none has a new, exciting agenda around which to rally the masses.

AN IDEOLOGY OF THE FUTURE

Imagine, for a moment, an obscure scribbler today in a garret somewhere trying to outline an ideology of the future that could provide a realistic path toward a world with healthy middle-class societies and robust democracies. What would that ideology look like?

It would have to have at least two components, political and economic. Politically, the new ideology would need to reassert the supremacy of democratic politics over economics and legitimate anew government as an expression of the public interest. But the agenda it put forward to protect middle-class life could not simply rely on the existing mechanisms of the welfare state. The ideology would need to somehow redesign the public sector, freeing it from its dependence on existing stakeholders and using new, technology-empowered approaches to delivering services. It would have to argue forthrightly for more redistribution and present a realistic route to ending interest groups' domination of politics.

Economically, the ideology could not begin with a denunciation of capitalism as such, as if old-fashioned socialism were still a viable alternative. It is more the variety of capitalism that is at stake and the degree to which governments should help societies adjust to change. Globalization need be seen not as an inexorable fact of life but rather as a challenge and an opportunity that must be carefully controlled politically. The new ideology would not see markets as an end in themselves; instead, it would value global trade and investment to the extent that they contributed to a flourishing middle class, not just to greater aggregate national wealth.

It is not possible to get to that point, however, without providing a serious and sustained critique of much of the edifice of modern neoclassical economics, beginning with fundamental assumptions such as the sovereignty of individual preferences and that aggregate income is an accurate measure of national well-being. This critique would have to note that people's incomes do not necessarily represent their true contributions to society. It would have to go further, however, and recognize that even if labor markets were efficient, the natural distribution of talents is not necessarily fair and that individuals are not sovereign entities but beings heavily shaped by their surrounding societies.

Most of these ideas have been around in bits and pieces for some time; the scribbler would have to put them into a coherent package. He or she would also have to avoid the "wrong address" problem. The critique of globalization, that is, would have to be tied to nationalism as a strategy for mobilization in a way that defined national interest in a more sophisticated way than, for example, the "Buy American" campaigns of unions in the United States. The product would be a synthesis of ideas from both the left and the right, detached from the agenda of the marginalized groups that constitute the existing progressive movement. The ideology would be populist; the message would begin with a critique of the elites that allowed the benefit of the many to be sacrificed to that of the few and a critique of the money politics, especially in Washington, that overwhelmingly benefits the wealthy.

The dangers inherent in such a movement are obvious: a pullback by the United States, in particular, from its advocacy of a more open global system could set off protectionist responses elsewhere. In many respects, the Reagan-Thatcher revolution succeeded just as its proponents hoped, bringing about an increasingly competitive, globalized, friction-free world. Along the way, it generated tremendous wealth and created rising middle classes all over the developing world, and the spread of democracy in their wake. It is possible that the developed world is on the cusp of a series of technological breakthroughs that will not only increase productivity but also provide meaningful employment to large numbers of middle-class people.

But that is more a matter of faith than a reflection of the empirical reality of the last 30 years, which points in the opposite direction. Indeed, there are a lot of reasons to think that inequality will continue to worsen. The current concentration of wealth in the United States has already become self-reinforcing: as the economist Simon Johnson has argued, the financial sector has used its lobbying clout to avoid more onerous forms of regulation. Schools for the well-off are better than ever; those for everyone else continue to deteriorate. Elites in all societies use their superior access to the political system to protect their interests, absent a countervailing democratic mobilization to rectify the situation. American elites are no exception to the rule.

That mobilization will not happen, however, as long as the middle classes of the developed world remain enthralled by the narrative of the past generation: that their interests will be best served by ever-freer markets and smaller states. The alternative narrative is out there, waiting to be born.

The Democratic Malaise

Globalization and the Threat to the West

Charles A. Kupchan

Foreign Affairs, January/February 2012

A crisis of governability has engulfed the world's most advanced democracies. It is no accident that the United States, Europe, and Japan are simultaneously experiencing political breakdown; globalization is producing a widening gap between what electorates are asking of their governments and what those governments are able to deliver. The mismatch between the growing demand for good governance and its shrinking supply is one of the gravest challenges facing the Western world today.

Voters in industrialized democracies are looking to their governments to respond to the decline in living standards and the growing inequality resulting from unprecedented global flows of goods, services, and capital. They also expect their representatives to deal with surging immigration, global warming, and other knock-on effects of a globalized world. But Western governments are not up to the task. Globalization is making less effective the policy levers at their disposal while also diminishing the West's traditional sway over world affairs by fueling the "rise of the rest." The inability of democratic governments to address the needs of

CHARLES A. KUPCHAN is Professor of International Affairs at Georgetown University and Whitney Shepardson Senior Fellow at the Council on Foreign Relations. This essay is adapted from his forthcoming book *No One's World: The West, the Rising Rest, and the Coming Global Turn* (Oxford University Press, 2012).

their broader publics has, in turn, only increased popular disaffection, further undermining the legitimacy and efficacy of representative institutions.

This crisis of governability within the Western world comes at a particularly inopportune moment. The international system is in the midst of tectonic change due to the diffusion of wealth and power to new quarters. Globalization was supposed to have played to the advantage of liberal societies, which were presumably best suited to capitalize on the fast and fluid nature of the global marketplace. But instead, mass publics in the advanced democracies of North America, Europe, and East Asia have been particularly hard hit—precisely because their countries' economies are both mature and open to the world.

In contrast, Brazil, India, Turkey, and other rising democracies are benefiting from the shift of economic vitality from the developed to the developing world. And China is proving particularly adept at reaping globalization's benefits while limiting its liabilities—in no small part because it has retained control over policy instruments abandoned by its liberal competitors. State capitalism has its distinct advantages, at least for now. As a consequence, it is not just the West's material primacy that is at stake today but also the allure of its version of modernity. Unless liberal democracies can restore their political and economic solvency, the politics, as well as the geopolitics, of the twenty-first century may well be up for grabs.

DEER IN THE HEADLIGHTS

Globalization has expanded aggregate wealth and enabled developing countries to achieve unprecedented prosperity. The proliferation of investment, trade, and communication networks has deepened interdependence and its potentially pacifying effects and has helped pry open nondemocratic states and foster popular uprisings. But at the same time, globalization and the digital economy on which it depends are the main source of the West's current crisis of governability. Deindustrialization and outsourcing, global trade and fiscal imbalances, excess capital and credit and asset bubbles—these consequences of globalization are imposing hardships and insecurity not experienced for generations. The distress stemming from the economic crisis that began in 2008 is particularly acute, but the underlying problems began much earlier. For the better part of two decades, middle-class wages in the world's leading democracies have been stagnant, and economic inequality has been rising sharply as globalization has handsomely rewarded its winners but left its many losers behind.

These trends are not temporary byproducts of the business cycle, nor are they due primarily to insufficient regulation of the financial sector, tax cuts amid expensive wars, or other errant policies. Stagnant wages and rising inequality are, as the economic analysts Daniel Alpert, Robert Hockett, and Nouriel Roubini recently argued in their study "The Way Forward," a consequence of the integration of billions of low-wage workers into the global economy and increases in productivity stemming from the application of information technology to the manufacturing sector. These developments have pushed global capacity far higher than demand, exacting a heavy toll on workers in the high-wage economies of the industrialized West. The resulting dislocation and disaffection among Western electorates have been magnified by globalization's intensification of transnational threats, such as international crime, terrorism, unwanted immigration, and environmental degradation. Adding to this nasty mix is the information revolution; the Internet and the profusion of mass media appear to be fueling ideological polarization more than they are cultivating deliberative debate.

Voters confronted with economic duress, social dislocation, and political division look to their elected representatives for help. But just as globalization is stimulating this pressing demand for responsive governance, it is also ensuring that its provision is in desperately short supply. For three main reasons, governments in the industrialized West have entered a period of pronounced ineffectiveness.

First, globalization has made many of the traditional policy tools used by liberal democracies much blunter instruments. Washington has regularly turned to fiscal and monetary policy to modulate economic performance. But in the midst of global competition and unprecedented debt, the U.S. economy seems all but immune to injections of stimulus spending or the Federal Reserve's latest moves on interest rates. The scope and speed of commercial and financial flows mean that decisions and developments elsewhere—Beijing's intransigence on the value of the yuan, Europe's sluggish response to its financial crisis, the actions of investors and ratings agencies, an increase in the quality of Hyundai's latest models—outweigh decisions taken in Washington. Europe's democracies long relied on monetary policy to adjust to fluctuations in national economic performance. But they gave up that option when they joined the eurozone. Japan over the last two decades has tried one stimulus strategy after another, but to no avail. In a globalized world, democracies simply have less control over outcomes than they used to.

Second, many of the problems that Western electorates are asking their governments to solve require a level of international cooperation that is unattainable. The diffusion of power from the West to the rest means that there are today many new cooks in the kitchen; effective action no longer rests primarily on collaboration among like-minded democracies. Instead, it depends on cooperation among a much larger and more diverse circle of states. The United States now looks to the G-20 to rebalance the international economy. But consensus is elusive among nations that are at different stages of development and embrace divergent approaches to economic governance. Challenges such as curbing global warming or effectively isolating Iran similarly depend on a collective effort that is well beyond reach.

Third, democracies can be nimble and responsive when their electorates are content and enjoy a consensus born of rising expectations, but they are clumsy and sluggish when their citizens are downcast and divided. Polities in which governance depends on popular participation, institutional checks and balances, and competition among interest groups appear to be better at distributing benefits than at apportioning sacrifice. But sacrifice is exactly what is necessary to restore economic solvency, which confronts Western governments with the unappetizing prospect of pursuing policies that threaten to weaken their electoral appeal.

ONE PROBLEM, THREE FLAVORS

In the United States, partisan confrontation is paralyzing the political system. The underlying cause is the poor state of the U.S. economy. Since 2008, many Americans have lost their houses, jobs, and retirement savings. And these setbacks come on the heels of back-to-back decades of stagnation in middle-class wages. Over the past ten years, the average household income in the United States has fallen by over ten percent. In the meantime, income inequality has been steadily rising, making the United States the most unequal country in the industrialized world. The primary source of the declining fortunes of the American worker is global competition; jobs have been heading overseas. In addition, many of the most competitive companies in the digital economy do not have long coattails. Facebook's estimated value is around $70 billion, and it employs roughly 2,000 workers; compare this with General Motors, which is valued at $35 billion and has 77,000 employees in the United States and 208,000 worldwide. The wealth of the United States' cutting-edge companies is not trickling down to the middle class.

These harsh economic realities are helping revive ideological and partisan cleavages long muted by the nation's rising economic fortunes. During the decades after World War II, a broadly shared prosperity pulled Democrats and Republicans toward the political center. But today, Capitol Hill is largely devoid of both centrists and bipartisanship; Democrats campaign for more stimulus, relief for the unemployed, and taxes on the rich, whereas Republicans clamor for radical cuts in the size and cost of government. Expediting the hollowing out of the center are partisan redistricting, a media environment that provokes more than it informs, and a broken campaign finance system that has been captured by special interests.

The resulting polarization is tying the country in knots. President Barack Obama realized as much, which is why he entered office promising to be a "postpartisan" president. But the failure of Obama's best efforts to revive the economy and restore bipartisan cooperation has exposed the systemic nature of the nation's economic and political dysfunction. His $787 billion stimulus package, passed without the support of a single House Republican, was unable to resuscitate an economy plagued by debt, a deficit of middle-class jobs, and the global slowdown. Since the Republicans gained control of the House in 2010, partisan confrontation has stood in the way of progress on nearly every issue. Bills to promote economic growth either fail to pass or are so watered down that they have little impact. Immigration reform and legislation to curb global warming are not even on the table.

Ineffective governance, combined with daily doses of partisan bile, has pushed public approval of Congress to historic lows. Spreading frustration has spawned the Occupy Wall Street movement—the first sustained bout of public protests since the Vietnam War. The electorate's discontent only deepens the challenges of governance, as vulnerable politicians cater to the narrow interests of the party base and the nation's political system loses what little wind it has in its sails.

Europe's crisis of governability, meanwhile, is taking the form of a renationalization of its politics. Publics are revolting against the double dislocations of European integration and globalization. As a consequence, the EU's member states are busily clawing back the prerogatives of sovereignty, threatening the project of European political and economic integration set in motion after World War II. As in the United States, economic conditions are the root of the problem. Over the past two decades, middle-class incomes in most major European economies have been falling and inequality has been rising. Unemployment in Spain stands at over 20 percent, and even Germany, the EU's premier economy, saw its middle class contract by 13 percent between 2000 and 2008. Those who slip through the cracks find a fraying safety net beneath them; Europe's comfortable welfare systems, which have become unsustainable in the face of global competition, are being dramatically scaled back. The austerity stemming from the ongoing debt crisis in the euro-zone has only made matters worse. Greeks are as angry about the EU-enforced belt-tightening as Germans are about having to bail out Europe's economic laggards.

Europe's aging population has made immigration an economic necessity. But the lack of progress in integrating Muslim immigrants into the social mainstream has intensified discomfort over the EU's willingness to accept more outsiders into its midst. Far-right parties have been the beneficiaries of this anxiety, and their hard-edged nationalism targets not only immigrants but also the EU. Generational change is taking its own toll on popular enthusiasm for European integration. Europeans with memories of World War II see the EU as Europe's escape route from its bloody past. But younger Europeans have no past from which to flee. Whereas their elders viewed the European project as an article of faith, current leaders and electorates tend to assess the EU through a cold—and often negative—valuation of costs and benefits.

The collective governance that the EU desperately needs in order to thrive in a globalized world rests uneasily with a political street that is becoming decidedly hostile to the European project. Europe's institutions could descend to the level of its politics, which would effectively reduce the EU to little more than a trade bloc. Alternatively, national politics could again be infused with a European calling, which would breathe new legitimacy into an increasingly hollow union. The latter outcome is much preferable, but it will require leadership and resolve that, at least for now, are nowhere to be found.

Japan, for its part, has been politically adrift since Junichiro Koizumi stepped down as prime minister in 2006. Thereafter, the Liberal Democratic Party (LDP), which had dominated Japanese politics throughout most of the postwar era, stumbled badly, losing power to the Democratic Party of Japan (DPJ) in 2009. The consolidation of a two-party system had the potential to improve governance but instead produced only gridlock and declining public confidence. Japan has cycled through six prime ministers in the last five years. This past summer, public approval of the DPJ stood at 18 percent. The DPJ and the LDP are as internally divided as they are at loggerheads. Policymaking has ground to a halt even on urgent issues; it took over 100 days for the Diet to pass legislation providing relief to the victims of last year's earthquake, tsunami, and nuclear disaster.

The trouble began with the bursting of Japan's asset bubble in 1991, a setback that exposed deeper problems in the country's economy and led to a "lost decade" of recession. Japanese manufacturers suffered as jobs and investment headed to China and the "Asian tigers." The country's traditional social compact, by which corporations provided lifetime employment and comfortable pensions, was no longer sustainable. The past two decades have brought a long slide in middle-class incomes, rising inequality, and a spike in the poverty rate from roughly seven percent in the 1980s to 16 percent in 2009. In 1989, Japan ranked fourth in the world in terms of per capita GDP; by 2010, its rank had plummeted to 24th.

It was to address such problems that Koizumi embarked on ambitious efforts to liberalize the economy and reduce the power of bureaucrats and interest groups. His charisma and ample parliamentary support made for significant progress, but his LDP and DPJ successors have been too weak to keep the process moving forward. Japan is therefore stuck in a no man's land, exposed to the dislocations of a globalized economy yet not liberalized or strategic enough to compete effectively.

BITTER MEDICINE

It is not by chance that the West's crisis of governability coincides with new political strength among rising powers; economic and political vigor is passing from the core to the periphery of the international system. And while the world's most open states are experiencing a loss of control as they integrate into a globalized world, illiberal states, such as China, are deliberately keeping a much tighter grip on their societies through centralized decision-making, censorship of the media, and state-supervised markets. If the leading democracies continue to lose their luster as developing countries chart their rise, the unfolding transition in global power will be significantly more destabilizing. Conversely, a realignment of the international pecking order would likely be more orderly if the Western democracies recouped and provided purposeful leadership.

What is needed is nothing less than a compelling twenty-first-century answer to the fundamental tensions among democracy, capitalism, and globalization. This new political agenda should aim to reassert popular control over political economy, directing state action toward effective responses to both the economic realities of global markets and the demands of mass societies for an equitable distribution of rewards and sacrifices.

The West should pursue three broad strategies to meet this challenge and thus better equip its democratic institutions for a globalized world. First, when up against state capitalism and the potent force of global markets, the Western democracies have little choice but to engage in strategic economic planning on an unprecedented scale. State-led investment in jobs, infrastructure, education, and research will be required to restore economic competitiveness. Second, leaders should seek to channel electorate discontent toward reformist ends through a progressive brand of populism. By pursuing policies that advantage mass publics rather than the party faithful or special interests, politicians can not only rebuild their popularity but also reinvigorate democratic institutions and the values of citizenship and sacrifice. Third, Western governments must lead their electorates away from the temptation to turn inward. As history makes clear, hard times can stoke protectionism and isolationism. But globalization is here to stay, and retreat is not an option.

None of these strategies will be easy to implement, and embracing all of them together will require extraordinary leadership and the political courage to match. But until such an agenda is devised and realized, the democratic malaise will persist.❷

The Strange Triumph of Liberal Democracy

Europe's Ideological Contest

Shlomo Avineri

Foreign Affairs, January/February 2012

Contesting Democracy: Political Ideas in Twentieth-Century Europe. BY
  JAN-WERNER MÜLLER. Yale University Press, 2011, 304 pp. $45.00.
How to Change the World: Reflections on Marx and Marxism. BY ERIC
  HOBSBAWM. Yale University Press, 2011, 480 pp. $35.00.

Any intelligent observer of Europe in the 1930s would have been
hard-pressed not to feel that its future belonged to either communism or fascism. Liberal democracy, besieged on the left by Stalin's
Soviet Union and on the right by Hitler's Germany and Mussolini's Italy, seemed to stand no chance of survival. Most central
and eastern European countries had already succumbed to
authoritarianism or different variations of fascism, and the Great
Depression suggested that the activist solutions implemented by
both extremes were better than the feeble nostrums liberalism
could offer. Back then, the notion that by the beginning of the
twenty-first century, Europe would be democratic from the Tagus
and the Ebro to the Danube and the Vistula would have seemed
utterly ridiculous.

SHLOMO AVINERI is Professor of Political Science at the Hebrew
University of Jerusalem and the author of, among other books, *The
Social and Political Thought of Karl Marx.* He served as Director
General of Israel's Foreign Ministry in the first cabinet of Prime
Minister Yitzhak Rabin.

And in fact, liberal democracy's triumph was hardly inevitable. Two recent books, by authors with greatly differing worldviews and methodologies, try to explain why history worked out as it did. In *Contesting Democracy*, Jan-Werner Müller, a German-born, British-educated political scientist who teaches at Princeton, traces the central ideological narratives of European politics during the century, arguing essentially that the postwar order emerged and has proved durable because it offered novel and satisfactory answers to major problems. In *How to Change the World*, meanwhile, the great Marxist historian Eric Hobsbawm grapples with why Marxism lost out and what it might still have to offer.

THE BATTLE FOR EUROPE

Müller's book is at once a political history of Europe since World War I, an inquiry into why Europe failed to achieve consolidated liberal democracies between the two wars yet was able to do so after 1945, and a collection of essays on some important European political thinkers. Although the volume's chapters show signs of their origin as separate articles, its overall message, complex and sometimes highly original, is clear. In a nutshell, post-1945 democratic development in Western Europe was not achieved easily, nor was it just the reestablishment of the previous political order. It grew out of the lessons learned from the brittleness of interwar democracy and the legacies of some of the nondemocratic interwar movements. It was helped, moreover, by the urgency and cohesion supplied by the broader Cold War environment.

As Müller tells it, the weakness of the post-1918 European democratic regimes derived primarily from the reordering caused by World War I. By suddenly bringing about the collapse of four empires (the Hapsburg, the German, the Russian, and the Ottoman), most of which were multiethnic, the conflict tore down a well-established conservative and hierarchical order and replaced it with a series of weak republican regimes. Many of these regimes were based on the principle of national self-determination, but at the same time, they were burdened with serious ethnic minority problems, irredentist movements, and contested borders.

Germany's Weimar Republic, created in 1919, was the prime example of such a troubled republic, and given his German background and the country's centrality in Europe, Müller naturally devotes significant space to it. Here was a defeated country that, having lost significant territories in the west and the east, adopted an extremely liberal democratic constitution, only to have its elites—bureaucratic, military, ecclesiastical, and academic—view the republican regime as illegitimate. Müller explores Weimar Germany through the prism of the thinking of the sociologist Max Weber, showing how now canonical and seemingly timeless works, such as the essay "Politics as a Vocation," were actually produced in response to the challenges of a unique political and historical context—the legitimacy crisis facing the Weimar Republic after 1919, exacerbated by violent left-wing revolutionary attempts, such as those in Bavaria.

At the time, Germany, like several other countries, was rapidly embracing a democratic ethos, just as the Great War and its aftermath had centralized much of the economy, expanded voting rights, and fostered Wilsonian ideas of national self-determination. It should have been no surprise that the newly established democracies would have so much difficulty juggling these contradictory realities and principles. Müller explains how under such conditions, ideologies—especially redemptive and totalistic ones, such as fascism and communism—could for the first time transcend merely intellectual discourse and capture the imagination of the masses, who thought the formalistic democratic structures failed to respond to their needs and aspirations.

In contrast to his respectful treatment of Weber's measured attempt to combine order, legitimacy, and representation in his theory of a modern nation-state, Müller offers a not very complimentary, but fascinating, characterization of the Hungarian philosopher György Lukács. Müller credits Lukács with an insightful and sophisticated reading of Karl Marx, which made him the preeminent Marxist philosopher of the interwar period, but also exposes his political immaturity during Hungary's 1919 communist revolution, his opportunistic turnarounds during the Stalinist period, and his final turn as a role model for the New Left in the 1960s. Müller also describes him as one of "many scions of highly assimilated Jewish businessmen . . . [who] became part of a free-floating, self-radicalizing intelligentsia moving around Europe on generous allowances (from their usually despairing fathers)." This may not be entirely wrong, yet such a stereotyping of the social origins of revolutionary intellectuals echoes, in gentler terms, what many right-wing anti-Semites were shouting from the rooftops at the time: that it was rich Jewish intellectuals, cosmopolitan and deracinated, who were undermining Europe's social order.

In his account of fascism, Müller rightly underlines the enormous impact that the philosopher Georges Sorel's ideas had on Mussolini and the French radical right, especially his concept that mass political action depended on a "social myth." As the historian Zeev Sternhell has shown, nationalist myths gave content and motivation to the deracinated masses, who felt alienated from the formal institutional structures of modern democracies. This popular foundation distinguished fascist mythmaking from elitist traditionalist conservatism, something many liberals and Marxists failed to see. Far from being agents of the conservative, bourgeois order, fascism and Nazism were revolutionary and supremely modern movements. Much of their appeal lay in their claim to be more democratic than the democracies.

After World War II put an end to fascism, Müller argues, Western Europe set about the task of political reconstruction. Political leaders understood that they had to do more than simply revive the interwar order, which had failed so miserably. So instead they crafted what he calls "constrained democracy," a system that took the formal institutions of parliamentarianism, universal suffrage, and multiple political parties and added a number of constraints. Trade unions negotiated directly with the state, which recognized them as legitimate constitutive elements of the political system (and not just as partisan representatives of socialist parties), allowing employers, employees, and the government to haggle over salaries and wages. Unelected constitutional courts acted as an elitist brake on the majoritarian vox populi, protecting human rights from unbridled populism. Last but not least, these constrained democracies adopted a modified Keynesian approach to state intervention in the economy, which added an element of security to the political structure—something that Europe had lacked before 1939.

In this context, Müller helps readers understand postwar Europe by highlighting the enormous contribution made by Christian Democrats. Italy's Alcide De Gasperi, Germany's Konrad Adenauer, and France's Robert Schuman transformed their parties from enemies of democracy into crucial pillars of it. Before 1939, many Christian parties had allied themselves with antidemocratic forces, and only the horrors of World War II and the Holocaust convinced them that such complicity with fascism ran contrary to their religious principles. Here, the writings of the French Catholic philosopher Jacques Maritain were crucial in reorienting Christian parties toward democratic liberalism. By joining with liberal and social democratic parties to embrace and even help lead the new order, Christian Democrats gave the system the sort of cross-class support of broad public majorities that the interwar republics had never had.

MARXISM'S TURN

One of the most surprising twists in Europe's political evolution is the reversal of fortunes that has befallen Marxism, a school of thought that once seemed a formidable ideological contender. Hobsbawm's latest book, *How to Change the World*, chronicles its influence over the twentieth century and tries to make a case for its contemporary relevance. Hobsbawm is one of the giants of the historical profession and the author of an impressive list of magisterial studies. Even those who disagree with his Marxist outlook know that his sophisticated use of Marxist theory has greatly enriched the study of industrialization, the modern working class, various revolutionary movements, and the emergence of empire.

No doubt his cosmopolitan background—from Alexandria through Vienna and Berlin to London—underpinned by his breadth of knowledge, generosity of spirit, and mastery of languages and topics, has helped him avoid the narrow and doctrinaire approach so common among lesser Marxist historians.

Yet as in the case of Goethe's Faust, there are, alas, two souls dwelling in his breast. There is Dr. Hobsbawm, the towering historian, using the tools of the Marxist tradition to explore history, and there is Comrade Eric, the revolutionary, who, despite distancing himself from debilitating party orthodoxies, is still captive to ideology. *How to Change the World*, which includes more than a dozen essays written between 1956 and 2009, some published here for the first time in English, brings out this duality. Although the volume's title is slightly misleading—this is not a compendium for revolutionary praxis—the book is one of the best accounts showing how Marx's thought did in fact change the world.

Hobsbawm traces Marx's influence on everything from politics to art in several countries from the late nineteenth century to the present. He shows how, despite Marxism's aversion to nationalism, Marxist analysis helped develop and sustain nationalist movements among some oppressed peoples. And his chapter on Antonio Gramsci will make this influential Italian Marxist thinker seem less esoteric and enigmatic to the English reading public.

Of greatest contemporary interest is the opening essay, "Marx Today," in which Hobsbawm brings his acute mind to bear on the post–Cold War era. He claims that the demise of Soviet-style Marxism has paradoxically made the study of Marx more relevant, liberating Marxism from the straitjacket imposed on it by its status as the official ideology of a repressive regime. Yet he also concedes that Marx's vision of the proletariat "expropriating the expropriators" is irrelevant today (although he contends that Marx's understanding of the dynamism of capitalist society is helpful in addressing capitalism's crises, such as the current global economic recession). Hobsbawm is determined not just to salvage Marx from the detritus of the Soviet catastrophe but also to help him regain his place in the pantheon of modern thinkers able to develop comprehensive and adaptive understandings of human affairs. Perhaps because he does not want to sound doctrinaire or old-fashioned, Hobsbawm refrains from calling this unique quality of Marx's thought "dialectical," but this is precisely its chief characteristic.

Still, as masterful as his analyses are, Hobsbawm remains unwilling to address certain problematic facts. Take ethnicity. Given his Jewish background, Hobsbawm is rightly sensitive to the role of Jewish intellectuals in various Marxist movements, focusing in particular on those in Germany and Austria-Hungary. He tersely castigates most non-Jewish intellectuals in Germany after unification, in 1871, for being "profoundly committed to the Wilhelmine Empire." This allegiance left the German social democratic movement bereft of intellectual leadership and thus thrust such Jews as Eduard Bernstein, Karl Kautsky, and Rosa Luxemburg into leadership positions. Similarly, the emergence of various nationalist movements within the Austro-Hungarian Empire in the late nineteenth century drove many Jewish intellectuals to socialism or Zionism, the only places where they could feel at home.

Hobsbawm describes all this with acuity but does not really grapple with the problem it poses for his broader framework. According to Marxist theory, class background should determine where people end up politically. But it was the Jewish background of these activists, not their identity as bourgeois intellectuals, that brought them to the shores of Marxism. This suggests that all history is not class history (as Marx would have had it), that national, ethnic, and religious affiliations matter, too. But if Hobsbawm admitted that, he would have to reject a major facet of theoretical Marxism, something he is unwilling to do.

A more serious omission concerns the Soviet elephant in the room. Hobsbawm's 2002 autobiography dealt with his changing attitudes toward the Soviet Union over the years, and in many cases, he acknowledged the inner tensions of his relationship to the Soviet experience and the havoc that experience created among Western Communists. But he shied away from grappling with the fundamental question: Did Russia's 1917

Leninist coup lead inexorably to Soviet tyranny, and was the attempt to force a socialist vision on a preindustrial society doomed from the very beginning? Readers will not find a definitive answer to this question in any of Hobsbawm's past work, nor in this volume, either.

This elephant casts other shadows. Hobsbawm discusses Marxist intellectuals in the 1930s without mentioning their re-actions to the 1939 Molotov-Ribbentrop Pact, between the Soviet Union and Nazi Germany. In his autobiography, Hobsbawm came to terms with the fact that he himself justified the pact at the time, with the usual language then prevalent among Communists. But he does not mention the pact here, and ignoring such an episode in a historical account of Marxism in the 1930s is simply inexcusable.

On a certain level, one can commiserate with Hobsbawm, a prominent member of the mainly (although of course not exclu-sively) Jewish interwar intelligentsia that believed in the redemp-tive vision of Marxism. The Soviet Union became a beacon of hope for this group after the slaughters of World War I and the collapse of European democracies and economies in the 1920s and 1930s. The tendency to close one's eyes at first to blemishes in the Soviet system was understandable. But this pose became an intellectual and moral prison when what initially could have been viewed as childhood illnesses of the revolution transmogri-fied into the hideous crimes of Stalinism. Some had the courage to liberate themselves; others clung to their hopes even as darkness descended at noon.

Hobsbawm tried to maintain both his integrity as a historian and his beliefs. He should be thanked for the historical gifts he has bestowed on his readers. But at the end of the day, he never ade-quately addresses the fact that Marxism failed utterly as a revolu-tionary movement, not once but three times—in the West, where no proletarian revolution occurred; in the East, where what was supposed to be an emancipatory redemption ended up as a hellish nightmare; and in the developing world, where communist regimes brought misery wherever they gained power.

THE CRISIS THIS TIME

The recent global financial crisis has once again shaken people's faith in the ability of capitalism to provide a sustainable flow of broad-based economic benefits to the public at large. It serves as a reminder of the fragility of the post–World War II order Müller describes. Recent demonstrations in Europe and the United States, meanwhile, attest to the failures of democratic governments to respond adequately to the crisis or satisfy public demands for action. Müller is aware that the hard-won postwar equilibrium should not be taken for granted, and he holds up the crisis of 1968 as an indication of its brittleness.

Today's economic crisis is also a reminder of the contemporary relevance of the issues that Marx and his disciples, including Hobsbawm, have agonized over. Dialectically (if one is still allowed to use the term), Hobsbawm's suggestions for how elements of Marxist thinking can inform solutions to the crisis might still rescue the approach from total relegation to the dustbin of history. As the crisis has made clear, market fundamentalism, radical privatization, and a universal fear of state power are overly simplistic answers to the question of how to sustain a modern, globalized economic order. One way of looking at Marx, after all, has always been to see him in the context of the Enlightenment project and the German tradition of *Bildung*, as a thinker who, when faced with the horrors of early industrial capitalism, tried to bring about a world of universal justice, solidarity, fairness, and humanity. In his own way, Hobsbawm continues to speak to that dream.

The two books are helpful in unsettling the ideological complacency of contemporary neoliberalism, which helped pave the way for the crisis even as it never imagined such a thing could happen. As both Müller and Hobsbawm show, the triumph of liberal democracy was made up of many ingredients, and neglecting any one of them is an invitation to trouble.◉

Acknowledgements

This book would not have appeared without the talent, judgment, and hard work of the *Foreign Affairs* staff: from Editorial, Andrew Bast, Stuart Reid, Justin Vogt, Joshua Yaffa, Jordan Hirsch, Benjamin Alter, Lorenz Skeeter, Ann Tappert, Belinda Lanks, Sarah Larson, Sarah Foster, and Elira Coja; from Publishing, David Kellogg, Lynda Hammes, Ed Walsh, Emilie Harkin, Michael Pasuit, Carolina Aguilar, Jonathan Chung, Daniel Schoenbachler, Christine Leonard, and Katie Sedgwick; and from Communications, Nadine Apelian. Associate Editor Katie Allawala played the largest role, expertly shepherding the project from start to finish. Here and in the magazine in general, their efforts consistently rise to the level of the subject matter they deal with, which is all that needs to be said.

Gideon Rose
Editor, *Foreign Affairs*

Jonathan Tepperman
Managing Editor, *Foreign Affairs*

December 2011

CPSIA information can be obtained at www.ICGtesting.com
Printed in the USA
LVOW090409270112

265687LV00007B/37/P